GCSE ICT for Edexcel

Ken Slee • Molly Wischhusen
Janet Snell • Jenny Johnson

Edexcel
Success through qualifications

Heinemann Educational Publishers,
Halley Court, Jordan Hill, Oxford OX2 8EJ
A division of Reed Educational & Professional Publishing Ltd

Heinemann is a registered trademark of Reed Educational
& Professional Publishing Limited

OXFORD MELBOURNE AUCKLAND JOHANNESBURG BLANTYRE
GABORONE IBADAN PORTSMOUTH NH (USA) CHICAGO

First published 2001
2004 2003 2002 2001
10 9 8 7 6 5 4 3 2

A catalogue record for this book is available from
the British Library on request.

ISBN 0 435 44802 1

Development editor Rosalyn Bass

Edited by Alex Gray

Picture research by Liz Savery

Designed by bigtop, Bicester

Illustrated by Linda Combi

Original illustrations
© Heinemann Educational Publishers, 2001

Printed and bound in Italy by Printer Trento S.R.L

Tel: 01865 888058 www.heinemann.co.uk

Contents

Acknowledgements

My sincere thanks go to Molly and Janet for suggesting to Heinemann that I be invited to join themselves and Ken in writing this book. Their support, encouragement and advice have been invaluable and it has been an immense pleasure to work with them. I would also like to express my gratitude to Margaret Berriman, Rosalyn Bass, Mick Watson and Alex Gray for their support, friendly e-mails and encouraging feedback and suggestions.

My thanks also goes to my colleagues Marcus Morris and Pam Gell who spent valuable time proofreading my work and making excellent suggestions.

Also, thank you to my wonderful sons Ian and Colin, and Ian's partner Helen, for their comments, constructive feedback, continual encouragement and endless cups of tea! Lastly, it goes without saying that the never-ending patience and support of my husband, Ray, whilst I have been ensconced in the study writing, contributed to the successful completion of my chapters.

Jenny Johnson, BA, MIITT

It has been my pleasure to work with Janet, Jenny and Molly on this book. Many thanks for all your boundless encouragement and really helpful ideas.
I would like to thank Rosalyn Bass, Margaret Berriman, Alex Gray and Mick Watson not only for their extremely professional guidance, but also for their understanding when deadlines were imminent!

Lastly, and by no means least, thanks to my family. Without their patience and good humour, my contribution to this book would not have been possible.

Ken Slee, BSc

I would like to express my sincere thanks to Margaret Berriman and Rosalyn Bass for inviting me to help write this book and also to Mick Watson and Alex Gray for their support in seeing it through to completion. It has been a delight to work with Molly on a second book and with Jenny and Ken – thank you all for your hard work and good ideas.

Finally, thank you again to my husband Bob for his continuing encouragement and to the rest of my family just for being there and putting up with me.

Janet Snell, BA

My very sincere thanks and appreciation to Margaret Berriman and Rosalyn Bass for once again inviting me to participate in writing a text book, to Mick Watson and Alex Gray for their invaluable advice and support with the proofs, and to Janet, Jenny and Ken who were a pleasure to work with.
Thanks again to all my family for their encouragement, but most especially to my husband, Peter, for his continuing patience and dinners cooked, especially as he thought book writing had just finished! It is no exaggeration to say that without his support it would not be possible to participate.

Molly Wischhusen, BA

The authors and publishers are grateful to the following for their permission to reproduce photographs and other material:
Amstrad plc, BBC, BMW, British Telecom, Camelot, CEC/Mark N Boulton, Corbis/Hulton Deutsch Collection, Corbis/Paul A, Dell, The Egg Group, Epson, Haddon Davies, Chris Honeywell, Microsoft, Penny-Giles Ltd. Reed Executive plc, Science Photo Library/Jim Olive, Peter Arnold Inc. Science Photo Library/Jerry Mason, Science Photo Library/John Greim, Souders, Stone, Techsoft and John Walmsley.

Introduction

Welcome to your GCSE in Information Communication Technology. You have made a very good choice in choosing this subject since computers, as you well know, are used in every aspect of life today. Whatever career you have in the future, it is almost certain that you will find the knowledge you gain on this course very useful.

You will learn about:

- Computer hardware and setting up the system.
- Computer software, including word processing, desktop publishing, spreadsheets, database, electronic communication, web page design and data logging.
- Networks and their topology or layout.
- Systems analysis – i.e. considering the needs of a business and designing a computer solution.

Introduction

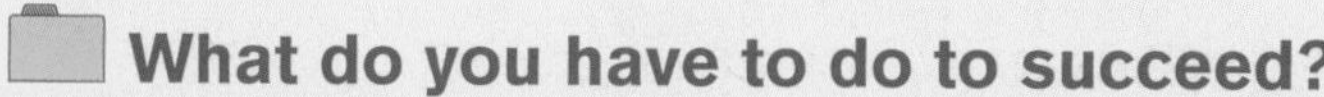

What do you have to do to succeed?

To be successful in your ICT GCSE you will have to complete four pieces of coursework and also pass a two-hour examination. The coursework consists of four projects, where you look at a business situation, identify the administrative needs of the business and design a computer solution to meet those needs.

You *must produce* a project for both:

- Spreadsheets

  and
- Databases

The other two projects may be selected from:

- Word processing
- Desktop Publishing
- Web Site Publishing
- Data Logging and Control
- Multi-media
- Programming
- Free Choice 1
- Free Choice 2

The examination has three sections:

Section A – Multiple choice questions

Section B – Structured questions based on an annually, pre-released Case Study

Section C – Structured questions.

Assessment

The coursework, which is assessed internally by your tutor, counts for 60% of the marks and the examination, which is externally assessed, counts for the remaining 40% of the marks.

Each of your projects should include the following sections:

Heading	Maximum mark
Identify	5
Analyse	9
Design	9
Implement	12
Evaluate	5
Total	40

A further *eight marks* may be awarded for the quality of your written communication when presenting your project.

Each question in the examination will indicate the number of marks that can be obtained. Clearly the more marks allocated, the more detail will be expected in the answer.

The layout of this book

The book starts with a scenario or case study on which the activities in the chapters are based. You will be able to use the scenario to consider computer solutions to business problems as practice, ready for finding your own projects for your coursework.

Chapters 1 to 9 cover the various aspects of computer hardware and software that you need to learn both for your projects and the examination. Chapter 10 explains what is meant by systems analysis and gives you guidelines on what should be included in each of the project sections. Within each chapter you will find:

The main text – which explains all the topics you need to learn.

Activities – which will help your understanding.

Key points

Key points – a list of key points that you should have learnt.

Did you know

Did you know? – small, interesting snippets of information which are relevant to the particular section, but are not necessarily essential.

Test your understanding – to check your understanding of the topics covered.

If you work through each chapter, completing the activities, you should gain the understanding required to pass the examination.

We do hope you enjoy your ICT GCSE and wish you good luck and every success both with the projects and the examination.

Jenny Johnson
Ken Slee
Janet Snell
Molly Wischhusen

Scenario: Greenfingers Garden Centre

Greenfingers is a garden centre managed by Pete and Sandra Wellings in Seahaven. Fifteen years ago they started the business from a small greenhouse and yard selling plants, shrubs, garden implements and flower pots.

The administrative side of the business is run by Rose Garland and an office junior, who use a couple of rather outdated computers for correspondence and customer records. Greenfingers also employs a full-time gardening advisor called Walter Butler who advises customers on garden design and is the plant and shrub expert. Salim Hassan runs day-to-day sales assisted by several part-time staff and additional weekend staff who attend the local college.

Over the years the business has grown and is about to move into new premises. The range of goods on sale will be expanded to include:

- Plants, shrubs and trees
- Cut flowers and gifts
- Garden tools, equipment and clothing (e.g. spades, lawnmowers, watering cans, wellington boots, waterproof jackets)
- Landscaping materials (e.g. rocks, paving and fencing)
- Garden furniture
- Tea room/restaurant
- Aquatics (e.g. fish tanks, ponds and water features)
- Garden design
- Wholesale nursery (where they grow their own plants and sell them on to shops/other garden centres).

The new premises will provide spacious accommodation for the office, a new indoor showroom/greenhouse, additional greenhouses for the wholesale business, together with a large outdoor plant display area with drive-through facilities for heavy items such as land-scaping materials. In addition, they are opening two further garden centres in the nearby towns of Dulton and Newford and will need to recruit some additional staff.

Sandra will manage the retail side of the new business and Pete will concentrate on the wholesale trade. Pete and Sandra know they must introduce ICT systems to ensure the new business runs efficiently and in the following chapters we will look at the ICT systems that will be able to help them.

CHAPTER 1

Computers and society

'I think there's a world market for maybe five computers'

This is a quotation made in the 1940s by Thomas Watson, chairman of IBM, manufacturers of the first large-scale calculating computer.

With the benefit of hindsight, we know this was a gross underestimation, but he was not alone in misjudging the impact information technology would have on all areas of society – commerce, industry, home, school, leisure and government.

Twenty or thirty years ago relatively few computers were in existence but throughout the 1980s and 1990s an explosion in the use of information technology occurred, and this has brought us into an information age where people need less supervision in their work, have increased leisure time and, as a consequence, the established traditions in work and leisure have seen significant changes in recent years.

There is no doubt that computers are here to stay and their presence will continue to influence our daily lives. Are the consequent changes to society for the better or worse?

In these opening pages we are going to look at the effect they have had on our way of life and the implications for the 21st century. By the end of the chapter you will have a greater understanding of the issues surrounding the use of information systems and should be in a position to form your own judgements as to whether they are beneficial or detrimental to society.

Computers and business

Did you know ?

Desktop computers first started to make an impact in the late 1970s/early 1980s when it was estimated that 2 million were in use. By 2000 that estimate had surged to around 500 million computers worldwide. (*Computer Active*, 15 January 2001, page 43.)

Activity

Look in a selection of newspapers and journals and make a list of the jobs advertised that require computer skills. Include salary details and any relevant information about experience. Can you reach any conclusions by looking at this list? For example, does your selection cover a wide range of commercial activities, is there evidence that one job might lead on to another, e.g. does an advertisement for one job call for existing knowledge/experience of another? Is there any evidence of salary progression? Write a brief evaluation of what you have found and save the data file as 'Employment Opportunities'.

Offices

Although the functions of an office are comparable to 20 or 30 years ago – i.e. to provide the administrative support to the business – the process by which they are achieved is very different. The advent of computerised office systems, such as database, accounting, word processing and desktop publishing, together with other automated office equipment, for instance the fax and computer-controlled telephone systems, heralded the era of the electronic office.

The early fears about mass unemployment were unfounded and whilst some jobs disappeared, many became much easier and more interesting. For example, typists have retrained as word-processor operators and have acquired new skills that enable them to edit and manipulate text, automate routine tasks, use mail merge and desktop publishing skills.

Account clerks no longer have to complete ledgers by hand or to repeat complicated calculations time and time again. Data is entered into the computer by data-processing operators, the software automatically performs the calculations and data analysis is much more efficient.

The paperless office

We hear about the paperless office and indeed in some businesses the traditional paper-based filing systems for payroll, stock, sales and orders, etc. have become redundant. Local and wide area networks provide the communication links that enable data to be held on one central computer system which is accessed by all departments, no matter whether they are in the same building or even in different towns or countries. The use of e-mail has reduced the time spent on the telephone and has made the exchange of information very much faster.

Figure 1.1 *A call centre*

Call centres handle many day-to-day routine tasks that were once undertaken by clerical staff. Nowadays, instead of writing letters to place orders, arrange insurance, etc., we speak to an operator who enters the details straight into the computer and can give an immediate answer to the enquiry.

Figure 1.2 *Videoconferencing*

Videoconferencing

Many managers find themselves spending a great deal of time away from the office attending meetings which can prove an expensive use of valuable human resources. **Videoconferencing** (or **teleconferencing**) is a system where video links enable delegates in different locations to see and speak to each other through their computers. A small camera is fixed to the top of each computer VDU and the image is displayed on the other computer screens.

Teleworking

Teleworking allows the employee to work from home with a PC or laptop that interacts with the company computer via a modem and the telephone network.

From the employee's point of view teleworking can offer a better quality of life since time is not wasted travelling to and from work and the flexibility in working hours is ideal for people who need to fit their work schedule around children/school or for disabled workers who find it difficult to commute. There is also an additional benefit to the environment because fewer commuters means fewer cars on the road, leading to a reduction in petrol consumption and pollution. However, home working can bring disadvantages. The employee may feel isolated and miss the support of colleagues, and there is always the temptation to put work off in favour of something more appealing.

The employer can rent less office space, resulting in lower rents, heating and lighting costs. In addition, staff can be recruited from a wider area because they don't need to live within commuting distance of the office. A negative aspect from the employer's point of view is that it can be difficult to control staff and encourage teamwork.

Key points

- Although office jobs were lost with the introduction of computer technology, many new jobs have been created.
- The computer now handles boring and routine tasks, leaving staff time to do more interesting work.
- We can get instant information or answers.
- Videoconferencing enables managers to spend more time in the office and reduce travelling expenses.
- Teleworking can offer a better quality of life, flexible working hours and provide employment opportunities for the disabled, whilst at the same time resulting in less expense for the employer.
- All workers need to be multi-skilled.
- There is a shortage of highly skilled IT professionals causing companies to look overseas for staff and to outsource data processing.

Computers and shopping

Did you know ?

Saturday 16 December 2000 was named 'Plastic Saturday' because over 40 million swipes created a record number of transactions using debit or credit cards in one day. This equated to approximately 250 swipes per second!

Did you know

Pizza Hut has installed a new computer system to help management monitor sales at individual shops. The system will give an instant overview of sales and will even indicate whether a shop is putting too much topping on the pizzas!

Did you know

Online credit card fraud in the UK was valued at £7 million in 2000. Online global purchases are expected to rise from $1.6 bn in 2000 to $15.5 bn in 2005 and fraud damages are expected to rise in proportion. Although secure systems are available to protect the consumer it is estimated that only 30% of Internet traders use anti-fraud technology.

Are you familiar with special offers in supermarkets such as 'Buy 2 and get 1 free' or 'Free sauce with every packet of fresh pasta', etc.? Offers such as these are only possible through the power of the computer and the use of computerised sales checkouts or **electronic point-of-sale** (**EPOS**) terminals that are found in many shops today. The label or packaging on most products carries a bar code which provides a unique reference number for the product. A bar code reader at the checkout scans the bar code and matches the product reference to the price in the shop's stock database. The product price is automatically generated and if it is a multi-save offer, appropriate discounts are deducted.

There is no need to price items individually – no need to employ assistants to stick labels on every product on the shelves. If the price changes, only the database needs updating. The computer systems provide management with instant and up-to-date information about daily sales figures. This in turn means decisions can be taken based on accurate information and makes it possible to predict market trends.

TESCO

			£
VALUE TISSUES	*		0.38
VALUE TISSUES	*		0.38
STILL WATER	*		1.49
MC MICROCHIPS			0.99
MC MICROCHIPS			0.99
MCCAIN PIZZAS			0.79
MULTISAVER		(-0.78)	
FZN MICROPZZA			0.79
MULTISAVER		(-0.78)	
CRUMPETS			0.49
CRUMPETS			0.49
MULTISAVER		(-0.49)	
CAKE BARS			0.95
ANGEL SLICES			0.99

Figure 1.3 *Tesco supermarket receipt*

Stock levels

The use of a database to record stock levels means store managers know instantly how much stock they have, which items are running low on the shop floor and which are selling well. Some computer systems are programmed to automatically raise a new order with the supplier when stock falls below a certain level. However, although it might appear intelligent, a computer database can only provide information based on the data fed into the system, and this means wastage and theft are not recorded. To rectify this situation a manual stock-take is still necessary in order to reconcile actual numbers on the shelf with the computer record.

Loyalty cards

Many supermarkets offer loyalty cards to their shoppers. In exchange for shopping regularly with the store, the customer receives money-off-vouchers and special offers. The store records customer details and creates a huge database of customers giving easy and instant access to valuable data on shopping and spending habits.

Shopping on the Internet

The **Internet** has added new expressions to our vocabulary – cyber shopping, e-shopping and e-commerce – and has opened up a totally new shopping experience both for customer and retailer. More and more well-known stores are offering the opportunity to shop online as they realise the potential of the international market place presented by the Internet.

This offers consumers a wider choice of goods 24 hours a day and the opportunity to shop around for the best buys from the comfort of their own home. It saves time, fares and parking charges and gives the housebound the same opportunities as the able-bodied. At the same time it poses a further threat to town centres which are already struggling to compete with large out-of-town shopping centres. Consumers do have serious concerns about the security of credit card details when shopping via the Internet. Retailers (or e-tailers) seek to reassure us that they operate secure sites and that online transactions are safe. As a result, sophisticated data encryption systems have been designed to encrypt data in transmission. A further development is a new facility whereby customers might soon be able to order over the Internet but have the balance added to their telephone account, thus eliminating the need to transmit credit card details. (*Computer Active*, 19 October 2000, page 7.)

For British expatriates there is even a web site where a selection of traditional British food can be ordered from anywhere in the world via the Internet. Have a look at www.expatshopping.com. (*Computer Active*, 16 November 2000, page 10.)

Figure 1.4 *The Internet makes it possible to buy goods from anywhere in the world no matter where you are*

Key points

- Electronic point-of-sale terminals linked to company databases provide accurate information to management about sales figures and stock levels which helps them to make accurate decisions.
- Computer systems enable shops to attract customers by offering special offers.
- Loyalty cards provide stores with valuable information on shopping habits.
- The Internet has made it possible to buy virtually anything from anywhere in the world 24 hours a day from the comfort of your own home.
- E-commerce has raised fears about the security of paying online with credit cards.

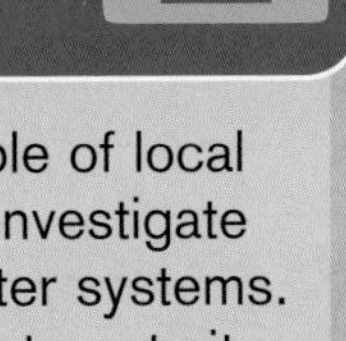

Activity

Try and visit a couple of local supermarkets and investigate their use of computer systems. Then look at their Internet sites and write a brief report comparing the use each store is making of information and communication technology.

Computers – banking and design

Did you know ?

In France a different system of recording credit card transactions is used. They do not use a magnetic strip and swipe the cards. Instead their credit cards contain a chip and customers must key in their Personal Identity Number (PIN) at each transaction to confirm their identity.

Computers and banking

We are fast becoming a cashless society and opting to use 'plastic' credit and debit cards when we shop in preference to cheques or cash. Salaries are paid by **bankers automated clearing system** (**BACS**) and bills are automatically settled by direct debit. We don't need to go anywhere near a bank to do any of these and as a result banks are closing branches and merging. The typical high street with a bank on every corner is now seeing an influx of trendy bars taking over empty bank premises.

More people are using remote systems for banking, such as the telephone and online or e-banking, rather than visit the bank. In fact, some banks only offer Internet banking. The customer has access to his/her account 24 hours a day, 365 days a year and can check their balance, pay bills and transfer funds to accounts paying better interest rates without leaving the house. We no longer need to queue at the bank to withdraw money because **automated teller machines** (**ATMs**) or cash-point machines provide access to our money 24 hours a day anywhere in the world.

The outcome of these changes to banking methods has brought new problems. As a result there are far fewer cheques in circulation and less staff are employed to process them. Furthermore, new computer systems are reducing the time it takes for a cheque to clear from three days to two. Credit card fraud was unheard of 20 or 30 years ago but today it is not uncommon. Some banks now issue cards with embedded photos as a further proof of identity. Rural communities in particular have been affected by the closure of smaller bank branches, causing inconvenience to customers. The elderly find it difficult to get into town because they no longer drive and cannot rely on public transport where services frequently do not run in country neighbourhoods.

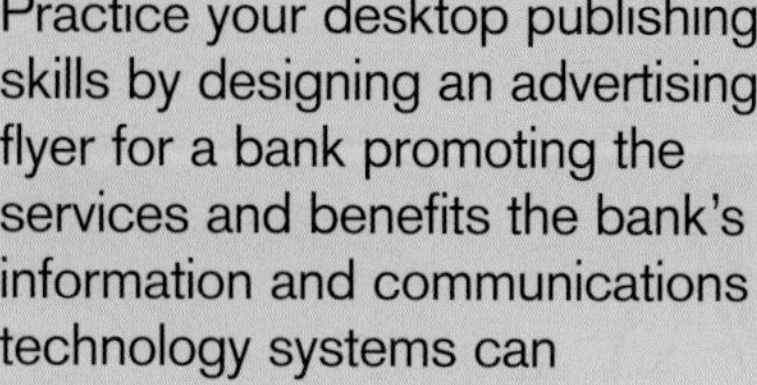

Activity

Practice your desktop publishing skills by designing an advertising flyer for a bank promoting the services and benefits the bank's information and communications technology systems can offer businesses similar to Greenfingers Garden Centre.

Computers and design

The use of computerised technologies such as **CAD/CAM** (**computer-aided design/computer-aided manufacture**) systems enable designers/engineers to develop new products and test them before investment is made in expensive new machinery. For example, a new car design can be tested to see how it will behave in a road crash before the first car is built. Modifications can be made to the design to overcome potential problems. Computer systems automatically produce precision designs for the dies that are made before mass production begins, resulting in better quality products.

Architects have transferred their design skills to CAD software and can produce clear, detailed drawings quickly and accurately. Changes in the designs can be made without the need to produce completely new drawings. 3D-CAD software will turn the drawing into virtual reality enabling the client to take a virtual tour of the new building – a very powerful marketing tool if you are trying to persuade backers to invest in a project.

Designers from other professions have benefited from computer-aided design too – fashion designers can visualise their creations in different fabrics/colours. You might have seen CAD software used in DIY stores for planning new kitchens.

Computer-aided design software is used in the design of sports equipment, such as racing cars, yachts, skis, and sports wear such as ski wear or football boots. Calculations can be made which will determine the maximum speed or durability of new designs and new materials. This is called computer modelling and you will learn more about this in Chapter 8.

Large projects, such as the development of new shopping malls or office buildings, are designed within a fixed budget. Computers support management of such projects, comparing actual costs with projected costs. This provides project managers with information that enables them to keep projects within budget and within the time scale.

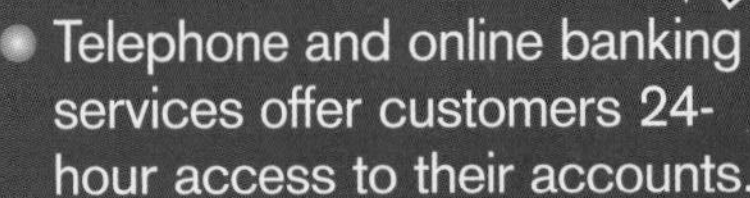

Key points

- Telephone and online banking services offer customers 24-hour access to their accounts.
- Money can be withdrawn from ATMs 24 hours a day anywhere in the world.
- A smaller quantity of cheques is being processed resulting in fewer jobs.
- The use of CAD/CAM software enables new products to be developed and tested before production begins.
- Computers can track the progress of an order all the way through production.
- Computers are used in the management of large projects.

Activity

Draw a sketch of a very simple logo for Greenfingers Garden Centre and scan it into your word-processing software. Create your design, import it into the word-processing file and describe the graphics tools you used to create the image.

Modify your image, import the new image into the file and describe the tools you used to manipulate the original image. Finally, write a paragraph describing the benefits of using a computer to design your image.

Computers – industry and publishing

Activity

Work in small groups and each of you look at the Internet site of a well-known manufacturer (e.g. Ford, Rover, Boeing, Rolls Royce, etc.) and see if you can find any information about their production methods and the role computers play in the processes. Compare your findings with the rest of your group. Are there any similarities in the information you have gathered?

Car manufacturing

If you were asked to suggest one way in which industry has been affected by the introduction of computers, you would almost certainly reply 'Robots', but computers are used to process orders and track their progress through the complete manufacturing process. Let us consider this in relation to car production at Ford.

Imagine a customer visiting a car showroom and choosing a new car. The dealer places the order with the manufacturer. The order is given a unique order number and full details are entered into the computer – e.g. customer, dealer, model, engine size, colour, number of doors, left-hand or right-hand drive, etc. At the same time an order is automatically generated for the seats to be made by another local manufacturer.

Each body shell is assigned a unique bar code during manufacture. Sensors read the bar code and computer programs generate instructions relating to that particular car. As a result, robots are programmed to weld according to each order and spray the right colour paint.

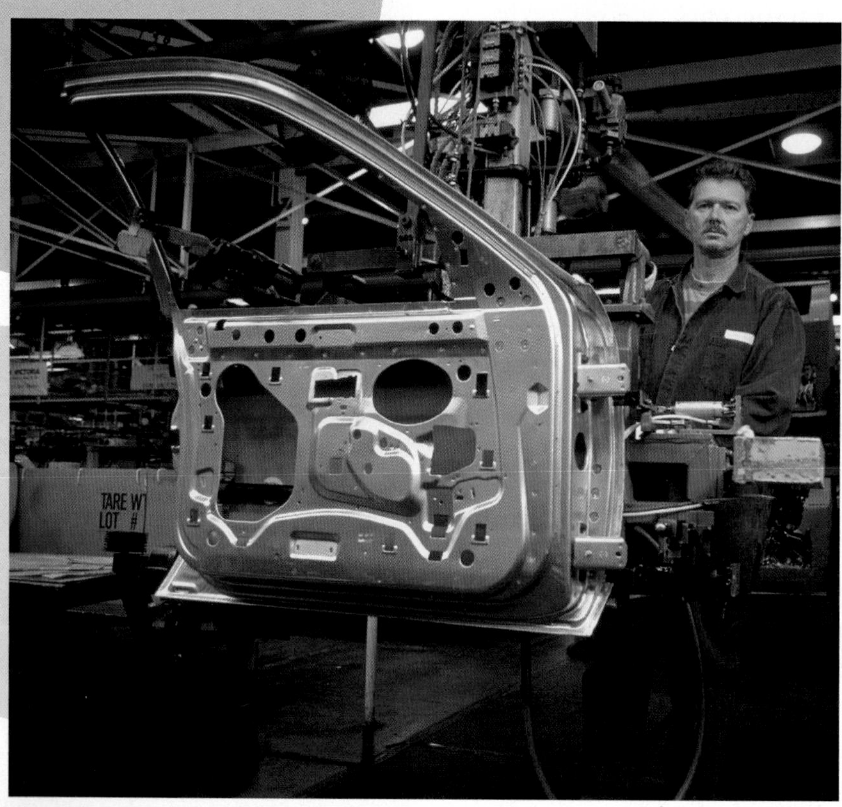

Figure 1.5 *Car production line*

Whilst all this is taking place the seats are being made down the road and are sent along an automatic conveyor from one factory to another to arrive at exactly the time they are needed.

One of the last stages in assembly is fixing the doors. Miraculously these too arrive with the right number of doors in the right colour for each car. The whole production process has been controlled by the computer, reducing the number of humans involved in production and ensuring that those who do work on the production lines are used in the most effective way possible.

Newspaper publishing

The production of newspapers has changed dramatically in recent years. Journalists were often portrayed huddled over an old typewriter rushing to get a story to the editor in order to meet a deadline. For example, there were many jobs for compositors who were employed to set the newspaper up ready for printing. Their job was highly skilled and they assembled the text, letter by letter, into blocks that would fit together to form the finished page. If a late story broke the whole page would need to be reset.

Today journalists word process their own stories and e-mail the copy to the editor from anywhere in the world. Desktop-publishing software is used to produce the final layout, import the pictures and arrange the columns. The design of a page can be easily manipulated if a late story has to be included; as a result the compositor's role has disappeared from newspaper production, an example of de-skilling.

Book publishing

We have made wide use of IT facilities in the production of this textbook. Chapters were produced using word-processing software and first drafts were saved. We have been able to edit the chapters to revise our ideas or add up-to-date snippets so that the text could be as current as possible when it went to print. We have used scanners to incorporate illustrations and e-mail to communicate with each other and to send the text to the editor at Heinemann. The final proofs were saved on CD-ROM and sent to the printer who has used desktop-publishing software to present the book as you see it now. The printing and binding of the book were handled by computer process control systems and another computer system produced the invoices that accompanied the books when they were despatched to your school, college or local bookshop.

Printing

The desktop publishing features of even a simple word-processing application enable news-sheets, business cards, invitations, programmes, etc. to be prepared in the office and photocopied. Many simple printing tasks of this nature that were once handled by the local printer are produced in-house.

Figure 1.6 *A newspaper journalist at work before computerisation*

Key points

- Robots have replaced the jobs of many manual factory workers.
- Robots can perform continuously to a consistent standard in any environmental condition.
- The use of desktop-publishing software has speeded up the production of newspapers, magazines and books.
- Word-processing software has desktop-publishing tools that mean jobs previously handled by a printer can be done in the home or office.
- Computer process control systems are used to monitor production.
- The print trade is a good example of de-skilling.

Activity

Use the desktop-publishing tools in your word-processing software to create a newsletter telling other pupils/students about your GCSE IT course.

Computers and health care

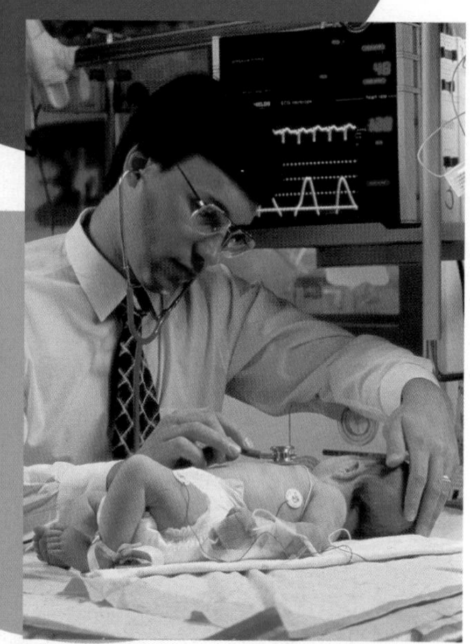

Figure 1.7 *A baby being monitored by computer*

Patient records

Most GP surgeries and hospitals now store patient records on a computerised database. This provides more accurate and up-to-date information because records of drugs taken, treatments, tests, etc. are kept in one place and are therefore less likely to get lost. A GP can use the database to search for patients of a specific age who perhaps need to be called in for screening or to find out which patients take a particular drug. He/she can then use the mail merge facility of the word processor to send individual letters to all the patients. A database of patients requiring transplants can quickly match a suitable patient with a donor. When an organ becomes available, doctors have to work very quickly to find a recipient and transplant the organ, and so every minute saved is vital.

Computer diagnosis

Computers are used to help diagnose disease by matching symptoms with illnesses. This can point towards a preliminary diagnosis, which can be confirmed by carrying out further tests. Scanners are regularly used in the diagnosis of illnesses such as cancer and early detection can improve a patient's chance of survival. Seriously ill patients are monitored by computer and medical staff are automatically alerted if the patient's condition deteriorates.

Computerised operations

Surgeons are now moving towards performing operations remotely with the use of robotic arms. A surgeon in one hospital can see an image of a patient in another hospital on the computer screen and can use a specially adapted mouse to control the actions of the robotic arm.

Computer prediction

Computers are also used to model new drugs and predict the possible effects. This speeds up the development time and makes eventual testing on patients safer. However, the advances in medicine do have underlying ethical implications. The new drugs and treatments are costly and the health service doesn't have the funds available to offer them to all patients. Who should decide who can receive treatment and who shouldn't?

Did you know ?

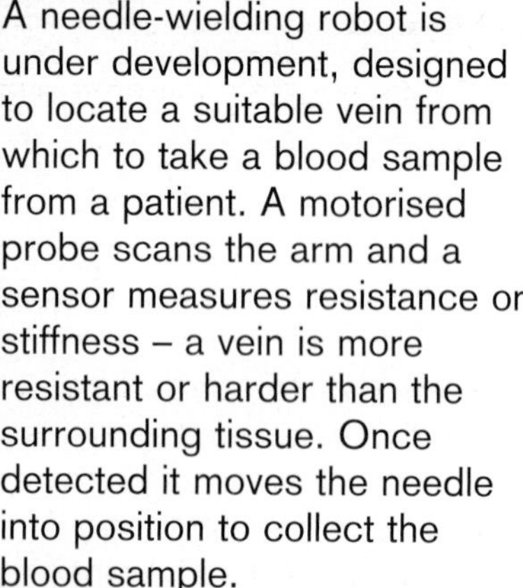

A needle-wielding robot is under development, designed to locate a suitable vein from which to take a blood sample from a patient. A motorised probe scans the arm and a sensor measures resistance or stiffness – a vein is more resistant or harder than the surrounding tissue. Once detected it moves the needle into position to collect the blood sample.

Computer interaction

Computers can improve the lifestyle of the disabled, offering them independence and opportunities for employment. We have already looked at the possibilities of teleworking. Robotic wheelchairs and robotic limbs can help physically impaired people regain mobility and dignity. Voice-recognition software converts speech to the printed word and conversely printed text can be converted to verbal output to help the visually impaired. Touch-sensitive screens and special pointing devices enable the physically impaired to interact with the computer. The use of e-mail (and text messaging on mobile phones) has opened up a new world of communication to the hard of hearing.

Computer monitoring

The computer is used to monitor sportsmen and women in training for important sporting events in order to determine their fitness levels. Similar monitoring techniques are also used for patients recovering from heart attacks, etc. as they follow exercise programmes designed to regain their fitness.

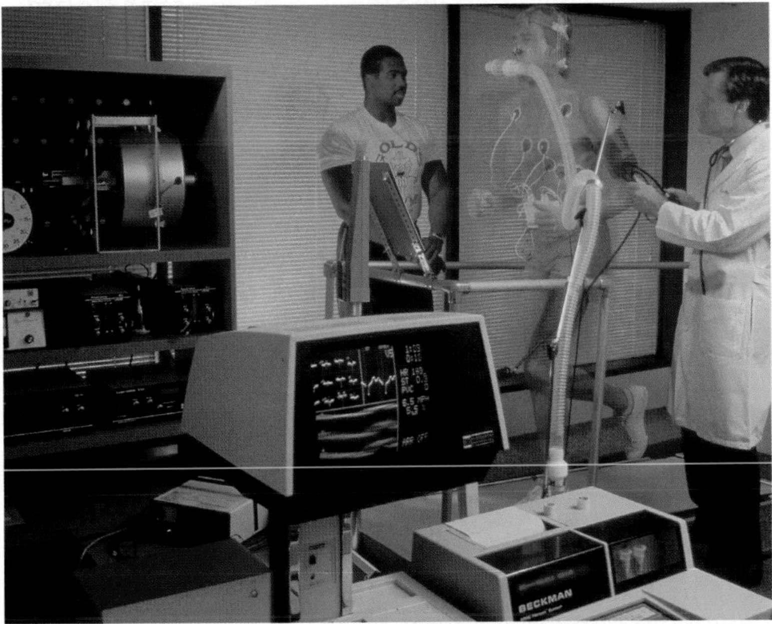

Figure 1.8 *Computers are used to monitor the fitness of sports people*

Key points

- Computerised medical records mean that patient information is up to date and readily available.
- Computers are used in the diagnosis of illness and to monitor a patient's condition.
- Surgeons can perform operations remotely by controlling a robotic arm through the computer mouse.
- Computers are used to monitor the development of new drugs.
- Computers can help to improve the lifestyle of the disabled.
- New treatments/drugs that are available may be denied to some patients because they are too expensive.

Activity

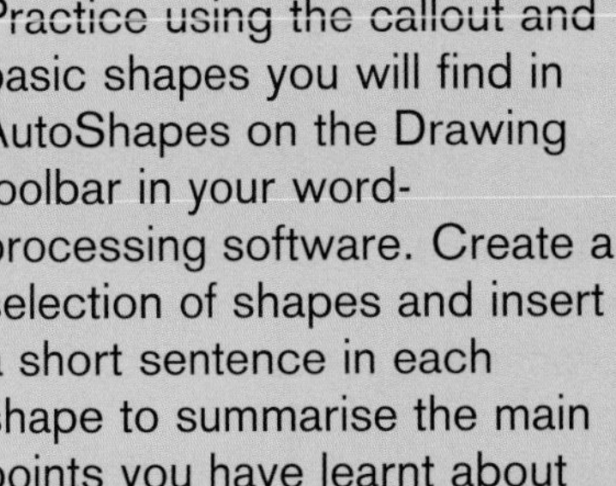

Practice using the callout and basic shapes you will find in AutoShapes on the Drawing toolbar in your word-processing software. Create a selection of shapes and insert a short sentence in each shape to summarise the main points you have learnt about computers and health care.

Computers and leisure

We have seen how the introduction of information technology in the workplace has improved working conditions and productivity. The use of **microprocessors** in domestic equipment to control washing machine and tumble dryer programmes, microwave ovens, central heating systems, etc. means that less time is spent doing household chores. A combination of better pay, more leisure time and lower prices made computers affordable to more and more people and as a result PCs started to appear in homes in the 1980s. The early computers were used mainly for games, word processing or household accounts. As more powerful computers were developed, their potential improved and they are now used for a wide range of activities.

The Internet has probably had the greatest impact on home-computer users. The introduction of digital telephone technology in the form of the **integrated services digital network** (**ISDN**) enabled voice, data and images to be transmitted through a digital line and suddenly the Internet became accessible. The new **asymmetric subscriber digital lines** (**ASDL**) will offer a much faster connection to the Internet and will enable you to receive telephone calls at the same time.

Digital televisions now offer access to the Internet, e-mail, online banking and shopping services, and the latest mobile phones also provide access to selected sites.

In addition to online shopping, the Internet provides a wealth of information in relation to travel and leisure interests. Before you leave home you can programme the on-board car computer to select the best route to avoid traffic jams or view the web cams on local information sites to check on travel conditions. When planning a holiday in the UK or overseas, you can download information about places to visit and make online bookings for travel and hotels. Many tourist locations have permanent cameras linked to a web site which transmit images over the Internet. These cameras are known as web cams and the images they obtain on a regular basis can be viewed through a web page. The regularity might be anything from one second to one hour but as soon as the image is refreshed you get to see it on the web page.

CD-ROMs offer a wide choice of multimedia software designed for leisure interests. Subjects range from games to garden design and from genealogy to German. If you are fortunate enough to have a

Did you know?

Some restaurants use electronic handsets at the table to take your order. Details are sent electronically to the kitchen and your waiter/waitress receives a message back when the meal is ready to be put on the table. This means the waiting staff can spend more time in the restaurant looking after their customers.

Did you know?

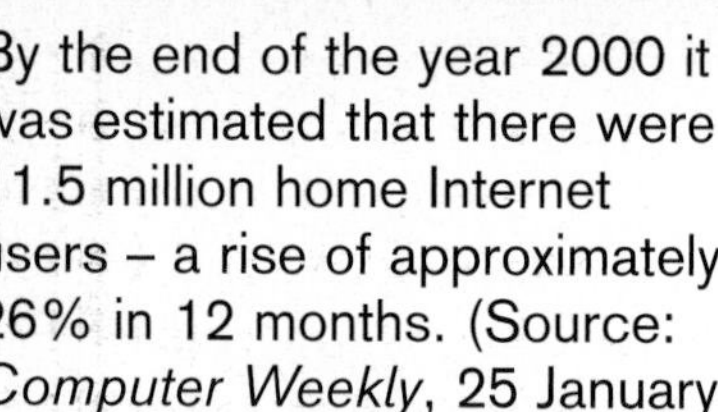

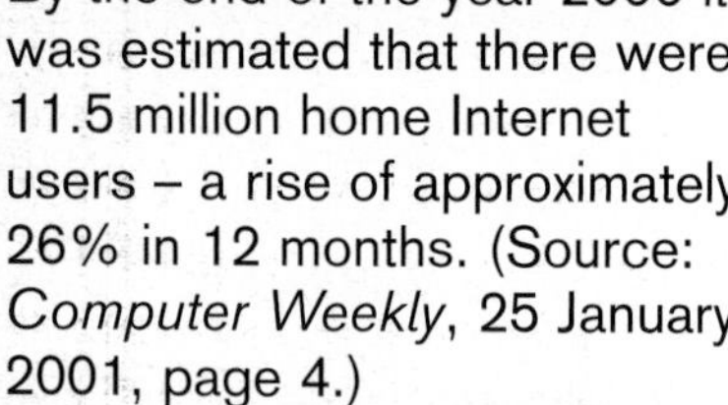

By the end of the year 2000 it was estimated that there were 11.5 million home Internet users – a rise of approximately 26% in 12 months. (Source: *Computer Weekly*, 25 January 2001, page 4.)

Activity

Use the Internet to see what information you can find that relates to a special interest or hobby or a place you hope to visit.

Activity

Start a new file with the heading 'Leisure Time'. Word process approximately half a page describing the use your family might make of a state-of-the-art computer system.

computer at home you might well have a selection of CD-ROMs to help you with your GCSEs.

Some children spend hours and hours at their computers either playing games, e-mailing their friends, logged onto chat lines or surfing the Internet. Many of the games they play contain violence that does not represent normal social behaviour. As a result some children are losing important interactive social skills and are at risk of becoming locked in an isolated cyber world. Lack of exercise means that more children are becoming obese and doctors are predicting that these children are more likely to experience health problems at an earlier age than would normally be expected. Another important issue for parents is control over their children's access to the Internet and we will consider this in more detail later in this chapter.

The use of web cams will make 24-hour security a realistic possibility for home computer users. While parents are at work they will be able to check on their children at home. While people are away from home they will be able to see that their houses are secure.

Key points

- Home computers provide the means to help with study or leisure interests either through CD-ROMs or the Internet.
- Some children risk losing social skills because they spend too long sitting in front of the computer screen.
- Digital televisions and mobile phones offer many Internet services without the need to buy computer equipment.
- Children risk becoming overweight by not spending sufficient time exercising.
- Computers can help plan journeys and check traffic conditions.
- Computers can be used to monitor home security.

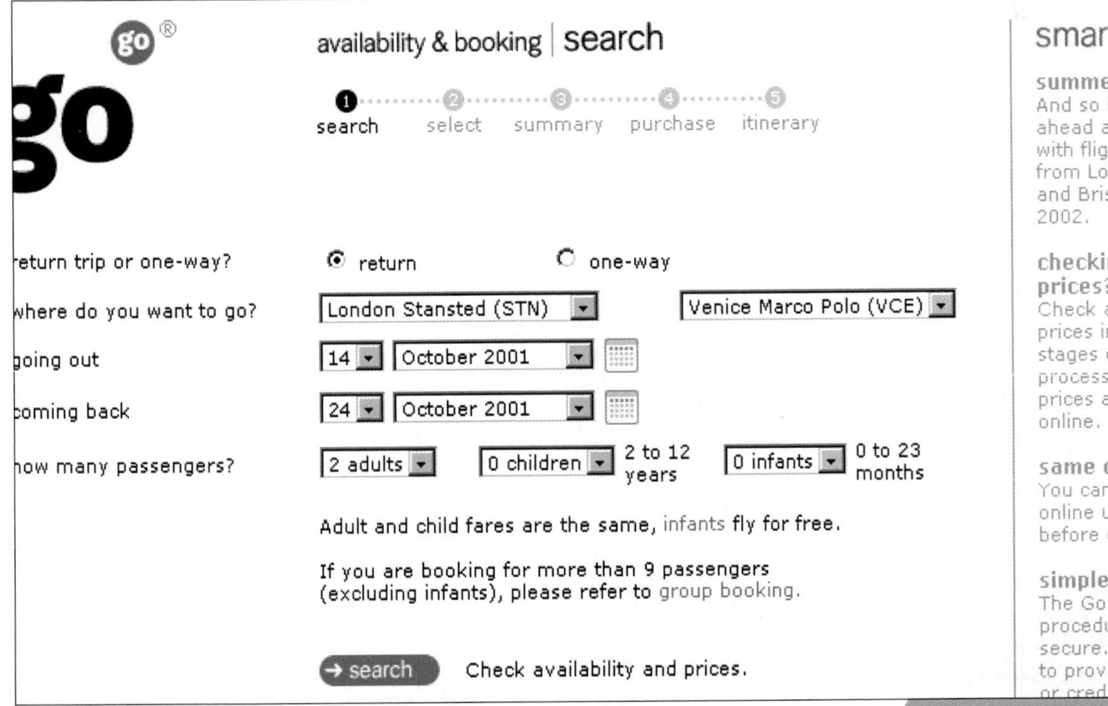

Figure 1.9 *The Internet can be used for obtaining travel information and making travel bookings*

Computers and education

Activity

Visit the BBC web site bbc.co.uk/education/schools/revision and check out the online revision pages that will help you prepare for your forthcoming written examinations. Copy the web addresses into a new data file and save in your revision folder so you can find them easily when you start to revise.

The first computers were introduced to schools in the 1980s. The rapid changes in technology and the cost of upgrading hardware and software means that some schools are still forced to use old, out-of-date equipment that is not sufficiently powerful to run modern software. However, information technology skills are essential if today's students are to compete in the workplace, and the government's wish for all secondary and primary schools to be online is almost realised.

Word-processing, graphic, desktop-publishing and spreadsheet software are widely used in the preparation of school projects and coursework. CD-ROM resources, such as multimedia encyclopaedias containing textual information, pictures, video and sound clips, help children to research school projects.

Computer-aided learning packages mean that students can learn at their own pace and can repeat lessons/exercises as many times as necessary. They also offer students the opportunity to study additional subjects when a specialist teacher is not available. However, learning without the aid of a teacher by sitting at a computer screen can be very boring and could prove to be a demotivating factor for some pupils/students. On the other hand, you might find yourself turning to an online teacher to help you with your homework or revision for your examinations.

Figure 1.10 *Computers are now an essential aid in education*

The Internet is also a valuable source of information for pupils/students when researching projects, but it must be used with caution. A search using suitable key words might bring up thousands of possible links and many of these might be rather dubious. Of course the disadvantage of searching is the amount of time it can take to look at the links, and many of them might be in foreign languages that are of no use at all. The use of a search engine such as

Lycos or Ask Jeeves will usually restrict links to the English language and help save valuable time, but you must be aware of the copyright issue since much information obtained from the Internet is not attributed.

In order to protect pupils from unsuitable web sites (e.g. pornographic) on the Internet, many schools manage their own Intranet sites. An Intranet is similar to the Internet but downloads selected pages only. This provides students/pupils with the opportunity to develop skills in using the Internet and e-mail whilst controlling the material available to them and preventing access to unsuitable sites. Some schools, colleges and businesses, both in the UK and overseas, have established links through the Internet to encourage students to share information and develop contacts with the community.

A trial is underway to develop the virtual classroom. The idea of pupils being able to log on from school and home to sign up for specialist lessons simultaneously, no matter where the teacher is based, is now a reality and your younger brothers and sisters may well experience virtual lessons in the not too distant future. (See *Computer Active*, 28 December 2000, page 6.)

Computers can help partially sighted students by the use of special software, which increases the size of the font to make it easier to read. Voice-activated software and touch-sensitive screens can help disabled students interact with the computer.

Some schools/colleges install entry barriers and issue students with swipe cards, which they must use to gain entry to the premises. This is a security measure to ensure only bona-fide students enter the building. Some schools make students swipe in and out of classrooms to record their attendance at lessons rather than have a register. This provides an instant record of who is at school and enables school welfare officers to check on missing pupils who might be playing truant.

Other schools use registers in conjunction with an **optical mark reader** (**OMR**). The teacher marks the register and the OMR enters attendance data into the computer. This system is not designed to highlight truancy but does provide quick and accurate statistics on student attendance.

Key points

- Computer-aided learning helps students learn at their own pace with increased motivation due to variety.
- School projects can be produced on the computer and research done via CD-ROMs and the Internet.
- Many schools have an Intranet where access to the Internet is restricted to suitable sites.
- Special software can help students with visual or hearing impairment.
- Computer software can reinforce school/college site security and provide accurate information on student attendance.

Activity

Create a 3-column table in your word-processing software with enough rows for the headings of each of the GCSE subjects you are studying. Head the first row as shown below.

GCSE Subject	School/ College	Public Library

Visit your school/college and local libraries and against each subject write down the titles of the CD-ROMs you can find that might be useful to you in researching your coursework.

Computers and government

Activity

The government maintains a very detailed web site that provides information on all aspects of government (www.gov.uk). Look at the web site and see what you can find out about the government. Can you find the Downing Street web site too? From time time to time the prime minister goes live and answers questions on line.

The government is elected to implement policies designed to secure the well-being of us as individuals and collectively as a nation. They oversee education, employment, law and order, defence, transport, trade and industry, the health service, science and technology, etc., and our details are held on computer by many government departments. Computers are used in all official departments for day-to-day business just like any other organisation.

The government is responsible for making sure the country can compete in the global market and they must therefore implement policies to make sure that the United Kingdom is competitive with the outside world.

National Curriculum and IT skills

We have already learnt that today's workforce needs to be multi-skilled and adaptable and the government must ensure that policies are in place to encourage people to acquire the IT skills that are a necessary part of their working lives. Information technology has been part of the National Curriculum for several years and the introduction of IT key skills as a compulsory part of the post-16 school curriculum is one way of trying to ensure that young people are equipped for the future.

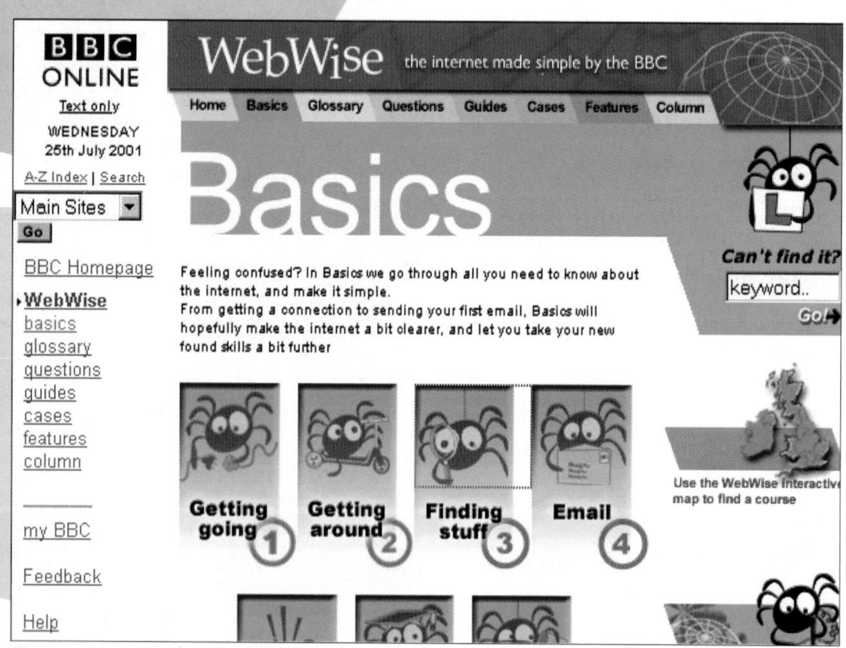

Figure 1.11 *The BBC helps beginners to learn how to use the Internet*

Adult learners are encouraged to learn IT through government-funded campaigns. For example, 'Computers don't Bite' and 'WebWize' are campaigns that have been advertised and run in conjunction with the BBC aimed at introducing beginners to computers and the Internet. Additional funding in the form of Learning Accounts is also available for students to attend courses to learn IT skills.

Another initiative to help families on lower incomes keep up to date with information technology is to provide cheap, reconditioned computer machines for those in receipt of benefit in order to bridge the gap between those who know about or use computers and those who don't.

Legislation

The government must ensure that legislation keeps pace with technology and over the last few years several new laws have been introduced to reflect society's use of information technology – see page 20.

Some government policies can be controversial. The decision to introduce plastic credit-card-type driving licences is seen by some as a first step towards national identity cards. The addition of a microchip would enable personal information such as a National Insurance number and medical details to be stored. This is viewed by some as an intrusion on civil liberty, whilst others believe ID cards would be a deterrent to crimes such as credit card fraud and benefit fraud.

This is just a glimpse at the responsibility the government has in the world of information technology. You must listen, read and ask questions to make sure you keep your knowledge up to date with current government initiatives as you prepare for your GCSEs.

Into the Future

The rapid growth in information technology means that to survive in the global economy of the 21st century we must all be multi-skilled and adaptable. In business today every worker from a junior data entry clerk to top management must be computer literate.

Whilst many traditional jobs have been lost, a new order of IT specialists has been created. These specialists can command very high salaries but, in spite of this, there is a serious shortage of e-commerce skills within the workforce. Some data processing, such as airline ticketing, is being outsourced to countries like India where there is a large qualified graduate workforce and where wages are much lower and therefore costs are cheaper. To overcome this shortfall, employers are being forced to look overseas to recruit qualified software engineers willing to work in the United Kingdom.

Activity

- In your word-processing software, create a new document headed 'The Government and Computers'.
- In half a page summarise the contents of this section and in the time leading up to your GCSE exam, add brief notes about any new government initiatives for information technology.

Key points

- Detailed records are held by government departments on all UK citizens.
- The government must ensure that legislation keeps pace with technology and that suitable laws are in place to protect individuals and organisations.
- Policies designed to ensure the United Kingdom is competitive in the global market must be implemented.
- Initiatives must be undertaken to ensure that IT skills are available to everyone.
- Some initiatives are controversial.

Computers, crime and the law 1

Did you know ?

Computers played an important part in helping to solve a recent murder case by providing the final piece of evidence needed to convict the suspect.
By checking credit card transactions police were able to prove that the suspect had bought petrol near the scene of the crime, even though he had denied being in the vicinity.

Did you know ?

One computer recently stolen from a car contained the medical records of a member of the Royal Family and another held important military secrets. In both cases the computers were eventually returned intact but we cannot be sure that copies of the data have not been made with the intent to use the information maliciously sometime in the future.

Rising crime

Computers have proved to be a valuable tool for the police in solving crimes. All the evidence is stored on a computer database. In addition, details of stolen vehicles, known criminals, their methods of operation, finger printing and DNA profiling, etc. are also recorded, and sophisticated analysis of the data can provide new leads which might result in eventual prosecution and conviction. Police computers are able to link those of other government departments together with Interpol to reconstruct the activities of known criminals they suspect are engaged in criminal activities.

Many town centres now have elaborate computer-controlled camera systems installed that help to detect and prevent crime. Speed cameras at the roadside record the registration numbers of speeding vehicles and automatically generate fixed penalty notices to the registered keepers of the offending vehicles by matching the numbers with the DVLA database.

Whilst using computers to help solve crime, the police also have to deal with crime arising as a result of computers. Theft of computer chips is growing at an alarming rate because chips are in short supply. In 18 months from the end of 1999, computer chips to the value of £18 million were stolen in the south-east of England alone.

Now that so many people have laptop computers we often hear of theft from cars – perhaps the back seat of a car is not the most sensible place to leave a laptop computer on display in an unattended vehicle!

Figure 1.12 *You need to take precautions against computer theft*

Internet crime

Internet crime is difficult to combat as the Internet is global and is not governed by the laws of any one country.

There is no control over the material that is posted on the Internet and it is impossible to prevent illegal material from appearing, for example pornography, racist material and political propaganda. However, certain measures can be taken.

- The use of online surveillance software is helping to track down people who use the Internet to peddle illegal material.
- A software robot can search newsgroups, chat rooms and web listings and follow a trail back to the source.
- An Internet scanner can uncover illegal pictures by recognising specific pixels and comparing them with files on a database. The software can scan servers to trace the person who downloaded the files.

Filtering software can offer some protection although any form of governmental control would be extremely difficult to enforce and the very high costs would inevitably fall to Internet users through their Internet service providers.

Consumers have little protection from rogue Internet traders who pose as legitimate businesses, take money from customers over the Internet and then fail to deliver the goods.

Hackers

We have become aware of computer **hackers** through their efforts to gain unauthorised access to computers and the files stored on them. Many hackers just want to try and outwit the authorities as a form of protest – in 1996 Tony Blair was given what has now become a well known facelift on the British Labour Party web site.

In this case the intent was mischievous but sometimes it is malicious, posing threats to national security. The United States web site owned by NASA (National Aeronautics and Space Administration) is thought to be one of the most targeted sites with an estimated 500,000 hacks in 1999–2000 (see *Computer Active*, 16 November 2000, page 19).

By contrast, some hackers are now employed legitimately by large organisations to test their computer security. The ex-hackers are actually paid to try and break into the systems!

Did you know ?

In the early 1990s a Russian called Vladimir Levin gained access to Citibank's computer and carried out an international bank robbery over the Internet. He obtained a list of customer bank accounts and passwords and transferred several million dollars to his own accounts.

Did you know ?

A team of 'cybercops' is being established in the UK whose purpose is solely to investigate Internet crime (see *Computer Active*, 14–27 December 2000, page 8) and a squad of police officers with expertise in IT has recently concluded a two-year investigation, painstakingly deciphering computer code in order to break up a ring of paedophiles and secure prison convictions. This operation relied on the close co-operation of police throughout the world.

Key points

- Computers help the police in crime detection.
- Theft of computer chips is a serious problem.
- Internet crime is very difficult to detect because no one country runs the Internet and success hinges on the co-operation of police forces worldwide.

Computers, crime and the law 2

Legislation

The increased use of computers and the new crimes that ensued demonstrated that existing laws were not sufficiently able to deal with the offences. Some contained too many loopholes or maximum sentences that could be imposed did not reflect the seriousness of the crime. As a result new laws have been passed or existing laws amended to address the situation. The relevant acts are summarised below.

- The **Copyright, Designs and Patents Act of 1988** was designed to protect the work of authors, artists and composers from being reproduced without permission. The Act was in existence before computers were widely used but it was extended to include computer software, to prohibit you or anyone else from making illegal (unlicensed) copies.

  European copyright lasts for 70 years after the death of an author or composer.

  The American courts acted to protect music copyright in the case of the Napster web site where music was freely exchanged over the Internet resulting in composers and songwriters losing royalty payments on their compositions. The courts closed down the web site and it is likely that exchange of music will in future be through subscription sites so that money can be raised to pay royalties to the composers.
- The **Computer Misuse Act of 1990** was established to deal with misuse of computer systems because existing laws were inadequate. Its primary purpose was to act as a deterrent to would-be hackers and those intent on planting computer viruses.
- The **Data Protection Act 1998** is an extension and strengthening of the first Data Protection Act of 1984 which was set up to take account of the increasing amount of personal data being held on computers and the potential misuse of that data.

  The Data Protection Act is a statutory code of data protection good practice designed to protect individuals whose personal data is held on computerised records by organisations. It requires companies to register with the Data Protection Commissioner and restricts the data they can hold. Individuals have a right to see the data held on them and to have it corrected if inaccurate. In

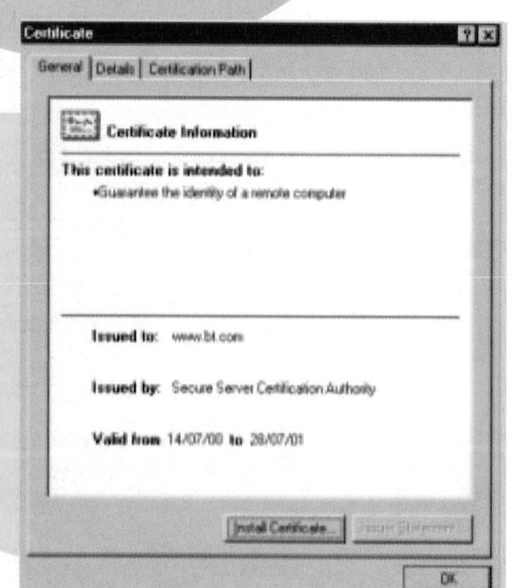

Figure 1.13 *A digital certificate in use by BT*

addition, the new Act gives individuals the right to know who is processing data and why, and prevents data users using the data for direct marketing.

Companies holding computerised data have a duty under the law to ensure that the data remains confidential and must also ensure that information is not disclosed, however, innocently.

- The **Electronic Communications Act 2000** was set up to provide security systems for those who send and receive electronic data. The need came about because of the increasing amount of e-business being carried out over the Internet. Firstly, if you send confidential data over the Internet you need to be sure that if the message is intercepted it cannot be read or tampered with, and secondly, if you receive an electronic communication you need to be sure that the sender is genuine.

  This is managed by a system of **cryptography**, which involves creating and using secure data encryption codes. Coded messages have been in use for many years. Simple codes might merely substitute letters for numbers or replace letters with alternatives. For example, information technology could be coded as 'jogpsnbujpo ufdiopmphz'. Can you work out, or break, the code?

The data encryption codes are generated by cryptography service providers who provide what are known as 'digital certificates'.

Ask your teachers for a more detailed handout about legislation from the Tutor's File.

Figure 1.14 *Confidential information must be protected against misuse*

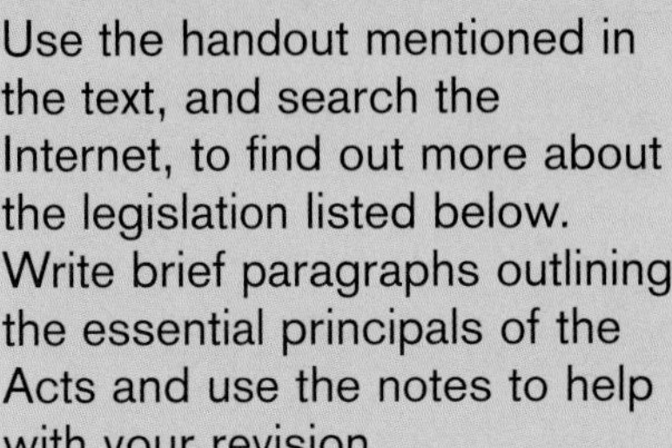

Activity

Use the handout mentioned in the text, and search the Internet, to find out more about the legislation listed below. Write brief paragraphs outlining the essential principals of the Acts and use the notes to help with your revision.

- Copyright, Designs and Patents Act of 1988.
- Computer Misuse Act of 1990.
- Data Protection Act 1998
- Electronic Communications Act 2000.

Add additional paragraphs to the page if you learn about any new legislation in the coming months.

Key points

- The Copyright, Designs and Patents Act of 1988 was extended to prohibit the illegal copying of software.
- The Computer Misuse Act of 1990 was established primarily to deal with hackers.
- The Data Protection Act 1998 was designed to protect individuals from misuse of data held about them on computer systems.
- The Electronic Communications Act 2000 has been established to create a secure system for the transmission of electronic messages.

Security 1

Activity

Talk to any grown-ups you know who use computers at work to try and find out the sort of security measures their companies employ to protect their systems. Produce a diagram similar to ours on page 25 to show how computer systems can be protected.

Security of computer systems is a major issue because not only is the equipment itself extremely valuable but also the data within the system. In fact it can be argued that the data is even more valuable because it can be difficult or impossible to replace, whereas the hardware and software is replaceable. Threats to computer security come from a variety of sources and can affect both hardware and software.

Theft

The most obvious threat is theft of computer equipment and peripheral devices such as microchips, keyboards, printers or even floppy disks. Most organisations now restrict access to buildings and issue staff with photo-identity cards which must be shown or swiped in order to gain entry. Visitors are usually required to sign in and wear a visitor's ID card. Once within the building some internal doors are kept locked and can be opened only by the use of swipe cards or alarmed keypads. Sometimes computers themselves are also alarmed.

System security

You will find that most companies use a system of login IDs and passwords and that many systems automatically call for changes to passwords at regular intervals. This is to ensure that passwords remain confidential and also to restrict unauthorised access should somebody have found a way into the system.

A database manager will have the responsibility for managing a large and complex system and for making sure that data is accurate, up-to-date and secure. The design of the database might restrict access so that only relevant information is available to database users. In addition, management of the system will ensure that only certain staff are able to enter or amend data in the system whilst others will be able to read it but not change it.

Some databases have time-restricted access that limits the time the user has to find information. Special software can be used to provide an audit trail to show which user has logged on to which files and for how long. This is a way of checking whether anyone has accessed information to which he or she is not authorised.

Did you know?

There are offices fitted out with complete computer systems that remain empty and unused but ready to function in an emergency. Every couple of years the computer systems are ripped out, even though they might have never been used, and replaced with the most up-to-date machines.

Security of data in transmission can be ensured by encryption, which means the data is coded before it is transmitted.

When you use your school or college computer system do you log on with a special number and password? When you enter your password it is almost certainly coded and you see a series of asterisks on screen ******. This is known as data encryption and the reason for this is to make sure nobody learns your password, so they cannot access your data files – in other words to keep your data secure.

When choosing a password it is important you choose something you will remember but not something that is too obvious to someone else. If somebody wanted to get into your account the first words they would try would almost certainly be your name, that of your favourite football team or pop star, etc. So remember – keep your password a secret and make sure you choose something you won't forget!

Staff

When a new member of staff is employed, references should be checked to ensure the applicant is genuine. Someone with a spiteful intent could try and gain employment in order to breach system security in some way.

Natural disasters

A natural disaster such as flooding is a potential threat that can be avoided by siting mainframe computer equipment away from basement or low-lying areas. Fire cannot always be prevented but the use of fire alarms and the provision of fire extinguishers can help to reduce risks.

Other disasters, such as explosion, might render the whole building unsafe and organisations must have contingency plans in place to ensure they can resume their business in alternative premises without delay. This is one reason for keeping backup tapes and disks in disaster-proof safes off the premises. Failure to do this would mean they could not continue trading and every hour they are not trading they are losing money.

Key points

- Threats to system security can come from inside and outside an organisation.
- Computer hardware and software are both at risk from theft.
- Organisations have a legal responsibility to ensure their systems are secure.

Activity

Look round your school or college and see what security systems are in place to protect the computer hardware and software. For example, access to the building, school office and computer rooms. Is the network set up with read-only drives? If so, why do you think this is?

Start a new document with the heading 'Security'. Word process a short report describing the systems you have observed and suggest any improvements you think could be made.

Security 2

Hackers

We have already reflected on computer hacking (refer to page 19) and have seen that determined hackers manage to get into what we would expect to be the most secure systems. As a result, organisations take active measures to ensure their systems are safe and are constantly striving to keep one step ahead of the hackers.

Viruses

Computer viruses are one of the most important risks to data security. A computer **virus** is a program written specifically to attack computer software. It can infect a system in various ways:

- by downloading software from the Internet
- from an attachment to an e-mail
- by transfer from one computer to another via a floppy disk
- by using pirate software which might be unreliable.

One of the dangers the web has introduced is the speed with which malicious programs or viruses proliferate via e-mail. There is usually no evidence that a virus is in the system until things start to go wrong. For this reason some organisations treat the risks very seriously, controlling e-mails being sent and received over the Internet and disallowing staff from taking disks between work and home and vice versa. Anti-virus software is therefore essential. It works by scanning files to detect and remove viruses from hard and floppy disks. The process of removing a virus is known as 'disinfecting'.

If you transfer data between your computer at school or college and your computer at home it would be wise to check that your anti-virus software is up to date. New viruses are continually being devised and they could miss detection by out-of-date anti-virus software. Remember that write-protecting your disks will help prevent the transfer of a virus to your equipment. Write-protecting will not prevent you reading data from the disk but will prevent anything being written to it. Additionally, back up regularly so that you can reinstall corrupt files.

Access to the Internet

The Internet can provide a valuable source of information to children but at the same time it can expose them to unsuitable sites.

Web software such as the family edition of Norton Internet Utility or Cybersitter can limit the sites accessible to children by applying blocking and filtering techniques. Blocking prevents access to specific web addresses and filtering refuses access to sites with key words. Another precaution parents sometimes take is to put a time limit on Internet access.

Activity

What can be done to protect a computer system from the threats illustrated on this page?

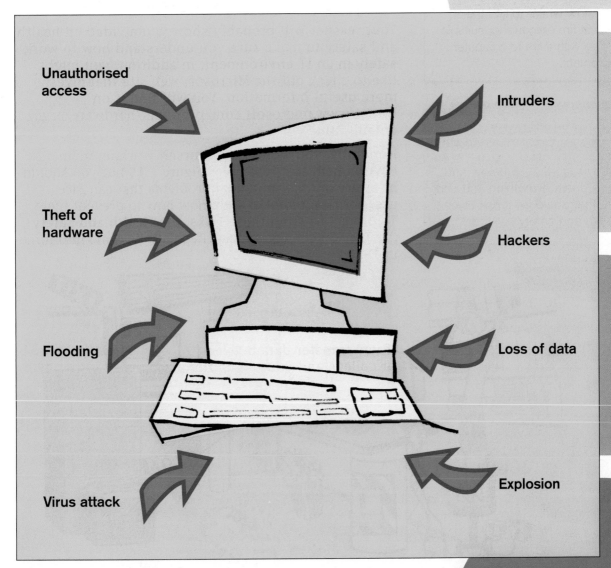

Figure 1.15 *Some of the threats to a computer system*

Health and safety 1

Whilst you are at school or college you are expected to behave in a way that does not harm yourself or your friends. Similarly, your school or college has a responsibility to maintain health and safety standards in order to ensure your well-being. For example, the computer equipment you use must be checked to prevent electrical faults and fire drills must be held to ensure everyone knows what to do in an emergency.

These responsibilities continue when you go to work and the Health and Safety at Work Act 1974 (HASAWA) and the Control of Substances Hazardous to Health Act 1989 (COSHH) require all employers to ensure that your place of work is a safe environment.

Your teacher will probably show you a video on health and safety to make sure you understand how to work safely in an IT environment. In addition, you might like to check out the Microsoft web site that gives more useful information. You will find it on http://www.microsoft.com/products/hardware/ergo/default.htm.

Hopefully, you won't find yourself working in an environment that resembles Figure 1.15 but you should be aware of other potential problems that can face users of IT equipment and know how to prevent them. To protect us from these risks, the Health and Safety (Display Screen Equipment) Regulations came into force in 1992.

Did you know ?

Different types of fire extinguisher should be used to extinguish fires in different situations. Make sure you know where to find the nearest fire extinguisher suitable to deal with a fire to computer equipment.

Activity

Study Figure 1.16 below and write down everything you can see that could be a risk to health and safety.

Figure 1.16 *Risks to health and safety*

The Display Screen Equipment Regulations specify regulations relating to the use of display screen equipment and lay down standards that must be adopted. The employer must carry out a regular analysis of workstations in order to ensure employees are operating in a safe environment. The employee in turn should use the workstation correctly and inform the employer of any problems so that they can be corrected.

Stress

Computers are often blamed for the increasing stress levels found in the workplace and indeed for many people the introduction of IT systems has been very worrying, especially if they haven't been trained to use the equipment or reassured about the security of their jobs. Some workers have a fear of computers and others fear that productivity will be monitored and, if they underperform, their jobs will be at risk. The software provided should enable workers to complete their work efficiently without presenting unnecessary problems or obstacles.

Laptop computers, mobile phones and pagers can all contribute to stress and make it difficult for workers to get any respite from the pressures of work. It is not an uncommon sight to see executives on train journeys conducting business conversations on their mobile phones or tapping away at their laptop computers. The train journey gives time away from the interruptions at the office and is viewed by some as an extension of their working day, leading many to become workaholics, i.e. unable to stop working. The problem is exacerbated by 'information overload' as workers are swamped with more information than they need.

Figure 1.17 *Today, the 'office' can be anywhere*

Did you know?

Some call centre workers are developing symptoms of a new industrial injury known as acoustic shock, where they experience sudden loud noises, pain, hearing loss or dizziness when using headsets. Headsets that filter out noise are being recommended to alleviate the problem.

Health and safety 2

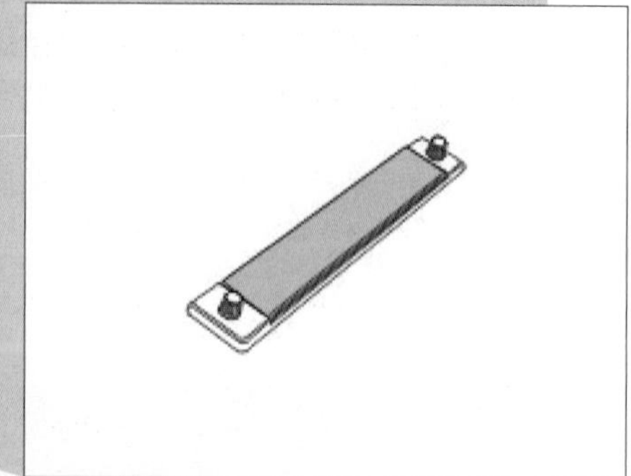

Figure 1.18 *Examples of health and safety aids for computer operators*

Eyestrain

Sitting in front of a VDU all day can pose the threat of eyestrain or headaches, however follow simple guidelines and you can reduce potential problems in the future.

- The office should be well lit with blinds at windows to keep the sun off screens and reduce glare. The ideal position for the computer is at right angles to a window and anti-glare shields should be available if required.
- Lighting should offer a contrast between the screen and surrounding area. If the light is too dim, documents will be hard to read.
- The image on the screen should be stable and should not flicker and the brightness and contrast should be adjustable.
- The screen should tilt and swivel and be positioned approximately an arm's length away.
- A copyholder at screen level will make it easier for the operator to move eyes from copy to screen and changes in activity will enable him/her to take his/her eyes off the screen and adjust the focus.
- The employer should offer free and regular eye tests to VDU operators.

Backache

Bad posture is the main cause of backache. There are guidelines that will help to reduce the risk of this.

- Operators should not be expected to work continuously at a VDU without regular breaks – ideally a 5–10 minute break away from the screen after an hour's continuous screen or keyboard work.
- The chair must be stable and allow the user freedom of movement.
- The seat should be adjustable in height so that the operator's eyes are level with the top of the screen and the backrest should also be adjustable in height and tilt.
- A footrest should be provided, if necessary, so that the operator's feet are supported if they don't reach the floor.
- Some form of exercise during lunch breaks (e.g. a walk to the local shops) is a sensible way to help prevent or relieve backache.

- Desks should be at the correct height and have sufficient space for the computer, mouse mat, telephone, and supporting documents and the desktop should be non-reflective.
- There should be enough space for the operator to change positions and vary movements.

Repetitive strain injury (RSI)

RSI is the name given to disorders resulting from repeated movements. It is not a new disease and has affected workers performing repetitive movements for many years. Symptoms can affect the neck, shoulders and upper limbs, cause numbness and tingling in the arms and hands, and in severe cases some sufferers cannot even lift a kettle or pour a cup of tea without suffering unbearable pain.

To reduce the risk of RSI, certain measures should be followed.

- Keyboards should be separate from the VDU and should be tiltable.
- The keyboard should have a matt surface and the symbols on the keys must be contrasted and legible.
- A wrist rest can be used to support the wrists.
- Ergonomic keyboards have been designed that place the hands at a more natural angle than the standard keyboard to help reduce the risk of RSI (see page 36).

Radiation

Evidence suggests that the radiation emitted from a VDU is less than that found in natural sources. From time to time concerns have been expressed that pregnant women are at risk of miscarriage as a result of radiation from VDUs but there is no conclusive medical evidence to support this. However, shields can be fitted to offer protection.

Remember

When you get into the driving seat of a car you automatically check your seat and mirrors before driving away. Get into a similar habit of checking your working position by adjusting your chair and screen before you start work at the computer.

Key points

- The Health and Safety at Work Act 1974 (HASAWA) and the Control of Substances Hazardous to Health Act 1989 (COSHH) make organisations responsible for maintaining a safe working environment.
- You are responsible for ensuring your actions do not cause hazards to your fellow students or workers.
- The Display Screen Regulations of 1992 lay down standards that should be adopted to ensure users of IT equipment are not at risk.

Activity

Design a poster for your computer room highlighting the safety measures computer users should take to look after their health.

Computers and ethics

Activity

Look at the Code of Ethics and Professional Conduct on the British Computer Society web site on www.bcs.org.uk.

If you run the word 'ethics' through the thesaurus in your word-processing software you will probably come up with a selection of words including:

- principles
- morals
- moral principles
- moral values.

Ethics is therefore a judgement of whether human behaviour is 'good' or 'bad' or 'right' or 'wrong'.

Computer ethics is an area of research and study that has evolved as a result of the dependency society has on ICT. Throughout this chapter we have seen how the use of computer technology has changed the way we work, shop, bank, learn, spend our leisure time, receive medical treatment, etc. We have also seen how new legislation has been needed to protect society from criminal activities that have arisen as a result of computer technology. The resulting issues don't always have answers but frequently raise a series of questions.

- Teleworking or home working can be expected to reduce pollution and road congestion but what effect will it have on the home environment? Can families afford to give up a habitable room for the office? If you are working at home and a social caller comes to the door should you ignore him/her as you would if you were out at work?
- The use of e-mail has revolutionised communication. Should employees be afforded the same degree of privacy as they have when using the telephone or should employers have the right to view their e-mail?
- The introduction of computer-aided learning packages means that students can learn at their own pace. However, students need to have some degree of computer literacy to use this material. Does this raise a question of equal opportunity? Is the material only to be made available to students who can use or have access to a computer? Cultural issues also arise. Students in school are frequently taught by teachers from a similar cultural background. Does this mean that computer-aided learning packages produced in the UK are not suitable for students from other cultures, e.g. Africa?

- A vast amount of data held on computers is about individuals. It is possible to track a person's activities by looking at credit card transactions, cash machine withdrawals, online ticket bookings and even CCTV footage. Is this an invasion of privacy? Who should have access to data stored about us?

Most professions have a code of ethics or standards that set out acceptable professional behaviour. The Code of Ethics and Professional Conduct laid down by the British Computer Society lists a number of 'rules' or 'standards' that IT professionals should follow in relation to public interest, their duty to employers, clients and to the profession.

What sort of ethical dilemmas might you find yourself faced with either now, whilst you are at school/college, or in the future when you go to work?

- Who would know that the essay you just handed in with your name on the bottom wasn't your work at all, but something you found on a disk left in one of the school computers?
- What does it matter if you use the office e-mail system to send the odd message in connection with a small business you run in your spare time?
- Why not make a copy of the graphics software on the college computer system to put on your home computer – after all you will be using it for college work?
- Will anyone know you are using the Internet to look for cheap airline flights rather than helping to clear the backlog of invoices?
- Your employer has been called out of the office and left his computer on with a confidential document on screen about a reorganisation in which your best friend looks likely to lose his job. Should you tell him?

It probably occurred to you as you read through this list that some of the actions were definitely wrong (and in some cases illegal) and that others were rather unsociable or unacceptable. As a general rule, your own conscience will direct you to the most appropriate course of action. If you ask yourself 'how would I feel if that was done to me' or think about the effect your action might have on someone else, you will generally come to the right decision.

What you have learnt in this chapter should help you to understand how society is managing the changes brought upon it by the information age.

Key points

- Computer ethics refers to a professional code of conduct that ensures we use computers in an acceptable way.

Test your understanding

Are the following statements True or False?

1 The introduction of ICT systems in offices has resulted in many people losing their jobs.

2 All computers must be fitted with an anti-glare screen.

3 It doesn't matter if software is a bit slow providing it does the job.

4 I cannot pick up a virus from my friend's computer if I use a new disk.

5 A computer hacker is given access to a company's computer system.

6 Bank branches are closing because more and more people are using remote banking systems.

7 Radiation emitted from VDUs is the same as that found in natural sources.

Fill in the gaps using the words below:

Videoconferencing web cam
CAD processing e-mail robots
database controlled

8 Information traditionally saved in paper-based filing systems is now held on a computerised ________________.

9 ________________ enables meetings to be held with delegates in different locations at the same time.

10 ________________ have replaced the jobs of manual workers and can work 24 hours a day in hazardous conditions producing goods of a consistent quality.

11 A journalist can ________________ his report from anywhere in the world.

12 A ________________ transmits images which can be viewed through a web site.

13 An architect uses ________________ software to produce clear, detailed drawings quickly and accurately.

14 Many town centres use computer ________________ camera systems.

15 Paper–based data input is undertaken by a data ________________ operator.

Multiple choice questions

16 An office making full use of automated systems might be referred to as:
a) an automatic office
b) a teleworking office
c) an electronic office
d) a computer literate office.

17 A company is running a software product on a computer network but only has a single user licence. Is the company:
a) in breach of data protection legislation
b) in breach of confidentiality
c) in breach of copyright
d) in breach of electronic communications legislation?

18 Data encryption is a system of:
a) scrambling messages
b) protecting copyright
c) removing computer viruses
d) sending e-mails.

19 VDU operators can avoid potential posture problems by:
a) using an anti-glare shield
b) adjusting the angle of the keyboard
c) adjusting the height and back support of their chair
d) keeping their desk clear.

20 The information age:
a) has affected the way old computers function
b) means that only people over the age of 16 can use the Internet
c) is where we store information about dates of birth
d) has significantly changed the way we work and spend our leisure time.

CHAPTER 2

Hardware and software

Figure 2.1 *A typical computer system*

In this chapter we are going to look at the make-up of a typical computer system and the ways that both the system and the data on the system can be protected.

A computer system is made up of several different components. Those that can be seen and touched are referred to as the hardware and those that can't be seen or touched are known as the software.

The components fall into categories that reflect the role they play in the overall system and can be summarised as:

- input devices that get data into the computer
- the main processor unit that manipulates the data
- the storage devices that save the data
- the output devices that display the data in soft or hard copy
- the operating system software that manages the running of the computer
- the applications software or programs that you use in the course of the day.

As you work through this chapter you will have a better understanding of the technical terminology – or jargon – used to describe these components and you will be able to select the appropriate hardware and software to meet the needs of different computer users.

Hardware

Pete and Sandra Wellings have been using two rather outdated stand-alone computers at Greenfingers Garden Centre over the last few years. They have been using the following equipment:

- Keyboard
- Mouse
- Central processing unit
- Monitor
- Printer
- Floppy disks.

These are the components of their system and they can be divided into four different categories:

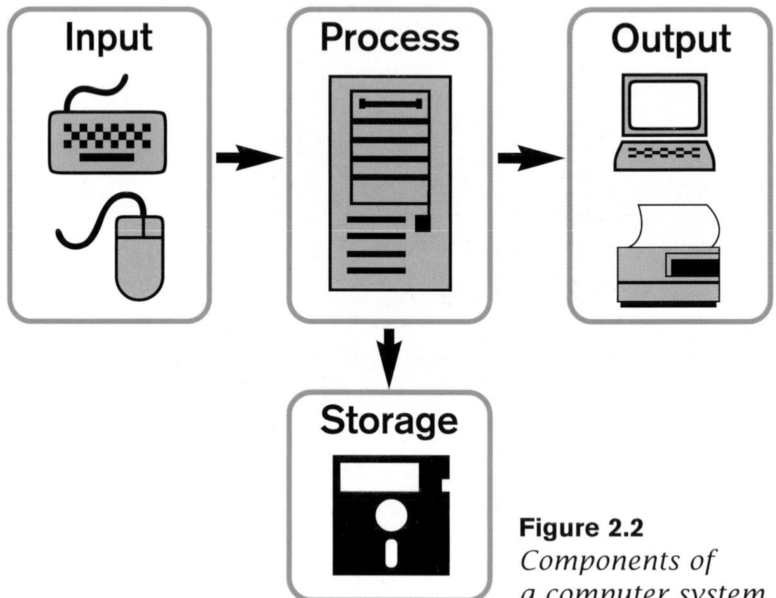

Figure 2.2
Components of a computer system

This is how it works.

1 Pete and Sandra input or feed data or instructions into the computer through the keyboard and mouse. For example, they type letters and words and then use the mouse to select an icon such as Print.
2 The central processing unit receives these instructions from the keyboard or mouse and acts on them, or processes them.
3 As a result of these processes the text is displayed on the screen or a copy is printed out. In other words, the results of the original actions are output to the screen or printer.
4 If Pete and Sandra wish to retrieve the text at a later date, they can store the data on the system hard drive or floppy disk.

This is known as the information processing cycle and all computer systems function in a similar way.

Input

Input devices enable you to enter data, commands and programs into the computer's central processing unit (CPU), its brain. The input devices you are most likely to come into contact with are:

- Keyboard
- Mouse
- Tracker ball
- Graphics tablet
- Scanner
- Digital camera
- Touch screen
- Optical mark reader
- Optical character reader
- Bar code scanner
- Magnetic stripe reader
- Microphone.

Process

The main processing unit of the computer system is housed in a case. Casings usually come in the form of a tower, mini tower or desktop case.

Located within the casing are the various components that link all parts of the computer system together. Each component has an important job to do and we will look at:

- Central processing unit
- Motherboard
- Ports
- Modem
- Network card
- Memory
- Disk drives.

Output

When you enter text through the keyboard or select a function through an icon or pull-down menu with the mouse, you usually see the result of your action on the computer screen. The computer screen outputs the result of the instructions that have been input into the system.

However, the screen is only one of a variety of output devices you are likely to come into contact with. These include:

- Monitor
- Printer
- Plotter
- Speakers
- Motors.

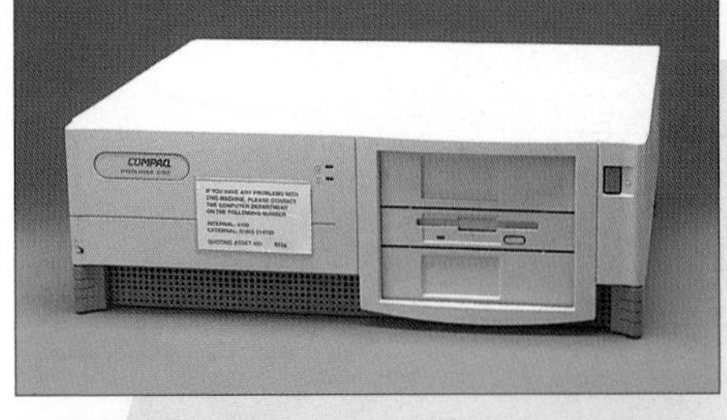

Figure 2.3 *Main processing units*

Input devices 1

Figure 2.4 *Traditonal keyboard and ergononic keyboard*

Keyboard

The **keyboard** is the most widely used input device and is used to enter data or commands to the computer. Touching or pressing a key sends an electronic signal to the computer which it interprets as a character or function.

A computer keyboard is similar to an ordinary typewriter keyboard but has extra keys for specialised functions. It is divided into four main areas:

- Function keys across the top.
- Letter keys in the main section.
- A numeric keypad on the right.
- Cursor movement and editing keys between the main section and the numeric keypad.

The standard layout of most typewriters and keyboards is called the QWERTY layout. The name comes from the first six keys on the top row of the alphabetic characters.

Some keyboards come with added keys for using the Internet and others have an integrated wrist support. Ergonomic keyboards have been developed to reduce the risk of repetitive strain injury to workers who use keyboards for long periods of time. Keys rely on finger pressure rather than hand movement and the keyboard has been split in two sections so that users' wrists are in a more natural and comfortable position.

Concept keyboard

You probably used a concept keyboard whilst at your primary school. It consists of a plastic surface where keys are replaced by designated areas which are programmed to input commands into the computer. Overlays are put on the keyboard with symbols to indicate the areas, and the commands are activated by pressure.

The concept keyboard is ideal for the young or disabled who cannot manipulate the standard keyboard and is useful in situations where, for example, dirt or liquids could damage a conventional keyboard. Some well-known fast-food outlets use concept keyboards to take your order. Next time you buy a hamburger watch the assistant select your choice by pressing the printed overlay.

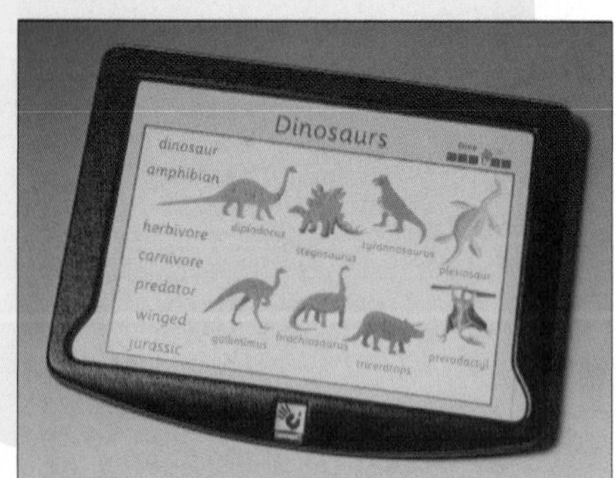

Figure 2.5 *Concept keyboard*

Mouse

Figure 2.6 *A computer mouse*

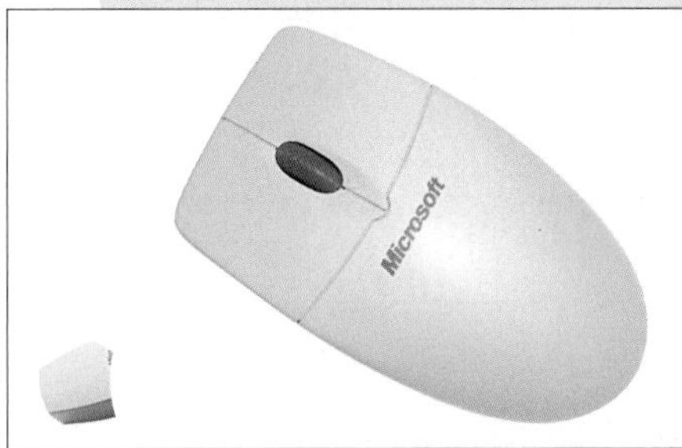

Figure 2.7 *Cordless mouse*

A **mouse** is a device that enables you to control the movement and position of the on-screen cursor by moving it around on the desk. To select an item you position the mouse pointer and press one of the mouse buttons. This produces a 'mouse click'. You might have heard the expressions 'double click', 'click and drag' and 'drag and drop'.

The standard mouse comprises casing, buttons and a base. The casing is designed to be held between the fingers and thumb of one hand with the bottom of the palm resting on a mat or other surface. The top generally has one or two buttons and most now have an added wheel for scrolling or zooming. Clicking the left or right mouse buttons offers a choice of different functions. The bottom is flat and has a 'multidirectional detection device', usually a rubber ball. Using a mouse mat gives you better control. When dust and dirt collect on the rubber ball clean it with a damp cotton bud.

There are alternative, more technologically advanced, designs of mouse available. For example, a mouse has been developed where the rubber ball has been replaced with an optical sensor that detects motion on the desktop. A tiny digital camera takes up to 1,500 pictures per second of the surface beneath the mouse and these pictures are translated into movement of the cursor on the screen. You don't need a mouse mat because the sensor works on most non-reflective surfaces – even your lap – and as there are no moving parts the mouse moves smoothly.

The cordless mouse relies on digital radio technology to send signals to a digital receiver. Radio waves enable communication with the CPU from a distance range of up to two metres regardless of any obstacles which might be in the way.

Activity

Experiment with your mouse and see what happens when you left click, double click, right click or double right click on the following parts of the screen in your word-processing software.

- Title bar
- Menu bar
- Toolbars
- Horizontal and vertical rulers
- The white area (the page)
- Each section of the status bar
- Task bar.

If you have a wheel mouse, what happens if you hold the left button down while you scroll?

Input devices 2

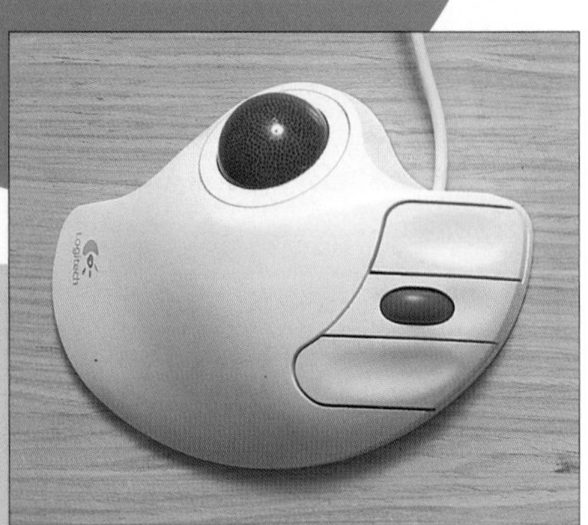
Figure 2.8 *Rollerball or trackerball*

Tracker ball

A tracker ball, sometimes referred to as a rollerball, is like an upside down mouse that allows the user to point and select items on screen by rotating the ball with the fingertips, rather than pushing a mouse around a desktop. It requires very little space to operate and is often used in conjunction with computer-aided design software. Sometimes you find a small trackerball built into laptop computers in place of the conventional mouse.

Graphics tablet

A graphics tablet is also referred to as a digitising tablet or digitiser. It is used in conjunction with a cursor (puck) and/or a pen (stylus). The tablet contains electrodes that detect the movement of the cursor or stylus and the movements are translated into digital signals that are sent to the computer. It is used for freehand drawing and sketching and is especially effective for tracing drawings.

Figure 2.9 *Handheld scanner*

Scanner

Scanners read words, symbols or other graphics from a printed page and 'translate' the pattern of light and dark or colour into a digital signal that the computer can store and manipulate. The quality of the image is dependent on the resolution of the scanner. For example, the image produced by a scanner with 600 dpi resolution will not be as sharp as that produced with 1200 dpi. However, you could expect to pay at least twice as much for the better quality.

The most popular type of scanner is a flatbed scanner which works in a similar way to a photocopier. Text and/or images are placed face down on a flat bed of glass and the lid is closed. The sensor moves across (scans) underneath the glass reading the information – very much like the operation of a photocopier. The scanned text or image can be edited on screen, imported into another document and, finally, saved in the usual way. Handheld scanners are usually only a few inches wide and are rolled across the document to be scanned. They perform the same job but the amount of information that can be scanned is limited by the width of the scanner and the images produced are not of the same quality as those produced by flatbed scanners.

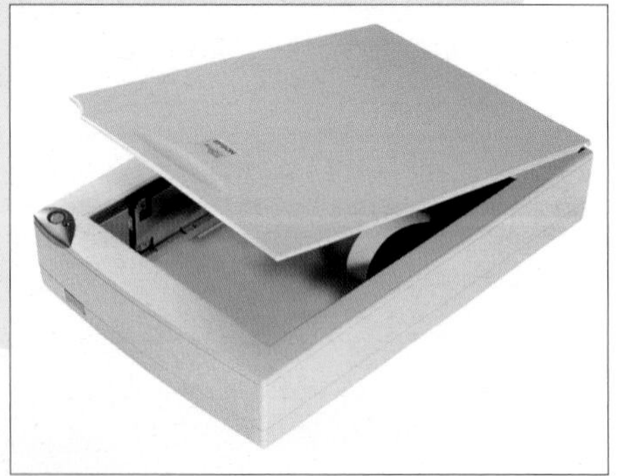
Figure 2.10 *Flatbed scanner*

Digital camera

A digital camera looks very similar to a traditional camera. However, rather than record the image on a film which needs to be processed, light intensities are converted into digital form that can be stored on a disk as a data file. Most digital cameras let you view the image as soon as you have taken the picture and, if you don't like what you see, it can be deleted. With the use of a computer, the digital image from the data file can be viewed on screen and edited with photo imaging software. It can then be imported into a document or printed. It can be printed on special photographic quality paper and will look the same as a traditionally processed photograph.

Digital video cameras work in a similar way and store the images on disk. Video editing software brings professional editing techniques within the grasp of amateur enthusiasts.

A web cam (world wide web camera) is a slow-scan camera. This means that an image will be collected once every few minutes, or periodically, rather than continuously. When a new image is received the picture is refreshed (or updated). The image is displayed on the Internet and can be viewed through the web page. Web cams have been put to many different uses. For example, you can log on to check out traffic flow in major towns and cities through the BBC web site (www. bbc.co.uk). Some holiday areas use web cams so that you can get an idea of what it is like before you go on holiday. One was even used by one family to show house renovation in progress!

Activity

Try and find a web site that has a web cam image of somewhere near you and see how frequently the image is refreshed.

Figure 2.11 *Web cams can provide helpful information about traffic conditions or holiday locations*

Input devices 3

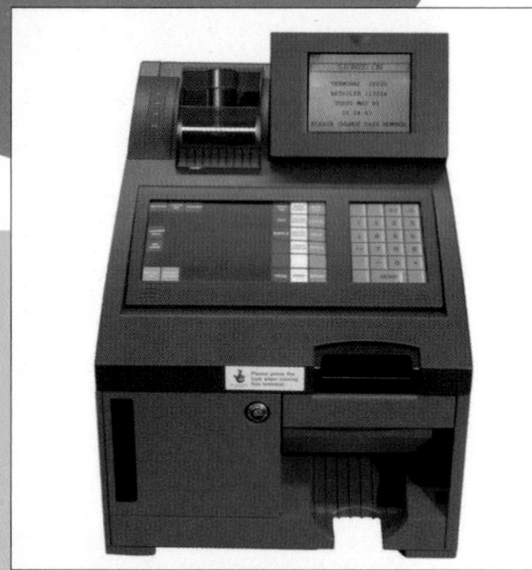

Figure 2.12 *Lottery terminal*

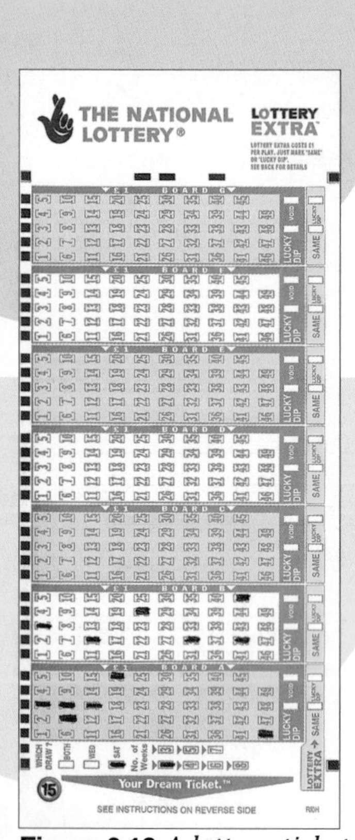

Figure 2.13 *A lottery ticket*

Touch screen

A **touch screen** is a display screen covered with a touch-sensitive transparent panel. To interact with the computer the user touches the screen on a display menu. This breaks an infrared light beam and generates an electronic signal which identifies the location on the screen. Computer software interprets the signal and performs the required operation.

You are most likely to come across a touch screen in a public place. For instance, BT have installed multimedia kiosks in shopping centres, airports and motorway service areas that, in addition to letting you make telephone calls, give access to the Internet and e-mail through a touch screen.

Optical mark reader (OMR)

An **optical mark reader** is a scanning device that reads carefully placed pencil marks on a specially designed form or document. You might have seen an optical mark reader in use if someone in your family has bought a lottery ticket. The chosen numbers are marked by a line drawn in the corresponding number box. The form is fed into the lottery terminal, sensors read the marks and the ticket is printed. They are also frequently used for questionnaires or multiple choice answer sheets where the computer can scan the answers, process and analyse the results very quickly.

Optical character recognition (OCR)

Optical character recognition enables the computer to identify written or printed characters. To illustrate this, a page of hard copy text can be scanned and the characters individually converted to their digital equivalent which are then displayed on screen in text format. The text can then be edited in exactly the same way as text that has been directly keyed in. This differs from scanning where the page is read as a graphics file and letters cannot be individually edited. Text scanned with OCR needs careful checking because some letters might be misread, particularly if the original text is indistinct.

Bar code reader

Most items offered for sale in shops will have a bar code printed on them somewhere – look on the back cover of this book for an example. The **bar code** is a strip of vertical bars of varying widths that establishes a unique reference code for the product. Groups of bars represent individual digits and most bar codes are made up of 12–13 digits. The last number is a check digit and this is used to verify that the number has been scanned in correctly. The computer applies a set of calculations to the individual digits and the answer should equal the check digit. If it doesn't, an error message will be generated.

Figure 2.14 *Bar code*

A **bar code reader** uses a visible red light to scan the bar code and it is interpreted through a decoder. The reference is matched to the stock list in the computer system and the appropriate price is displayed. Have you noticed that sometimes an item will not scan and the assistant has to key the number in manually? The numbers are always printed beneath the vertical stripes just in case the bar code reader is unable to read the code.

A great advantage of using the bar code system is that any price change only needs to be made to the computer system and not each individual item. In addition, supermarkets in particular can run special promotions to attract customers – '3 for the price of 2', etc. The computer system can be programmed to recognise when three items with the same bar code have been purchased and will automatically deduct one price from the bill.

Your library ticket probably contains a bar code that recognises you as a member. All the library books will also have bar codes. When you borrow a library book, both your ticket and the book are scanned. The library computer system can then match the borrower with the book. When you return the book it is scanned again. The computer system removes the link between you and that book. This enables the system to keep track of books on loan and to generate letters automatically to remind members that their books are overdue.

Did you know ?

BE WARNED! A telephone bill can be scanned and imported into a spreadsheet. There it can be sorted by telephone number and the call charges totalled to see just how much you have cost your family in telephone calls to your best friend's mobile!

Input devices 4

Magnetic stripe reader

Cards that are 'swiped' contain a magnetic strip and the action of swiping the card enables a **magnetic stripe reader** to read information that has been magnetically stored on the black strip. If you have a bank account you will almost certainly have a card containing a magnetic strip that you use to withdraw cash from your account. When you insert the card into the automatic teller machine (ATM) the magnetic stripe reader reads the data stored on the strip and knows which account is being accessed. To verify the authenticity of the user you will be asked to enter your PIN (personal identification number) which the computer will match with the stored data – this is why it is so important to keep your PIN secret.

Magnetic stripe readers are widely used in conjunction with electronic point-of-sale (EPOS) terminals in shops. If you pay for goods with 'plastic money', the card is swiped and the amount is automatically taken from your bank account. Debit and credit cards must be signed on the reverse and the shopkeeper is obliged to check that the signature the customer signs on the slip matches the one on the card. If cards are stolen the loss must be reported to the bank or credit card company as soon as possible so that the card cannot be used. Stolen card numbers are programmed into the computer and if someone tries to use the card the shopkeeper will automatically receive a message to contact the bank or credit card company.

Did you know ?

Biometric security is under development that will authenticate the identity of an individual by measuring physical characteristics. For example, the index finger can be placed in a fingerprint scanner or the retina of the eye can be scanned. The computer will analyse the fingerprint or eye and authorise access if the scanned data matches that which is already stored.

Microphone

Microphones are sensors that detect sound. Some microphones are used with voice-recognition modules that take spoken words and translate them into digital signals for the computer. The computer is trained to match voice patterns with those that are stored in the system.

If you want to use voice-recognition software it will probably be necessary to record your commands several times over so that the computer will recognise your spoken voice and will be able to respond when you issue your commands. This technology makes it possible to operate a computer without using hands, which is a major development for people who suffer physical limitations.

Sensors

In a computerised control system, **sensors** are used to detect environmental conditions such as temperature, light, humidity or pressure. Electronic signals recording the current conditions will be sent to the computer and if a condition changes, the system will react accordingly.

For example if the temperature falls below a pre-determined level, the computer program will respond by activating heaters to bring the temperature back to that level. When the level is reached the computer will issue an instruction to turn the heaters off. You will learn more about sensors and computer control systems and computer control systems in Chapter 9.

Did you know ?

The trial of a biometric voice-based offender tracking system is under way. This has been designed as an alternative to electronic tagging or a custodial prison sentence. Offenders will record a series of passwords to provide a voice pattern. They will be required to phone in at certain times during the day when a computer will match their voice pattern and trace the call to ensure they are telephoning from their home. In due course the same principle might be applied to check that teleworkers are at home. (Source: *Computer Weekly*, 15 February 2001.)

Key points

- An input device is used to enter data, commands and programs into the computer.
- Input devices include keyboard, mouse, scanner, OCR, OMR, sensors, etc.

Activity

Greenfingers Garden Centre needs to identify suitable input devices for the following areas:

- the office
- the sales floor
- the checkouts
- the greenhouses.

Make a list of suitable input devices against each heading and justify the reason for your choice. Try and find a picture to illustrate each one. You can scan images from magazines or books or alternatively you might be able to search on the Internet.

Process 1

Central processing unit (CPU) or processor

The **central processing unit** (**CPU**) is the part of a computer that controls all the other parts. It is often referred to as the computer's brain.

The key role of the central processing unit is to:

- carry out instructions within the software
- handle control signals
- store data
- perform arithmetic and logic operations.

The CPU is a microprocessor – a chip of silicon – composed of tiny electrical switches. The speed at which the processor carries out its operations is measured in megahertz (MHz) or millions of cycles or pulses per second. The Intel Pentium is probably the most well known processor. Cheaper alternatives are the Athlon, Celeron and Duron.

Did you know ?

The first Intel 8088 chip had 28,000 transistors on it, the latest Intel chip, the Pentium IV, has 42 million. (Source: *Financial Mail*, 12 August 2001.)

Process capacity

The higher the number of MHz the faster the computer can process information. In 1965, Gordon Moore, founder of Intel, accurately predicted that the capacity of memory chips would double every 18–24 months. To give you an idea of how quickly technology has moved forward, in 1995 you might have expected a speed of 90 MHz to be adequate but in 2001 we have seen the introduction of Intel's Pentium IV chip with speeds of up to 1.5 GHz. For average, everyday processing requirements in 2001 a minimum speed of 600 MHz is adequate. To handle large and complex graphic processing requirements you would need something more powerful.

Did you know ?

In the late seventies, the world's fastest super-computer was in a building at the University of London, and cost £2.5 million. Nowadays a machine costing £599 calculates six times more quickly! If cars had developed at the same rate, a Rolls Royce would now cost £2.75 and travel three million miles on a gallon of petrol! (Source: *Financial Mail*, 12 August 2001.)

Interpreting instructions

Every time you press a letter on the keyboard, an electrical signal is generated which passes between the keyboard and the processor. The processor interprets the signal and displays the appropriate letter on screen. Similarly, when you click an icon with your mouse the instruction is carried from the mouse via the cable to the CPU, which reacts to the signal and carries out your instruction, for example when you click . The CPU will interpret other instructions you make, such as create an automatic backup copy, password protect or make a file read only.

In a computerised control system a signal from a sensor, for example, is received by the CPU and acted upon. The resulting action might be something simple like increasing the temperature or something more complex like activating a robot.

Arithmetic logic unit

The arithmetic logic unit within the CPU handles the **arithmetic** and **logic operations**. Quite simply, the arithmetic unit enables the computer to add up (+), subtract (-), multiply (*) and divide (/) – or perform standard arithmetic functions such as =sum, =average, maximum, etc. The logic unit handles more complex queries, for instance equal to (=), greater than (>) or less than (<). A typical query in a database might be to show all girls aged over 12. The logic operators you would be using are =girls and >12.

Memory

Within the main processing unit is an area allocated to the working memory of the computer where data and instructions are stored for fast access. It comprises ROM and RAM.

ROM (read-only memory) is a permanent memory that is available whether the computer is switched on or off. The start-up procedure (or boot program) when you switch your computer on is stored in ROM. It is installed when the computer is manufactured and can be read from but not over-written (i.e. changed). It is the memory that brings you to the desktop whenever you switch on.

RAM (random access memory) is a fast temporary working memory where programs and data are stored when the computer is running. For example, when word-processing your homework you are working in RAM, but documents must be saved permanently on a hard or floppy disk or they will be lost when the computer is switched off. For this reason RAM is known as volatile memory – memory that is non-permanent.

To enable the computer to run the advanced applications you are familiar with today, the amount of RAM that is needed has increased from approximately 16 MB in 1995 to the 64+ MB of RAM needed to run programs simultaneously today. In fact many computers are sold with 128 or 256 MB.

Key points

- The central processing unit is the 'brains' of the computer which controls all the other parts.
- The CPU handles arithmetic and logic operations.
- The computer memory comprises ROM and RAM.
- Permanent memory can be stored on the hard drive, floppy disk, optical disk or tape.
- The read-only memory (ROM) contains the start-up instructions.
- The random access memory (RAM) is a fast, temporary working memory but is lost when the computer is turned off.
- The operating system is a program that controls and organises the general operation of the computer system.

Storage capacity

The size of data or storage capacity of a computer is measured in bytes. One byte contains 8 bits – bit stands for binary digit and is the smallest unit of data that can be stored. A bit is represented by a 0 or 1. Standard alphanumeric characters (e.g. A, B, C, and 1, 2, 3) are represented as numbers from 0 to 127. The numbers are translated into 7-bit binary code which is used by most computers and enables text-only files to be transferred between different kinds of computer systems. The code is called the **American Standard Code for Information Interchange** or **ASCII**. Each binary digit represents an electronic signal where 1 means 'on' and 0 means 'off'. Different patterns of signals represent different characters, e.g. the letters a, b, and c are represented in binary code by 110 0001, 110 0010 and 110 0011. Your teacher has a copy of the full code in the Tutor's File.

We normally refer to the storage capacity of a computer in terms of Kilobytes (kB), Megabytes (MB) and Gigabytes (GB).

Bit	smallest unit of data with a value of 1 or 0
Byte	equal to 8 bits – approximately equivalent to one character
Kilobyte (kB)	equal to 1,024 bytes or 2^{10}
Megabyte (MB)	equal to 1,048,576 bytes or 2^{20} (equivalent to approximately 500 double-spaced pages of text)
Gigabyte (GB)	equal to 1,073,741,824 bytes or 2^{30} (equivalent to approximately 500,000 double-spaced pages of text)
Terabyte (TB)	equal to ~1,099,000,000,000 bytes or 2^{40}

Figure 2.15 *A motherboard*

Motherboard

The **motherboard** is the main printed circuit board of the computer which usually forms the 'floor' of the system. All the other electrical components are plugged into the motherboard, e.g. CPU, memory. The components are linked by 'buses' which are etched into the motherboard and carry signals from one component to another.

Ports

Ports are the 'sockets' at the back of the main processor casing which are used to attach peripheral devices such as the printer, monitor, keyboard, mouse, scanner, etc. Cables from each peripheral device plug into the ports allowing data to be sent and received between the peripherals and microprocessor.

- The **universal serial bus** (**USB**) supports peripheral devices that can be plugged in or unplugged without having to reboot the PC and provides a much faster transfer of data than the traditional serial and parallel connection ports.
- IBM developed the PS/2 port (or mouse port) for connecting a mouse and keyboard and most PCs will have at least one.
- A parallel port transmits data in or out in parallel and is the printer connection favoured in most PCs.
- A serial port is a general purpose interface that transmits data in one direction, one bit at a time, and is therefore much slower than a parallel port. With the emergence of USB and PS/2 it is now becoming redundant.

Modem

If you want your computer to provide access to the Internet or e-mail you will need a **modem**. Modems come ready installed on most new computers but some older computers have a separate external modem which plugs into the PC. The modem converts the computer's digital signal into an analogue signal that can be carried over the telephone network. You will learn more about these in Chapter 6.

Network card

If you are at school or college your computer is probably connected to a network. Networks allow the sharing of resources and information by users, and to access the network each PC must be fitted with a **network card**. This is similar to a printed circuit board, which slots into the CPU, and contains all the necessary electronics and connections to allow the PC to link into the network. Again, you will find out more about networks in Chapter 6.

Storage devices 1

We have already looked at RAM and ROM and seen that they don't provide the means to store permanently either the applications software (e.g. word processing, spreadsheet) or the data you have input and spent time working on. Disk drives enable you to do this. A disk drive is a storage device that transfers data to and from magnetic or optical disks. Your PC will probably have 1 hard drive (typically referred to as Drive C), 1 floppy drive (referred to as Drive A) and a CD-ROM drive (referred to as Drive D or E). You might also have a zip drive and DVD-ROM.

The hard disk drive

The **hard disk drive** is the storage area, rather like a filing cabinet, where all the applications software you use and documents you create are kept. It is the main memory of the computer and data can be transferred to the hard disk much quicker than a floppy disk. The hard drive houses one or more rigid magnetic disks that rotate about a central axle. Each surface of each disk is divided into a number of concentric circles or tracks which the read/write heads access. The tracks are divided into sectors.

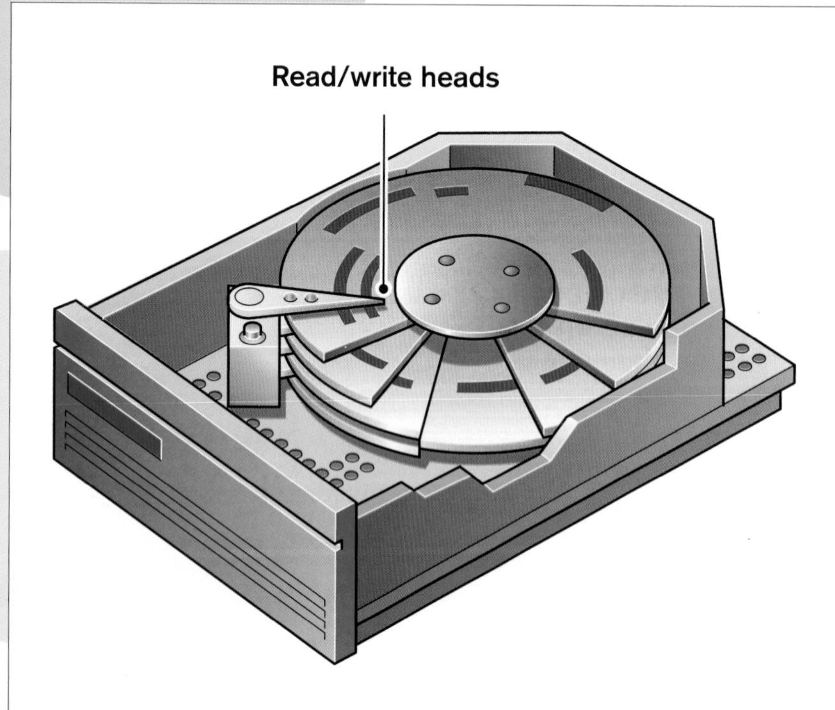

Figure 2.16 *Hard disk*

Hard drives today are measured in gigabytes (GB). The most expensive computers will have the largest hard drives – over 50 GB. In 2001 a capacity of at least 10 GB will be required if you want to play high quality games, although 5 GB should be enough for average use. This is an enormous increase from 1995 when you would have expected a hard drive to be about 800 MB. The application software we run today is far more complex, offering the capability to perform more complicated functions and as a result requires much greater storage space.

The floppy disk drive

Figure 2.17 *A 3.5 inch floppy disk*

The **floppy disk drive** enables you to save files onto a floppy disk so that you can take data files between home and school or college and make backup copies of your data files as a security measure.

Floppy disks are round, flat and made of a flexible substance called Mylar. They have a magnetic surface which allows the recording of data and they are covered in a hard, protective plastic case. The disk turns in the drive allowing the read/write head to access the disk. Most PCs take a 3.5 inch floppy disk which can store up to 1.44 kB of data. This is approximately equivalent to 300 A4 pages of straightforward text. The size of a data file containing graphic images and complex formatting will be much larger and consequently will reduce the number of pages that can be stored on disk.

Floppy disks are formatted before data can be written to the disk. Formatting establishes tracks and sectors into which data files are stored. Use the write-protect tab to protect the data on your disk from accidental deletion. A write-protected disk can only be 'read from' and not 'written to'. This means that you can retrieve the files stored on the disk but they cannot be accidentally overwritten or deleted. It also protects the disk from infection by a computer virus from another computer.

Care should also be taken when handling disks to protect data. If you are carrying disks to and from home and school/college store them in a protective case to keep them clean and away from dust and moisture. The surface of the disk should not be touched and they should be kept away from extreme temperatures and not stored near magnetic fields (e.g. telephones, televisions) which could erase the data from the disk.

Zip drive

The **zip drive** is similar to a floppy drive but can store 100 MB of data, at least 70 times more than a floppy. Some zip disks store as much as 250 MB. The zip disk is slightly thicker than a floppy disk and needs a separate drive. Data is compressed, thereby reducing the size of files that are too large to fit onto a floppy disk. In this way they can be backed up or transferred from one machine to another.

Storage devices 2

Figure 2.18 *There are various ways to store information*

Optical storage

The **CD-ROM drive** (compact disk-read-only memory) has, as the name suggests, a read-only memory, which means you cannot alter or store data. It uses the same technology as CD music discs and CD players where a laser beam reads the data from an optical disk rather than a magnetic disk. A typical CD holds around 650 MB of data, which is equivalent to about 450 1.4 MB floppy disks.

The entire contents of a text-based encyclopaedia takes up only 25% of one standard-sized CD-ROM. This has allowed publishers to fill up the other 75% with video sequences, animations, photographs, sound and interactive programs. The result is an interactive multimedia encyclopaedia. If you look at most of the software on offer today you will see that it comes stored on a CD-ROM. The shelves in computer superstores are lined with CD-ROMs on every subject imaginable – route planners, lessons in how to speak a foreign language, design for the home or garden and how to pass your driving test.

The **CD-RW drive** enables data to be read from and written to CD. Many new computers have these in place of the CD-ROM and they enable you to both read from CDs in the usual way and to save onto compact disk. For example, you can compile your own music CDs as well as providing an alternative method for transporting large data files and backing up.

The new **DVD-ROM** (digital versatile disk or digital video disk read-only memory) is the same diameter as a CD but holds nearly 10 times the data. A DVD can hold between 4.7 GB and 15.9 GB data and has afforded the means for digital quality movies or other home entertainment that you can watch on your PC (or television with a DVD player). It is still generally available as read-only and requires its own drive, but if you only have a DVD-ROM you can still use it for your CD-ROMs.

Magnetic tape

The amount of work you do on your computer at home can easily be backed up on floppy disks for safety. However, most organisations need to back up large volumes of data and floppy disks are not the best method for doing this. Mainframe computers therefore use **magnetic tape** to create backup copies of the computer's hard drive.

Magnetic tape consists of a thin plastic strip with a magnetic coating to one side which is stored on a reel or cartridge. The tape is read to and written from by a tape drive which winds the tape from one reel to another past a read/write head. The backup procedure is often scheduled at night when the computer is not in use.

Access to data on tape is known as '**serial access**' which means that the tape must be run from one end to the other to find the data you might be looking for. This is ideal as a method of backing up but not as a general storage method for files you work with every day. In this way it differs to the system of '**direct access**' used by the PC to locate data files on the hard, floppy or CD drive.

To make this clearer, compare a cassette music tape with a music CD. If you want to find a particular piece of music on cassette you have to run through the tape until you find the right track. It can be difficult to stop in just the right place first time and you often find yourself rewinding and winding to get to the beginning of the track. This is the same principle as serial access applied to tape backup. With a music CD you can go directly to the track you want to listen to – in other words you have direct access.

Activity

Look at the specification of the two computers illustrated below.

700 MHz Intel Celeron Processor
20 GB Hard Disk
64 MB SDRAM memory
15" SVGA Colour Screen
CD-ROM Drive
Intel 810e Graphics
3D sound

Special Offer

Includes Epson 480 Colour Inkjet Printer
Portable 3 in 1 digital camera
Windows ME
Microsoft Works 2000

£799 + VAT
Total price £979.79

1 GHz AMD Athlon Processor
40 GB Hard Disk
256 MB SDRAM memory
17" SVGA Colour Screen
CD-RW Drive
DVD-ROM
Zip Drive
32 MB NVIDIA TNT2 Graphics Card
Creative Soundblaster 128 Sound
Z12 Colour Printer
600 dpi Colour Scanner
Windows ME

£999 + VAT
Total price £1218.83

Fergul is writing a book and Faye is working on the illustrations for it. Which computer do you think would suit Fergal and which would suit Faye? Why did you come to this decision?

Suggest another suitable user for each of the models described and say why you think each model would suit each user.

Output devices 1

Figure 2.19 *Traditional monitor*

Figure 2.20 *TFT LCD flat panel display*

Activity

Type the letter **R** on a clear screen. Highlight the letter and change the font size to 450. Compare the **R** in Arial with the **R** in Times New Roman and the **R** in Comic Sans. Can you see the jaggedness of the curved edges of the letters? This is formed by the individual pixels.

Monitor

A monitor or visual display unit (VDU) consists of a computer video display and its housing. The monitor displays images (characters or graphics) generated by the computer's video adapter. The image on the screen is referred to as 'soft copy', i.e. you can't touch it.

Most monitors use a cathode ray tube (CRT) similar to your television set. Size is determined by measuring the distance between the diagonal corners of the screen, e.g. 15", 17", 19" and 21".

Laptop computers use **TFT LCD** (**thin film transistor liquid crystal display**) flat-panel display screens which take up much less desk space. However, they are very expensive. In March 2001 a 15" traditional screen might cost little more than £100, compared to £700 upwards for a 15" TFT screen.

The sharpness or clarity of the image on a VDU is determined by its resolution. Resolution is measured in pixels (short for picture elements). If you look at your computer monitor closely, you will see that the image is made up of tiny dots. Each dot is called a pixel. The more pixels per square centimetre of screen the better the resolution.

Most computers come with super video graphics adaptor monitors (SVGA) with resolutions measured in pixels across and down the screen. Resolutions vary between 1024 x 768 pixels, 1280 x 1024 and 1600 x 1200. The higher the number of pixels the clearer and crisper the display.

Printers

If you need a permanent (or hard) copy of the information on screen you will need a printer. Although the dot matrix printer is useful for some printing, laser and inkjet printers are the most widely used and are known as non-impact printers because no part of the printer touches the page to form the image. They print in black and white and/or colour.

The quality, or resolution, of the image is measured in dots per inch or dpi. The more dots per inch the more detailed the output. The speed of the printer is rated by pages per minute (ppm) or by characters per second (cps) – the higher the value, the faster the speed.

Laser printer

Laser printers are based on the technology used by photocopiers – lasers produce an image on an electrically charged drum, dry ink or toner sticks to the electrical charge and is fixed by heat. They have a high resolution of 1200 or more dpi, can reproduce complex graphics, are almost silent and operate at reasonably high speeds of between 8 and 30 or more pages per minute – depending on their cost. Files containing graphics are more complex and will slow the printer down.

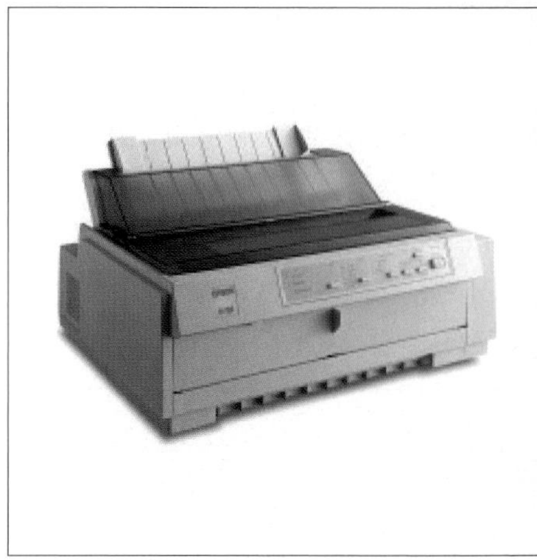

Figure 2.21 *Dot-matrix printer*

Inkjet printer

Inkjet printers use liquid ink to spray characters onto a page and provide a similar high resolution of up to 1200 dpi and are also quiet to operate. It can be difficult to tell the difference between a print from a good quality inkjet and a standard laser printer. However they operate at much slower speeds of between 6 and 10 ppm for black and white copies and half the speed if printing colour. They are generally cheaper in price than a laser printer but when used with inexpensive copier paper the ink has a tendency to smudge.

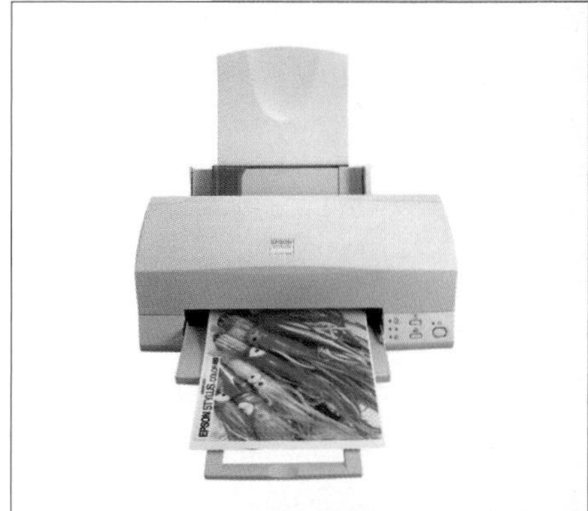

Figure 2.22 *Inkjet printer*

Dot-matrix printer

Dot-matrix printers are known as impact printers because the dot-matrix print head hits (or impacts on) the paper and for this reason they are noisy in operation. The characters are made up of dots using a 9, 18, or 24 pin print head. The pins hit or impact on the paper through a ribbon, making patterns of dots in the shape of letters and numbers. They can print different fonts and sizes. The print quality depends mostly on the number of dots in the matrix. Dot-matrix printers are useful when more than one copy of a document is required. For example, a company might want several copies of an order:

- One white copy to be despatched with the order.
- One blue copy for the warehouse.
- One green for the accounts department.
- One pink copy for the file.

By using NCR (no carbon required) stationery the dot-matrix print head will strike the page and the imprint will be made on all copies.

Figure 2.23 *A laser printer*

Output devices 2

Plotter

There are two types of graph plotter in use – the flat-bed plotter and drum (or rolling) plotter. The advantages of the drum plotter are that it can work with very large sheets of paper and produce neat accurate results. Drum plotters therefore justify their size and cost for large high-quality items such as posters, wallcharts and reference drawings. They are often used in combination with computer-aided design software to produce technical drawings where precision is essential, for example in engineering and architectural applications.

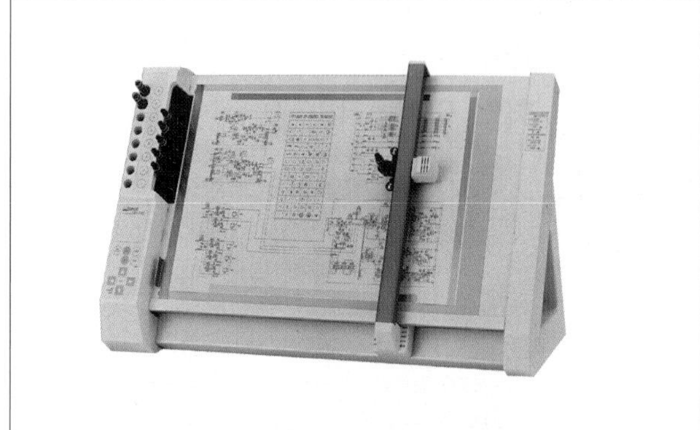

Figure 2.24 *Flat-bed plotter*

Figure 2.25 *Drum or rolling plotter*

A plotter differs from a printer in that it draws images using a pen that can be lowered, raised and moved across the page to form continuous lines, whereas a printer simulates lines by a series of closely spaced dots. Lines and curves are drawn on the page by a combination of horizontal and vertical movement of the pen or paper. The pen (or pens in multicolour plotters) produces horizontal lines by moving along a horizontal bar. With the flat-bed plotter, movement of the bar enables the plotter to draw vertical lines, whereas with the drum plotter, the paper moves.

Speakers

Most computers are fitted with a small internal speaker that will beep to draw your attention to an error – for example if you hit the wrong key. On multimedia PCs additional speakers are attached to the computer to provide better quality sound. The development of audio technology is enabling blind people to share the possibilities of information systems that we all take for granted. A sound card enables the computer to output sound through the speakers and a soundblaster has become the standard for PCs.

Figure 2.26 *Multimedia PC with speakers*

Motors

Computer control systems do not generally need the same output devices that you are familiar with. Although they might have a VDU, they would probably not require a printer. The most likely output device would be a motor or actuator. For example, a greenhouse would need a motor to automatically open the window if the temperature became too high or a robot would need a motor to make it move.

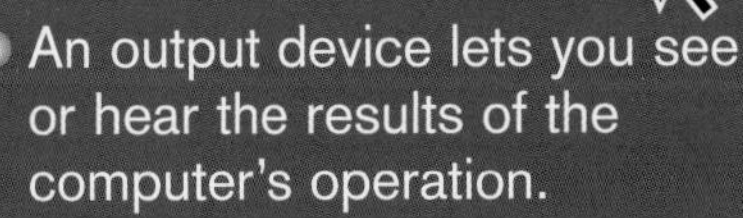

- An output device lets you see or hear the results of the computer's operation.
- Output devices include monitors, printers, plotters, speakers and motors.

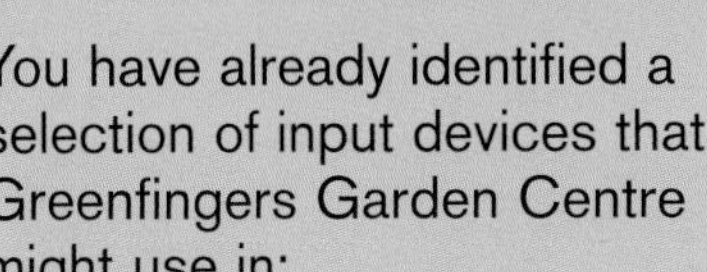

You have already identified a selection of input devices that Greenfingers Garden Centre might use in:

- the office
- the sales floor
- the checkouts
- the greenhouses.

Under the same headings, consider the output devices they might also require and justify your choices. Try and find an illustration for each one.

Software 1

Figure 2.27

Software programs are sets of instructions that make the hardware work. A computer can't do anything on its own. Instructions are input by the user, using perhaps the keyboard or mouse, and the software reacts to these instructions. This is why you shouldn't blame the computer if things go wrong. It is only doing what you (the user) have told it to do!

Whereas you can see and touch computer hardware (monitor, keyboard, mouse, etc.), you can't see or touch computer software. Some software comes pre-installed on your computer (the start-up program) and some comes on disk or CD-ROM (operating systems and application software) that you or your computer supplier must load onto the hard drive before you can use the computer.

The different types of software include:

- ROM (read-only memory)
- Operating systems
- Applications software
- Programming languages.

The ROM-BIOS chip

The software that enables the computer to start up is permanently stored in the read-only memory chip on the motherboard. When the computer is turned on or restarted, it looks for the start-up instructions in the **ROM-BIOS chip**. BIOS stands for 'basic input-output system' and is a set of instructions that tell the computer how to handle the flow of information between the computer and its input and output peripherals.

Operating system

The operating system is the most important program that runs on the computer and provides the basic user interface when no applications are open. The computer you are using probably offers you the desktop as your starting point.

The operating system:

- schedules tasks
- recognises data input from the keyboard, mouse or sensor
- keeps track of the directories and files on the disks
- controls peripheral devices such as the printer.

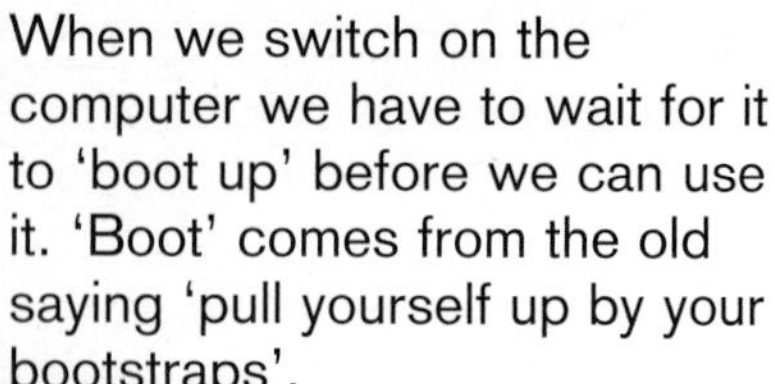

Did you know?

When we switch on the computer we have to wait for it to 'boot up' before we can use it. 'Boot' comes from the old saying 'pull yourself up by your bootstraps'.

If you are lucky enough to have your own computer you probably had to load the software from a set of disks or a CD–ROM. The operating system generated the instructions that led you through the steps and allocated an area on the hard drive for the software. Directories and folders are created through the operating system, and the commands to rename, delete or move files are acted upon by the operating system.

If you send a document to print and the printer is switched off or out of paper an error message will come up on screen to warn you of the problem. These messages are produced by the operating system.

This makes the operating system the foundation that application software, such as word-processing and spreadsheet programs, are built on. The most common operating systems for PCs are MS-DOS and systems that use windowing environments such as Windows ME or Windows 98. Apple Macs have a different operating system known as the Macintosh OS/2.

MS-DOS

MS-DOS was developed by Microsoft and introduced as a standard operating system in all IBM-compatible computers from the early 1980s, and for many years was the most popular system in use. MS-DOS stands for **M**icro**s**oft **D**isk **O**perating **S**ystem. It controls many internal computer functions such as how to process information, how to manage files and how to interpret commands. For this reason it is described as a 'command led' system.

The command processor – or command interpreter – receives and carries out the operating system commands. When the command prompt C:\> is displayed the command processor is waiting for a command. For example, typing 'dir' at the command prompt and pressing Enter will display the contents of the C drive. The command **copy c:\letter.doc a:** would be required to copy a file called 'letter' from the C drive to a floppy disk. DOS is difficult to work with because commands have to be typed in an exact way and there are too many different codes for the ordinary everyday user to remember. You might have used a computer that required you to enter **c:\>win** to access Windows. If so you were giving a command in MS-DOS to load the Windows environment.

Software 2

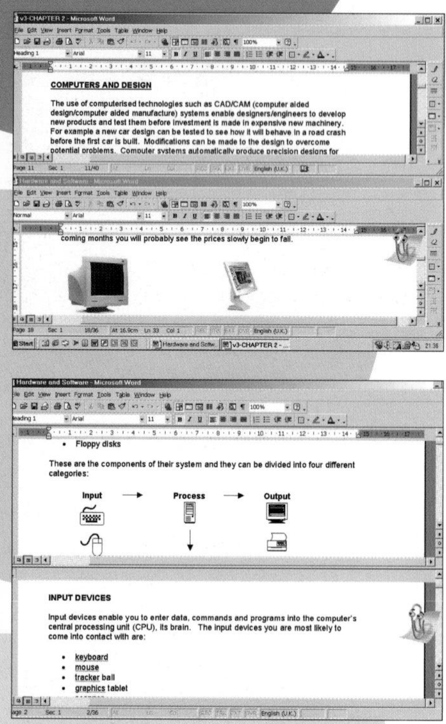

Figure 2.28 *The windows environment enables you to split the screen and work in both sections at the same time. The top illustration shows two different documents and the bottom illustration shows two sections of a long document*

Windows

Windows was first introduced in 1985 and is now the most popular PC operating system. The name comes from the computer term 'windowing environment', which is an operating system that can divide the screen into independent areas called windows. Each window has its own frame that can usually be resized and moved around on the screen. Individual windows can contain different documents or messages, or even their own menus or other controls.

The advantage of Windows is the **graphical user interface** (**GUI** – pronounced 'gooey') which is a user-friendly method of showing information on screen graphically. It lets you start programs, select menus, choose commands and other options by using the mouse to click on the menus or icons. You no longer need to remember complicated commands. For example, to copy a file from the hard drive to a floppy disk you can use My Computer and drag and drop the file from one folder to another.

Mainframe computers

In addition to meeting the same basic requirements as a PC, the operating system of a large mainframe computer must be able to handle many programs and operations simultaneously. To help you understand, try and imagine the day-to-day operations of Getaway, a travel company selling holidays. Getaway's head office is based in Luton and they have retail outlets in the high streets of most major towns.

In Getaway's head office each member of staff has a computer terminal on their desk linked to the mainframe

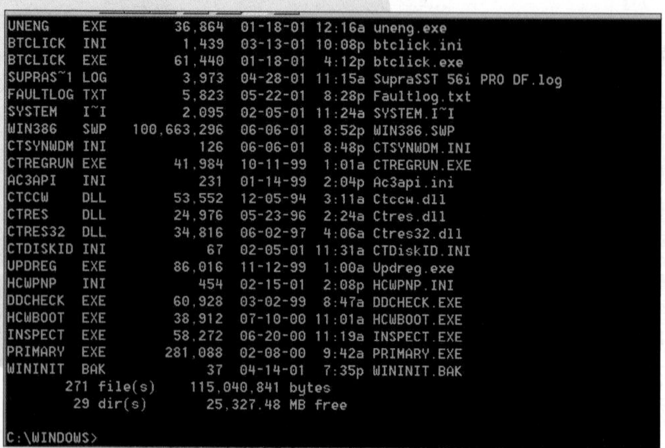

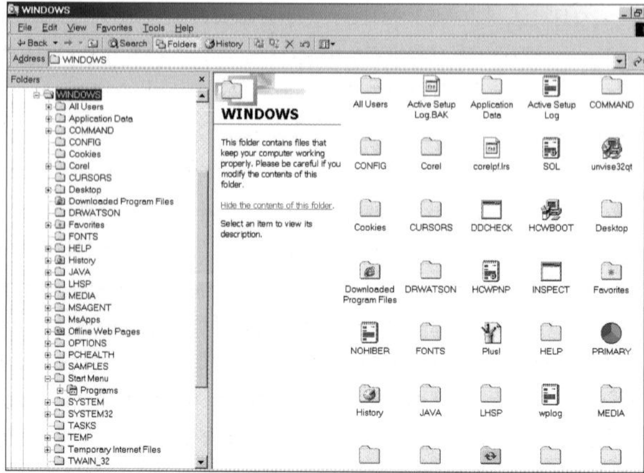

Figure 2.29 *The contents of C drive viewed in MS-DOS and Windows*

computer. A terminal consists of a VDU, keyboard and mouse and is known as a dumb terminal since it relies on the processing power of the mainframe computer. The operating system must be capable of dealing with multi-access or multi-user operations.

Sahida works in the accounts department and is processing invoices, Peter is using the database to produce a list of customers travelling to Majorca on a particular flight the following week and Mary is printing a mail-merge letter to accompany tickets she is sending out later that day. The computer is running several different applications at the same time. This is known as multi-tasking. Each user is given the impression that he or she is the only person using the system but in fact the computer is processing one operation while somebody else is keying in their data. The operating system is prioritising the jobs and switching from one to another. Because the processing time is so fast it appears that it is doing more than one thing at a time.

Meanwhile, Jane in Bristol is trying to find a holiday for a customer. Jane has a permanent connection to the Getaway mainframe computer in Luton and can see the up-to-date availability of holidays and flights. The customer decides to book a two-week holiday to Florida for himself, his wife and two children. Jane enters his details into the computer system to confirm the booking. The computer records the booking and immediately changes the availability of that holiday and reduces the number of seats available on that flight to Florida. The computer is processing in real time.

A real-time processing system responds to data input immediately. Real-time processing is used in computer-control systems where an immediate reaction is required, for example industrial processes, computers in space travel, traffic lights, as well as travel bookings. Real-time processing is essential for Getaway because the sales staff throughout the country must have accurate information on holiday and flight availability.

Finally, it is pay day this week and Ellie is preparing data for the payroll. Every week she enters details of the hours worked by staff and the computer stores this information. Today she must enter the data for the last week of the month and overnight the computer will process the data for all four weeks and print the salary slips. This is known as batch processing and is a system of collecting all the information together over a period of time before processing it in one go.

Figure 2.30 *Getaway's computer system*

Applications software

Applications are sometimes referred to as packages. They are programs designed to help people perform certain types of work by manipulating text, numbers and graphics, or all three together. All the popular software applications are now written to work in the Windows environment. This is beneficial for the computer user because the applications look very similar on screen and this makes it much easier to use the different applications.

The various types of application software include:

- word processing
- spreadsheet
- database
- desktop publishing
- graphics
- utilities such as virus checkers.

Word processing

Word processing enables you to manipulate text-based documents – for example you can enter text, edit and format it, change the presentation, etc. The simplest features make typing and basic editing tasks, such as deleting and inserting, easier. The more complex check your grammar, find synonyms, allow you to drop text, graphics or calculations created with another program into your text, record macros that simplify difficult or repetitive operations and merge documents created in one program with data files created in another. You will probably use word-processing software to present your coursework for IT and possibly some other subjects too. Read Chapter 3 to learn more about the characteristics of word-processing software.

Spreadsheets

Spreadsheets are used to process numbers in a similar way to the word processor processing text, and they are particularly helpful for financial forecasting. You will be looking at the features of spreadsheet software in Chapter 4. Spreadsheets can be used to enter text, numbers and formulas into cells and those cells can be formatted to display their contents as whole numbers or currency, etc. Spreadsheets can automatically produce charts and graphs to display trends and make comparisons clear. These can then be imported into word-processed reports.

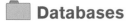

Databases

A **database** contains data which can be processed in various ways to produce information. For example, the database in a video store contains the names and addresses of members and the titles of videos. It can manipulate this data to produce information to show which member might have a particular video on loan or how many times that video has been borrowed. This information helps the store maintain a selection of videos that will appeal to the public. You will be looking at the power of the database in Chapter 5.

Desktop publishing

A **desktop-publishing** (**DTP**) package is more sophisticated than word-processing software because it has the capability of implementing complex page layouts. For example, the text for inclusion in a newsletter would be created in a word-processing application, spell checked, edited and saved. It would then be imported into the DTP program together with graphics that would have been created in a graphics program.

Newspapers and magazines are produced using DTP software. To achieve the best results from a DTP application you would need to use a high-resolution monitor and colour laser printer.

It is not necessary to have high-level DTP software if you want to produce fairly basic newsletters or brochures because your word-processing software has many of the features of desktop-publishing programs. For instance, text formatting enables you to change the font size and style, page layout features make it possible to change the page orientation and put the text into columns, and graphic attributes help you to add lines and borders, and position and resize graphics.

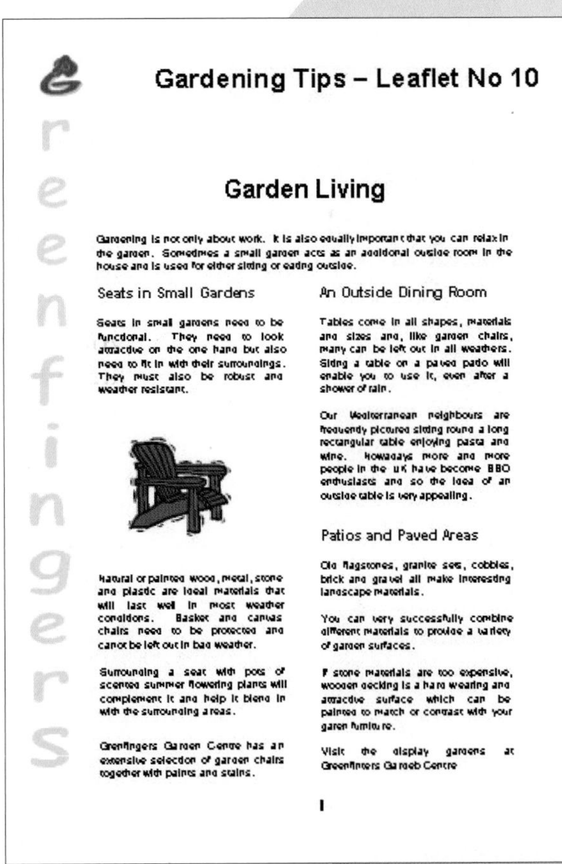

Greenfingers

Gardening Tips – Leaflet No 10

Garden Living

Gardening is not only about work. It is also equally important that you can relax in the garden. Sometimes a small garden acts as an additional outside room in the house and is used for either sitting or eating outside.

Seats in Small Gardens

Seats in small gardens need to be functional. They need to look attractive on the one hand but also need to fit in with their surroundings. They must also be robust and weather resistant.

Natural or painted wood, metal, stone and plastic are ideal materials that will last well in most weather conditions. Basket and canvas chairs need to be protected and canot be left out in bad weather.

Surrounding a seat with pots of scented summer flowering plants will complement it and help it blend in with the surrounding areas.

Grenfingers Garden Centre has an extensive selection of garden chairs together with paints and stains.

An Outside Dining Room

Tables come in all shapes, materials and sizes and, like garden chairs, many can be left out in all weathers. Siting a table on a paved patio will enable you to use it, even after a shower of rain.

Our Mediterranean neighbours are frequently pictured sitting round a long rectangular table enjoying pasta and wine. Nowadays more and more people in the UK have become BBQ enthusiasts and so the idea of an outside table is very appealing.

Patios and Paved Areas

Old flagstones, granite sets, cobbles, brick and gravel all make interesting landscape materials.

You can very successfully combine different materials to provide a variety of garden surfaces.

If stone materials are too expensive, wooden decking is a hard wearing and attractive surface which can be painted to match or contrast with your garen furniture.

Visit the display gardens at Greenfinters Gareb Centre

Figure 2.31 *Desktop features in your word-processing software enable you to produce newsletters, leaflets, etc., similar to this example*

Software 4

Figure 2.32 *A bitmap image before enlarging*

Figure 2.33 *A bitmap image loses clarity when enlarged*

Graphics

Most PCs now have a graphics card installed which permits the computer to display pictures. Graphics software includes:

- paint programs
- illustration and design programs
- presentation graphics (e.g. charts and graphs)
- animation software
- CAD software.

Graphics software comes in two formats – bitmap and vector. A bitmap image is made up of small squares called pixels which can be edited pixel by pixel, but when enlarged the image loses it sharpness. Paint and photo-editing programs are typical examples of bitmap applications. Vector graphics is a way of representing pictures by designating coordinates and drawing lines or geometric shapes in relation to them. A vector graphic is stored as a file containing instructions for drawing it and can be enlarged or reduced without losing quality. Drawing packages are examples of vector graphics.

It can be very confusing trying to understand the difference between the various file formats available for graphic images. The most common way of storing an image on a computer is as a bitmap, i.e. as a grid of pixels. However, the more detailed the image the larger the file size, and certainly when a graphic is intended for the Internet the larger the file, the slower it will take to download. To overcome this problem files are compressed so that they can be transmitted as quickly as possible. The two file formats suitable for the Internet and e-mail are JPEG (.jpg) and GIF (.gif).

JPEG (pronounced 'jay peg') is named after the Joint Photographics Experts Group that formulated its specifications. A JPEG image format is best for photographic images to be viewed on the web or to be sent via e-mail since it supports a maximum colour depth of 24 bits or 16.7 million colours.

GIF format supports a maximum colour depth of 8 bits or 256 colours and is ideal for web graphics and animations but not photographs.

Both **JPEG** and **GIF** images can be interlaced. That is, a low-resolution representation of an image can be downloaded first and then be gradually replaced by a more detailed version, giving the illusion of faster downloading.

The two other graphics formats that you will probably come across are TIFF (.tif) and windows bitmap (.bmp).

TIFF files support 24 bit or 16.7 million colours and so are the preferred format for desktop publishing, print and photography uses. The file sizes can be very large, particularly images that are large enough to fill an A4 page, which may be many megabytes in size, and so you need a very powerful PC to handle the files efficiently. A TIFF image is compatible with both PCs and Apple Macs, which is why it is the preferred format in publishing.

Bitmap files with the .bmp format are specific to Windows and cannot be viewed easily on other operating systems. Windows has traditionally used bitmap images for small graphics, desktop icons and tiled backgrounds for desktop wallpaper. They support 24-bit colour depth and are therefore equally as good as TIFF files for quality, but they cannot be compressed and create very large files. Files created in Paint are typical bitmap files and if you save too many on your hard drive you might run the risk of running out of space!

Figure 2.34 *A vector image before being enlarged*

Figure 2.35 *A vector image after being enlarged*

Utilities

Utility programs help computer users recover data that has been lost as a result of damaged disks, virus attack or accidental deletion. They provide diagnostic and measurement routines that check the performance of the system and are built into the memory to continually monitor the executable files (the main applications) for any damage or change. If any change is detected the file is prevented from being run and a user message is given.

The increasing use of the Internet and e-mail has greatly added to the risk of picking up a virus and you should install anti-virus software in order to scan files, detect and remove viruses from your hard and floppy disks. This is known as 'disinfecting'.

If you tend to transfer data between your computer at school or college and your computer at home (or even a friend's computer), you would be very wise to make sure your anti-virus software is up-to-date. New viruses are continually being contrived and you could miss detecting them if you are using out-of-date anti-virus software.

Did you know?

In 2000 the 'Lovebug' virus caused an estimated £6.7 billion in lost business and productivity.

Backing up

Activity

Create folders and directories within your area of the school/college computer system to organise your own data files.

Create a folder for each of your GCSE subjects. Within the IT folder create sub-folders for word processing, spreadsheet, database and graphics class work and for each of the four pieces of coursework you will be doing. An additional folder named Revision will also be useful. It might look similar to this when you have finished:

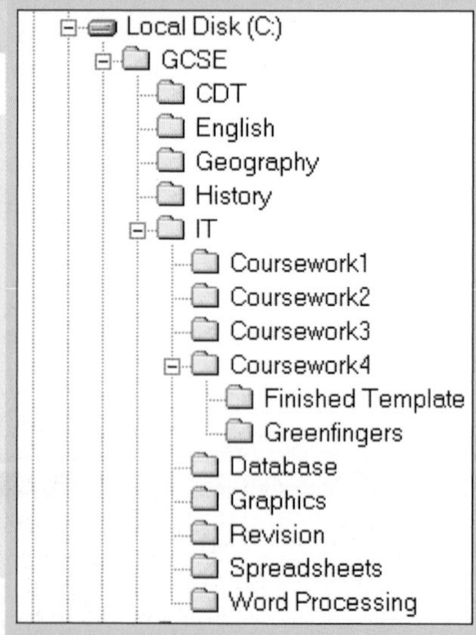

Figure 2.36

Data security

Have you ever experienced your computer system 'freezing up' for no apparent reason? Sometimes it is because the system is being asked to do more than it can cope with. All you can do is reboot your computer and hope that your work will be recovered. If you had saved your work regularly, however, you wouldn't have a problem because you could revert to the saved data file and continue. However, if the problem was due to hard drive failure you wouldn't be able to resume your work unless you had a very recent backup copy of your work on a floppy disk.

Hard drive failure and the subsequent loss of data could spell disaster for any organisation that relies on the computer to process their day-to-day functions such as purchasing, stock control, accounting, production, etc. Loss of data means loss of business. Protection of data is therefore an essential operation within any organisation. The obvious way to protect data is by regular backing up of the system.

Backup methods

Although a floppy disk might provide a suitable method of backup for your coursework, most businesses have far too much data for disks or CD-ROMs and they generally use magnetic tape (see page 50). All systems should be backed up at regular intervals and this is generally carried out overnight when the system is not busy. In this way, if disaster strikes, the business can recover data and resume trading. Although the company would not have a record of every transaction since the last backup, they would not lose everything.

Backup tapes or disks, together with software, should be stored in special 'disaster-proof' safes. These are usually stored away from the main business premises so that if the premises are destroyed the tapes and disks will still be safe. Less valuable data could well be kept in a locked filing cabinet which might also be bolted to the floor.

Nowadays more and more people use laptop computers in addition to the main company computer system. Backing up data stored on the mainframe computer will not help if the data is only on a laptop, which might get damaged, lost or stolen, so it is just as important to ensure that data on a laptop is saved both internally on the hard drive and externally on a floppy disk or CD-ROM.

Remember that even if you have set your computer to automatically back up your work, the backups will also be on the hard drive and it could be equally disastrous for you if your hard drive crashed and you lost everything on your machine. So be warned – save your work **regularly** on both the hard drive and a disk or CD-ROM!

Activity

You can take simple measures to secure your own data files. Have a look at the File, Save As menu and select Tools and General Options (or use Tools, Options and Save).

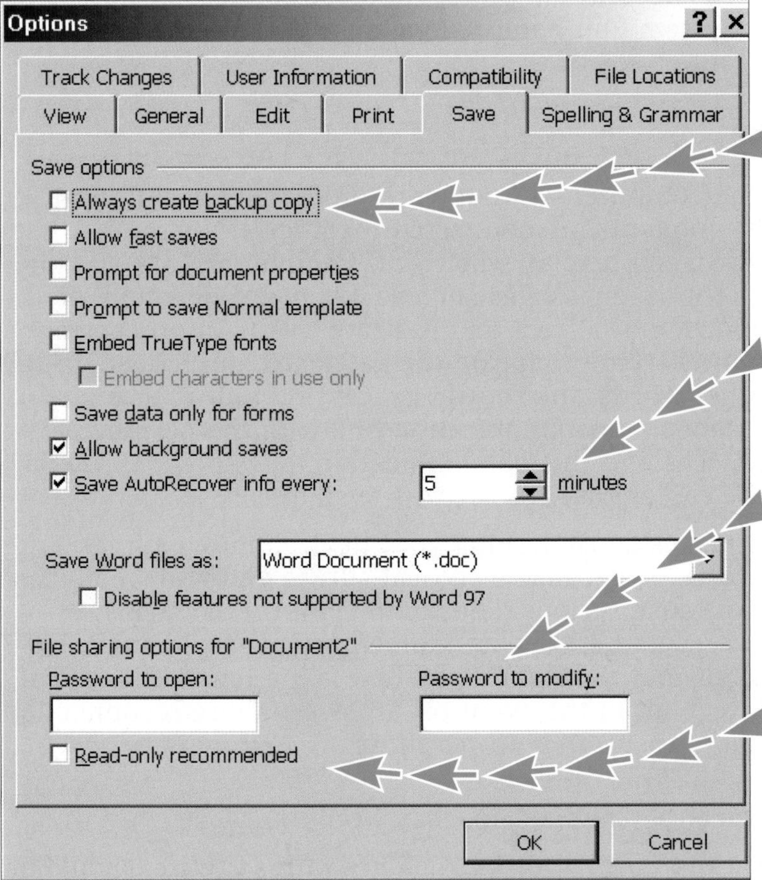

Figure 2.37 *Automatic backup and making files secure*

Creating data directories or folders

When software is installed on a computer the operating system ensures that directories/folders are created to keep all the relevant program files together. It is equally as important when saving your work as it is to create directories/folders to separate data files from program files. If we didn't do this we would end up with a very long, muddled list of data files.

Key points

- Utility programs protect the system from virus attack and check the performance of the computer.
- Passwords should always remain secret.
- Back up regularly and store backup disks safely.
- Use directories and folders to organise your data files.

Setting up the system

There are some very important things you should remember whenever you are working with a computer system. They may appear to be common sense but it is worth pointing them out to you again:

1 To avoid damaging a computer, never plug in or unplug a cable when the system power is on.
2 Never handle a live connector – it could kill you.
3 Connect all the power cables to the rear of the system unit before plugging them into the wall outlet or power strip.

Cables and connectors

The computer will not work unless all the different components are connected together. If you look at the on-screen display when your computer boots up you might see messages such as 'keyboard detected' or 'mouse initialised' that indicate the main processing unit is trying to locate the keyboard and mouse. In other words, the central processing unit is trying to establish a communication link with the peripheral devices and this communication takes place through the cables that connect the system.

It makes sense to plug your devices into a surge protector because electrical surges and voltage spikes can cause serious damage to computer systems. Surges and spikes are momentary overvoltages of up to several thousand volts that last a few millionths of a second. In the event off a power failure reconnection might result in a power surge.

Powering up

When you power up you should hear the hard disk beginning to spin and see the monitor flicker into life. If nothing happens, switch off the computer and check the power cables to make sure they are still plugged in securely. If you are using a surge protector, make sure it is switched on. Check that the monitor is turned on and adjust the brightness control if necessary.

Installation

Once you have the basic system connected, powered up and running smoothly, you are ready to install the software and prepare the system for use. Almost all systems come with the operating system pre-installed and configured. From this point you may have to install drivers for the display, the printer and any other peripherals, as well as the application software.

Device drivers are programs that enable a computer system to communicate with a device. A printer driver, for example, translates computer data into a form that is understood by the specific type of printer you have connected. In most cases, device drivers also manipulate the hardware involved in sending data to the device.

Accessing the applications

To ensure that your software has been loaded successfully and each application is functioning correctly, you need to test it. The following procedure will be adequate.

1. Open the application.
2. Type 'Test1' with your initials and the date.
3. Save the file as Test1 with any appropriate extension.
4. Exit the application.
5. Re-open the application.
6. Open the file.
7. Print a copy.
8. Save and close the file and exit the application.

System configuration

The system will be set up with standard settings which, for most people, will be quite acceptable. However, some people will find the system much easier to use if some small adjustments are made. This is called configuring the system. For example, the left-handed user will find the mouse more comfortable to use if the button functions are reversed.

Systems can be configured in several ways:

- by creating data directories or folders
- through the Control Panel
- through the pull-down menus
- through style sheets.

Additionally, the creation of templates and macros will make the system easier to use.

Test your understanding

Are the following statements True or False?

1 The rubber ball in an optical mouse needs regular cleaning.

2 The central processing unit controls all other parts of the computer.

3 Memory is measured in MHz.

4 A typical CD-ROM can store data which is equivalent to about 450 floppy disks.

5 A JPEG file is the preferred format for saving animations to the Internet.

6 Data folders and directories serve the same purpose as a filing cabinet.

7 Always turn the computer off before unplugging a cable.

8 RAM is used for storing the start-up instructions on the computer.

9 A floppy disk can be taken from one computer to another.

10 Setting my computer to automatic backup is all I need to do to ensure my data files are safe.

11 My computer comes with Windows ME. I don't need to buy additional software.

12 Loss of data due to hardware failure can be minimised by regular backups.

13 The use of data folders (or directories) will make my computer work faster.

Fill in the gaps using the words below (you can use words more than once):

unit input central data output
process commands processing
storage programs graphical central
operating interface user device

14 The four stages in the information processing cycle are i________, p________, o________, and s________.

15 The c________ p________ u________ is sometimes referred to as the computer's brain.

16 Input devices enable you to enter d________, c________ and p________ into the computer's central processing unit.

17 Windows is a g________ u________ i________.

18 The o________ s________ software manages the running of the computer.

19 An o________ d________ displays the results of commands fed into the computer.

20 Computer terminology is full of abbreviations. Look at the list below, write the abbreviation in full and try and decide into which category (or categories) it falls.

Abbreviation	Meaning	Input	Output	Process	Storage
OCR					
RAM					
SVGA					
MHz					
TFT LCD					
DVD					
OMR					
NCR					
ROM					
MB					
CRT					
CD-RW					
VDU					
dpi					
USB					
GB					

CHAPTER 3

Word processing and desktop publishing

Word processing is the use of a computer to enter, edit and manipulate text to produce letters, business reports, memos – in fact, any kind of written work which is mainly **text**. A text letter or report produced using a word processor is called a **document**.

The word-processing application (or program) can be used to:

- correct or **edit** text
- set out the text in different **formats**
- store or **save** the edited text
- **print** the text.
- check automatically for spelling and grammar
- create a file for attachment to an e-mail document
- send multiple copies of the same document
- show pictures, graphs, tables and charts alongside the text.

The latest word-processing applications have many of the features of a desktop publishing (DTP) program and allow you to import text, graphics and tables created in other programs.

Desktop publishing is the use of a computer system to produce page layouts for printing. The contents of the pages are prepared using:

- a word processor for the text
- a graphics package for pictures, diagrams and other illustrations

and imported into the desktop publishing package to adjust the layout and appearance.

Word processing

Activity

Use a word processor to set up this page:

- paper size = A4
- orientation = portrait
- page margins:
  top/bottom = 1.25"
  left/right = 1.5"

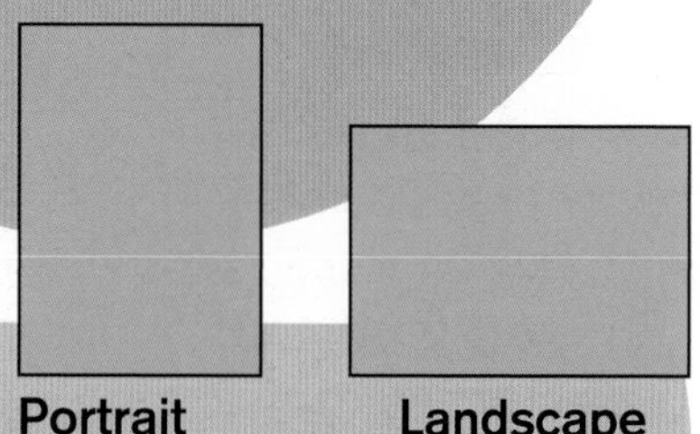

Figure 3.1 *Page orientation*

Portrait is the normal (default) setting and is used for letters and business reports.

Landscape is often used when an A4 page is folded to create an A5 booklet. It is also used whenever wide tables are created in a spreadsheet program.

Setting up a new document

When using a word processor before any text is entered, some properties of the page should be set. These are called **page attributes** and are: paper size and orientation.

Paper size

The most commonly used paper sizes are

- **A4** 297 mm x 210 mm
- **A5** 210 mm x 148 mm

All modern printers will print to A4 paper, but for other sizes, you will need to check your printer.

Page orientation

A document can be set up to be either **portrait** or **landscape**. Portrait has the longest side vertical and landscape has the longest side horizontal.

Page margins

The margin is the space around the outside of the page which is not printed on. Leaving margins is necessary as most printers cannot print right up to the edges of the paper. The size of each margin can be set individually.

The text can be made wider or narrower by altering the left and right margins. By adjusting the top and bottom margins, the text can be made longer or shorter.

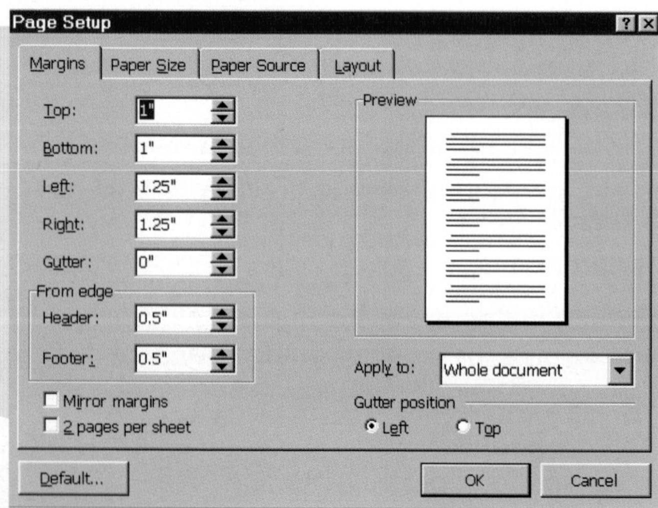

Figure 3.2 *Setting up page margins*

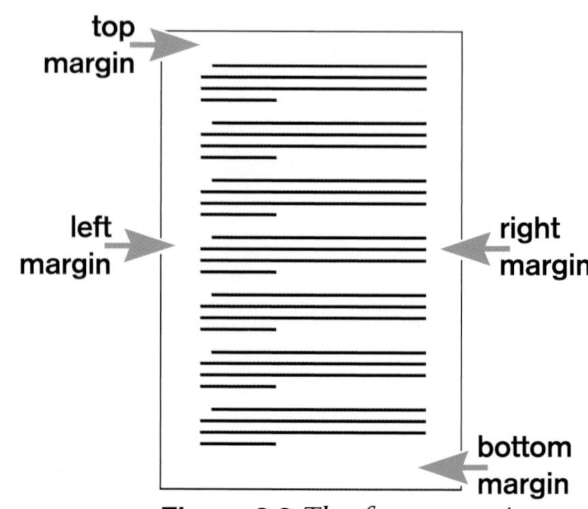

Figure 3.3 *The four margins*

Line spacing

Text is normally printed using **single line spacing**:

Text is normally printed using single line spacing.
Text is normally printed using single line spacing.
Text is normally printed using single line spacing.

Sometimes documents are produced using **double line spacing**. This option is usually available in a typical word processor.

This is double line spacing, with a gap between lines.

This is double line spacing, with a gap between lines.

This is double line spacing, with a gap between lines.

Double line spacing is often used in word-processed essays and business reports.

Figure 3.4 shows the line spacing options in a typical word processor.

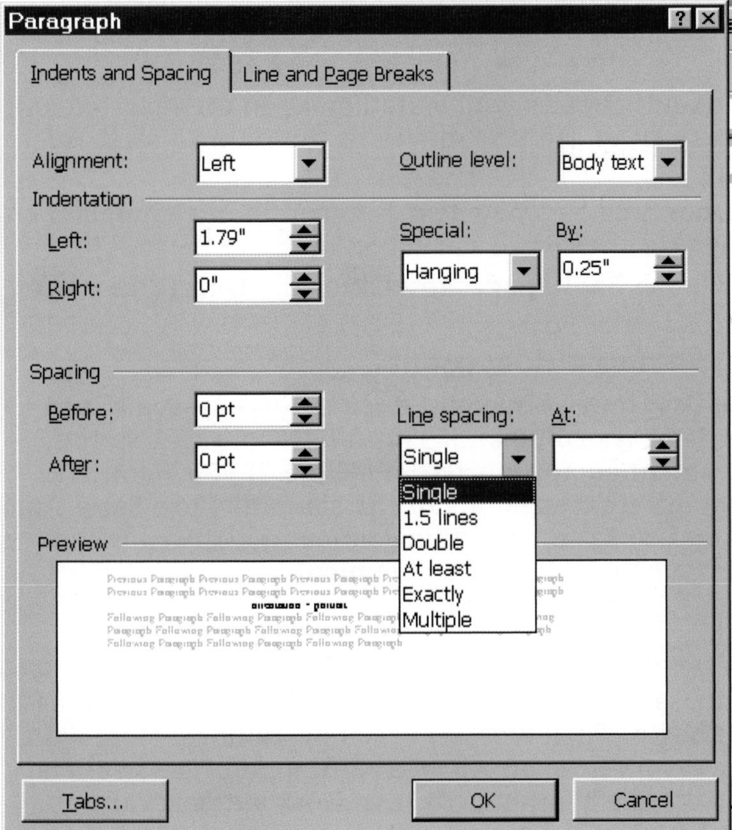

Figure 3.4 *Setting line spacing*

Key points

- Set page attributes before entering text.
- Use double line spacing for essays and reports.
- Save the document you are working on every few minutes.

Entering and saving text

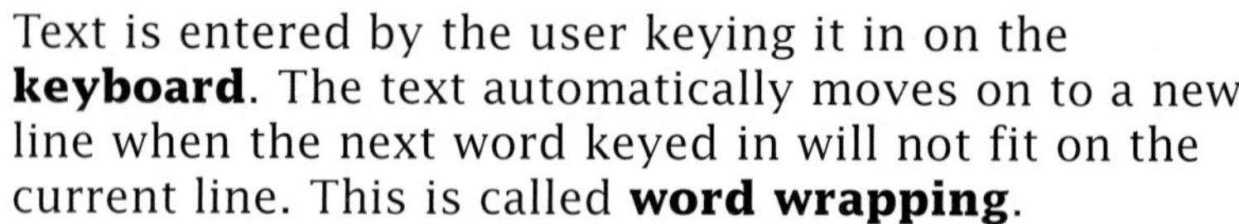

Text is entered by the user keying it in on the **keyboard**. The text automatically moves on to a new line when the next word keyed in will not fit on the current line. This is called **word wrapping**.

To end a paragraph the user presses the **Enter** key once. To leave a line space between paragraphs, the **Enter** key must be pressed a second time.

Tab key

To type one empty character space the Spacebar is used. To move more than one space at a time, the Tab key can be used. When the Tab key is pressed, the cursor moves several places to the right, usually about 5 character spaces or about $\frac{1}{2}$" to the next Tab stop position. The default tab width can be changed.

Editing text

To edit text means to change the text in some way, e.g. moving text around and/or correcting mistakes in the text.

To move to the part of the text which is to be edited the user can use the arrow keys or the mouse (or touchpad on a laptop). Once at the correct place in the text, the edit can be done in a number of ways:

- **Insert** – letters which are keying in are inserted and the rest of the text moves to the right to make space for the added text.
- **Overtype** – as new text is keyed in, the character next to the cursor is rubbed out.
- Use the **Backspace key** ← or the **Delete key** Del

Saving a document

The first time you save a document you usually use the **Save As** command. This allows you to give the document an appropriate filename. If you want to have different versions of the same file, use **Save As**. If you use **Save**, then this command overwrites the previous version of the document.

When saving work:

- Decide where to save the work

To be safe, save a new document as a file as soon as you begin. Then resave every few minutes. Most word processors have an **AutoSave** function. The user can instruct the computer to save work automatically at regular intervals, e.g. every five minutes.

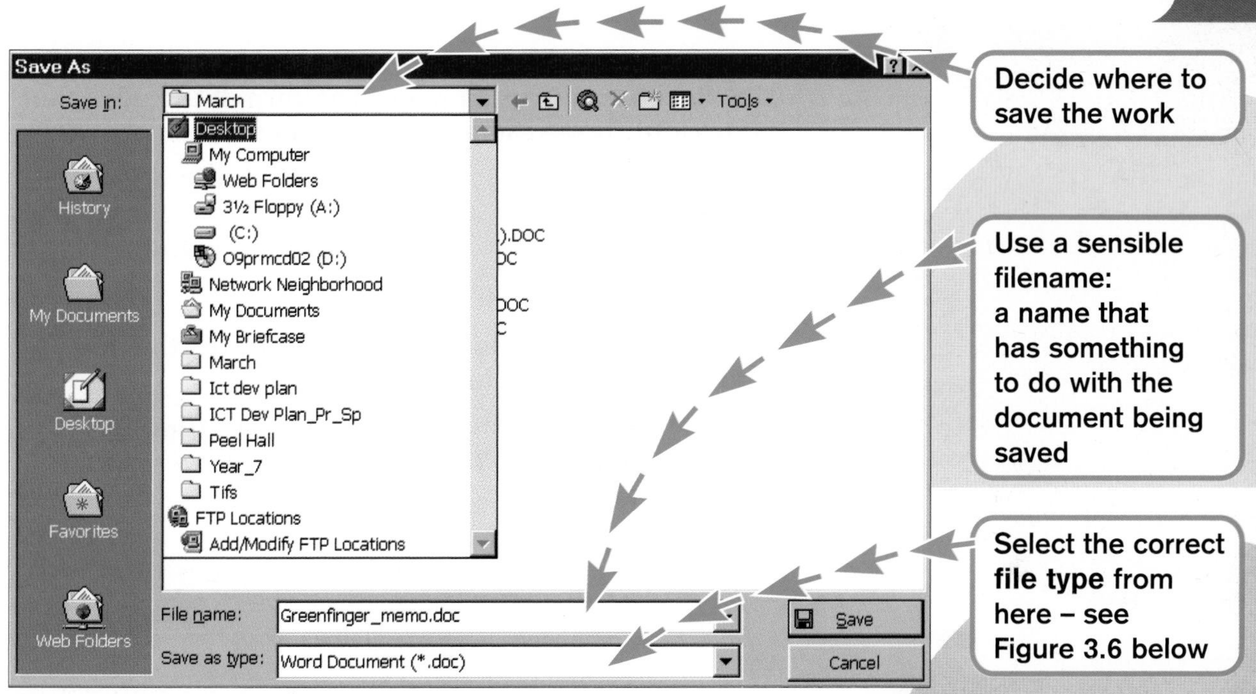

Figure 3.5 *Saving work*

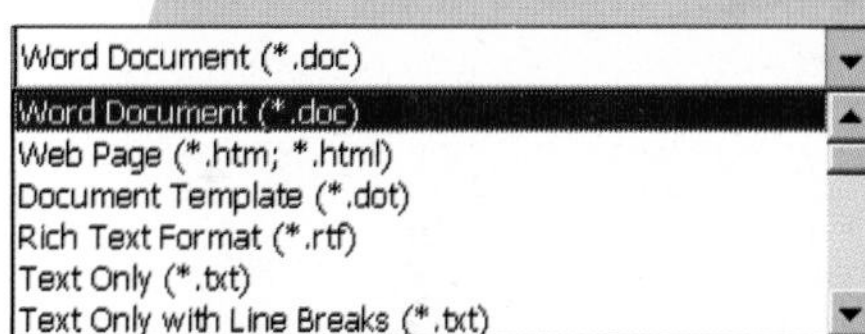

Figure 3.6 *File types*

Working with blocks of text

A word processor will allow a block of text, e.g. a sentence or paragraph, to be marked for:

- deletion of the marked text
- the movement of a block of text from one part of the document to another
- a copy of the marked text to be placed at some other point in the document
- text to be cut and pasted from one document to another.

These functions are known as **cut** and **paste**.

Cut: to delete selected text from a document. The cut is temporarily stored in the Clipboard, from where it can be pasted elsewhere or deleted.
Paste: to move the material from the Clipboard to its new location.

Printing a document

Before printing:

- make sure the work is saved
- use the Print Preview facility of the word processor to check what the document will look like when printed
- if the document does not look right, edit and resave before printing!

Key points

- Text can be moved using cut and paste.
- The text must be marked before it can be moved.
- Use Print Preview to check the appearance of text before printing.
- Use a laser printer to give fast, high quality copies.

Formatting a document 1

Format describes the appearance of the document on the screen and printed page. The format includes the style, font, text spacing and alignment.

Text style

The style of the text can be changed in many ways.

For example, text can be:

- emboldened – **This text is made bold, the letters are darker and thicker**
- underscored – This text has a line drawn under it
- italicised (italic) – *This text leans forward*
- superscript or subscript text:

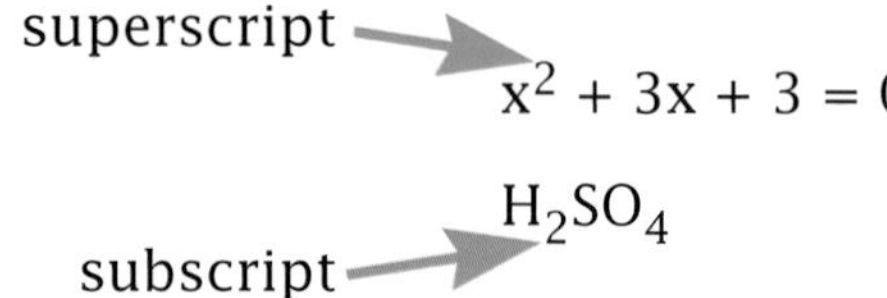

Fonts

A font is a complete set of characters with the same typeface.

It is best to use fonts that are clear and easy to read. Ornate fonts are best left for posters and design work. Each font comes in a range of sizes.

Examples: This is Arial 12 point

This is Courier ITC 14 point

This is Sand 9 point

Sans serif and serif fonts

Serif fonts have small strokes at the top and bottom of letters. Serif fonts help the eye of the reader to flow through the text as it is read. They are often used in newspapers and magazines.

- This text is written in a serif font – this is Times New Roman.

Sans serif fonts do not have any strokes and are simple and plain in appearance. Sans serif fonts are often used in children's books and on application forms.

This text is written in a sans serif font – this is Arial.

Figure 3.7 shows a typical dialogue box from which the font, font style, size and effect can be chosen:

Key points

When choosing font styles and sizes don't forget:

- your **audience** – the person or people who will be reading the document.

  Young children will need a simple font – so choose a sans serif font.
- your **message** – what you are trying to say.
- that using too many different fonts and styles will stop the reader from getting the message.

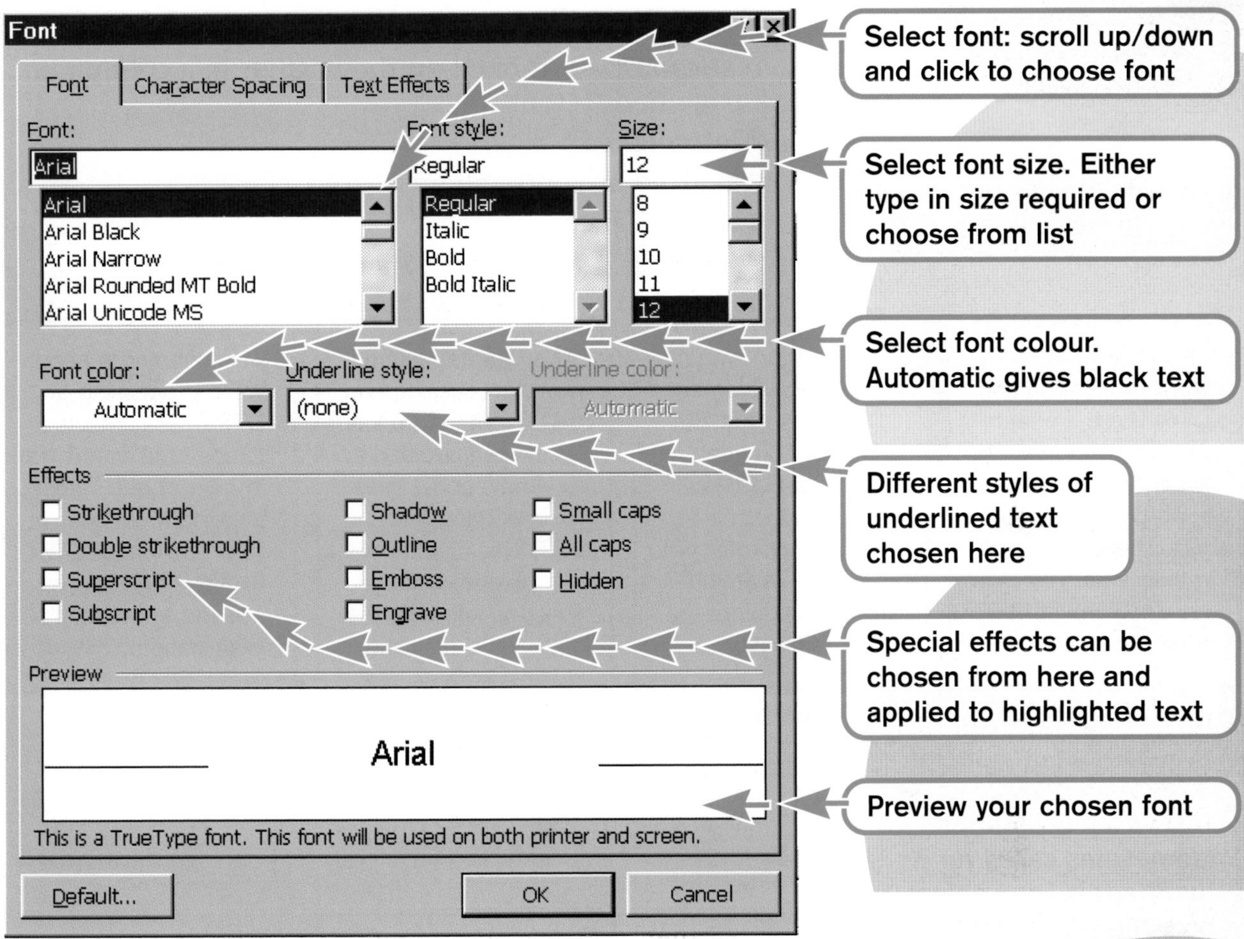

Figure 3.7 *Selecting fonts and styles*

Activity

- Using the document you have set up on page 70, enter the following extract from a Geenfingers' brochure.

> Autumn shades are vivid oranges, yellows and browns.
> Spring sees bulbs beginning to break through, with the garden coming to life after a long winter sleep.
> Winter has the garden looking very sad apart from the odd snowdrop and evergreen tree such as the holly with its bright red berries.
> Summer brings almost everything into full bloom, with the garden full of life and brilliant colours.

- Set the line spacing to double line spacing.
- Use cut and past to move the sentences so that they are in the correct order of the seasons.
- Save the file as 'GREENFINGERS'.
- Check the appearance using Print Preview. Edit if necessary and print the document.

Format the text as shown below.

Seasons in: Arial, **Bold**, 14, black. All other text: Times New Roman, Regular,11, black.

Font colour to match word, e.g. 'oranges' to be shown in orange colour

CHAPTER 3

Formatting a document 2

Text alignment

Text can be positioned on the page or in a column on a page in different ways:

- left aligned
- centred or centre aligned
- right aligned
- justified – sometimes called fully justified

This chapter is about word processing and DTP. There are lots of things you need to know about these important topics in ICT. This chapter will explain what you need to know for the examination.	This chapter is about word processing and DTP. There are lots of things you need to know about these important topics in ICT. This chapter will explain what you need to know for the examination.	This chapter is about word processing and DTP. There are lots of things you need to know about these important topics in ICT. This chapter will explain what you need to know for the examination.	This chapter is about word processing and DTP. There are lots of things you need to know about these important topics in ICT. This chapter will explain what you need to know for the examination.
Left aligned	**Centred**	**Right aligned**	**Justified**

Figure 3.8 *Text alignment*

Text which is justified (sometimes called fully justified) is lined up against both the left- and right- hand margins of the page or column. The word-processing program checks the length of each line of text, line by line. If the text is less than the line length, the text is stretched along the line, with additional spaces added where required.

Head Office
44 Meryview Way
SEAHAVEN
SE4 8HV
Tel: 076 2883 4621 Fax: 076 2883 4633 E-mail: Greenfingers@userve.co.uk

Ref: PW/VR/CD324

01 January 2001

Mrs J Price
Landscapes Direct
21a Lloyd Place
Sheepstone
SH12 4PV

Dear Mrs Price

I am pleased to enclose our latest catalogue as requested. You will see that we are currently offering a 10% discount on all trade orders placed before the end of the month. If you wish to take advantage of this offer please contact me as soon as possible.

I look forward to hearing from you.

Yours sincerely

Pete Wellings
Wholesale Manager

Centred

Left aligned

Justified

Figure 3.9 *A business letter showing alignments*

Key points

- Text can be aligned to the left, centre or right of the page.
- Text can be justified – the text is stretched out to fill the line.

Columns

Today's word processors allow pages to be created with columns as shown in Figure 3.10.

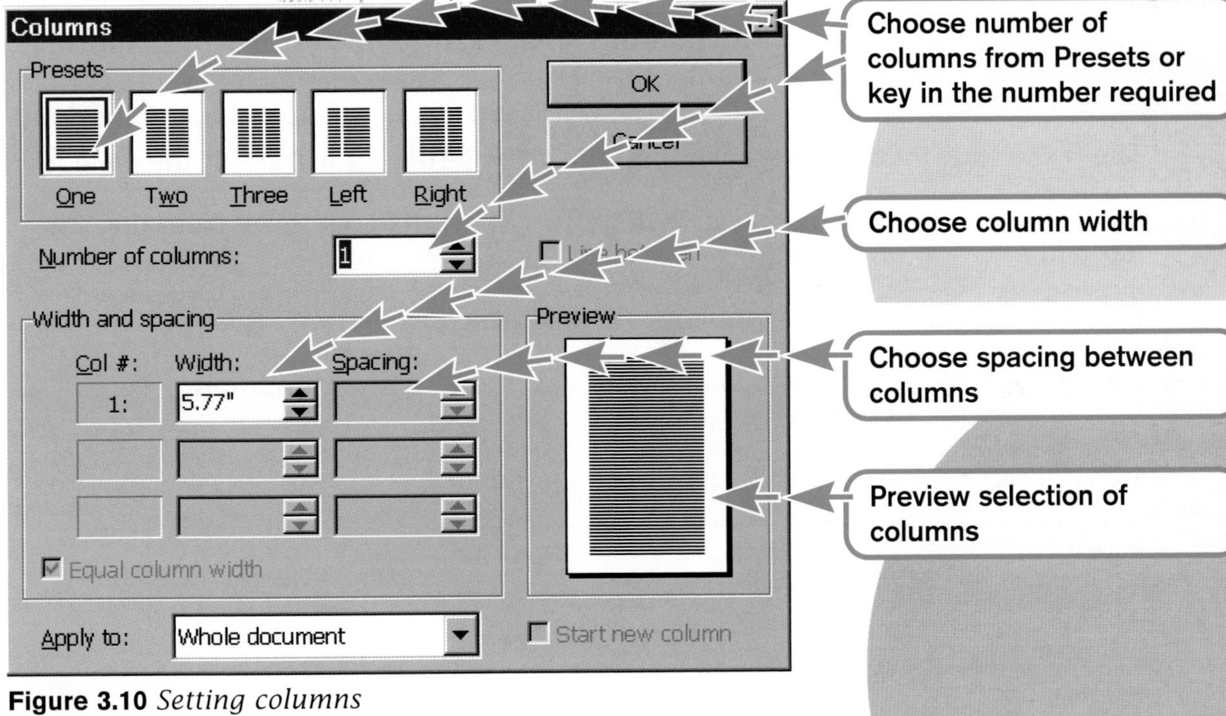

Figure 3.10 *Setting columns*

Columns are often used within a word-processing program when a simple newsletter is being produced. For more complicated newsletters **desktop publishing** would be used.

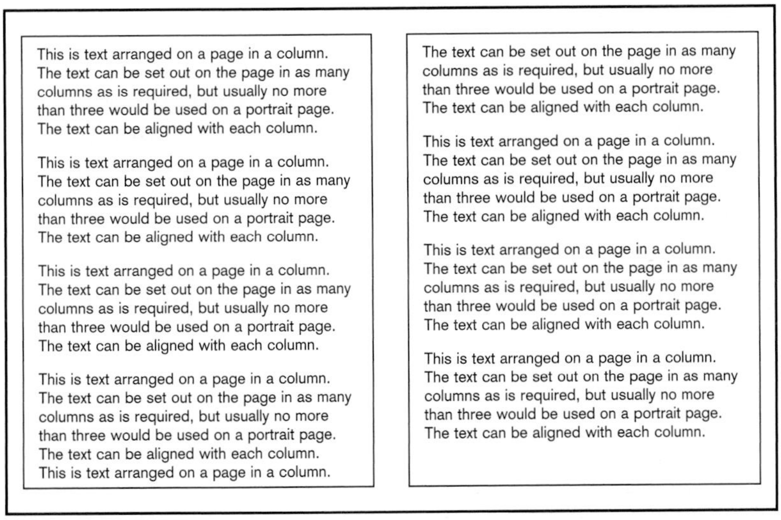

This is text arranged on a page in a column. The text can be set out on the page in as many columns as is required, but usually no more than three would be used on a portrait page. The text can be aligned with each column.

This is text arranged on a page in a column. The text can be set out on the page in as many columns as is required, but usually no more than three would be used on a portrait page. The text can be aligned with each column.

This is text arranged on a page in a column. The text can be set out on the page in as many columns as is required, but usually no more than three would be used on a portrait page. The text can be aligned with each column.

This is text arranged on a page in a column. The text can be set out on the page in as many columns as is required, but usually no more than three would be used on a portrait page. The text can be aligned with each column. This is text arranged on a page in a column.

The text can be set out on the page in as many columns as is required, but usually no more than three would be used on a portrait page. The text can be aligned with each column.

This is text arranged on a page in a column. The text can be set out on the page in as many columns as is required, but usually no more than three would be used on a portrait page. The text can be aligned with each column.

This is text arranged on a page in a column. The text can be set out on the page in as many columns as is required, but usually no more than three would be used on a portrait page. The text can be aligned with each column.

This is text arranged on a page in a column. The text can be set out on the page in as many columns as is required, but usually no more than three would be used on a portrait page. The text can be aligned with each column.

Figure 3.11 *Columns in a simple newsletter*

Formatting a document 3

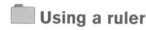

Indents

To **indent** text means to move it in from the margin. Indents are used to emphasise or separate text to make it easier to read.

The **indent** is the distance the text is moved in from the margin.

The text is **not** indented because it starts at the left-hand margin of the page.

    This text **is** indented because it starts a short distance away from the left-hand margin of the page.

In business reports hanging indents are often used as below:

1.1 This is an example of a hanging indent. It allows the paragraph numbering to be clearly seen.

1.2 This is a second paragraph of hanging indent.

Figure 3.12 *Indents*

Using a ruler

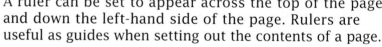

Figure 3.13 *A ruler*

A ruler can be set to appear across the top of the page and down the left-hand side of the page. Rulers are useful as guides when setting out the contents of a page.

Bullets

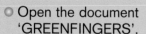

Bullets are used to make a list or a number of lines stand out from the rest of the page. A **bullet** can be any character, but the most common is the filled in circle: •

Bullets are used when listing items whose content is of similar importance.

A **numbered list** is similar to a bulleted list, except that numbers are used instead of bullet characters.

Activity

- Open the document 'GREENFINGERS'.
- Make each sentence start with a bullet point.
- Set the Page Number to be:
  Bottom
  Centre
- Save the document and print it.

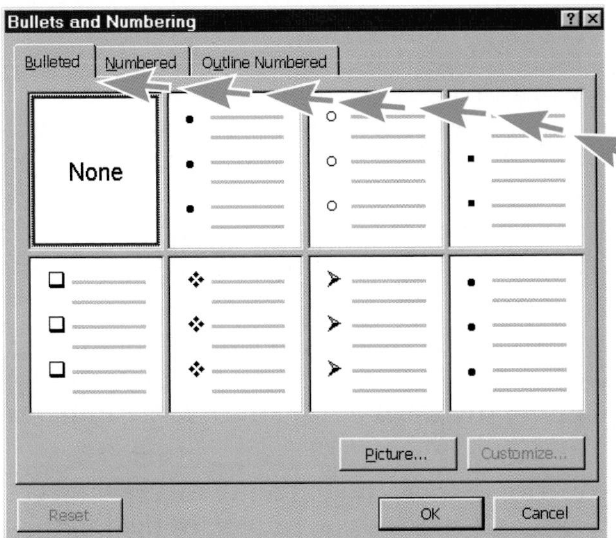

Figure 3.14 *Choosing a Bulleted list*

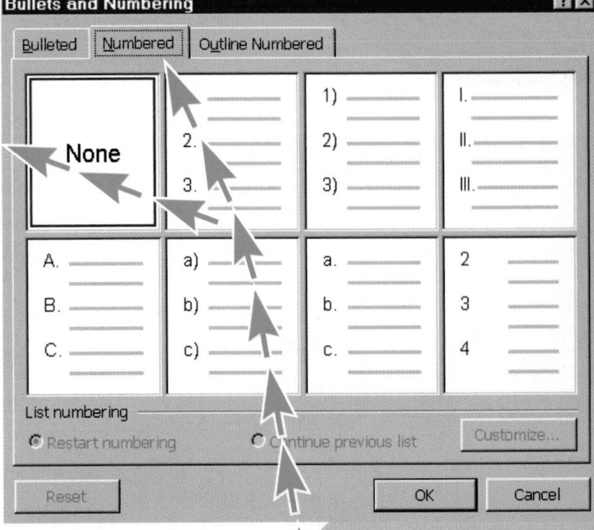

Figure 3.15 *Choosing a Numbered list*

Page numbering

In a document with more than one page, **page numbering** is often used. Figure 3.16 shows a typical dialogue box from which page numbers can be added to a document.

Once page numbering has been set up and **OK** selected, then page numbers are added automatically to pages as they are created in a document. Page numbers will then appear on both the screen and printed versions of the document.

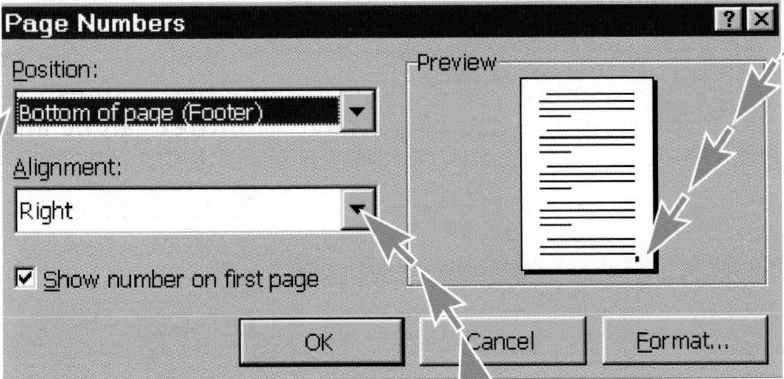

Figure 3.16 *Adding page numbers*

Key points

- An indent moves text in from a margin.
- A ruler can be used as a guide when setting out the contents of a page.
- Bullets make lines of text stand out from the page.
- Page numbers should be used on documents with more than one page.

Proof reading

Proof reading is checking a document to see if there are any errors. These errors may be in the layout, spelling, grammar or the number of words allowed in the document. A word processor can be programmed to check spelling, grammar and the number of words used.

Checking spelling

Most word processors have a built in **spell checker** program which allows text to be checked to make sure that it is spelt correctly. The program checks for the correct spelling of words in a document by comparing each word against a stored, dictionary file of correctly spelled words. The dictionary contains a large number of commonly used words.

A spell checker can display suggestions for the correct spelling of a word and enables you to replace the misspelt word with the correct one. It is important to remember that the spell checker will not show words which are correctly spelt but used incorrectly. For example:

My bike has **too** wheels	'too' is a correctly spelt word, but the sentence should have read, 'My bike has **two** wheels'.

Words can be added to the spell checker's dictionary. These words might include real names, address names and technical words not normally found in a dictionary.

In Figure 3.17, some text has been entered and the spell checker has been used.

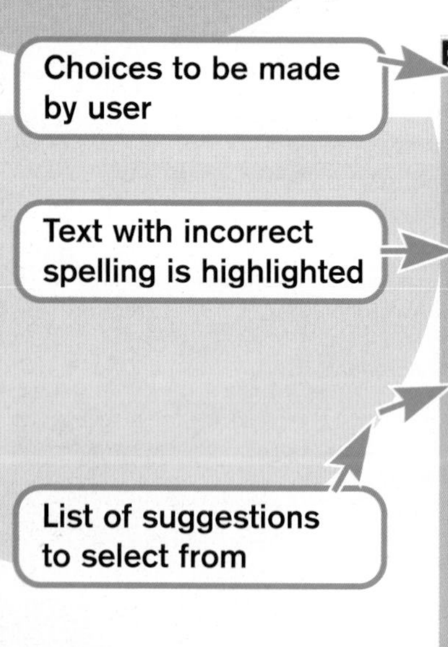

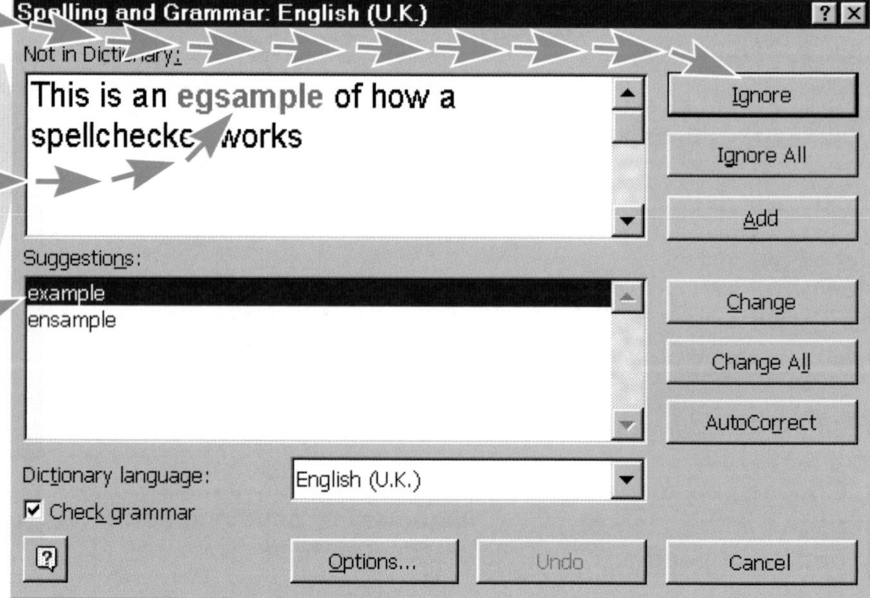

Figure 3.17 *Checking spelling*

Checking grammar

In this check, the software looks at the way a sentence is written. It compares the sentence with sets of rules for writing style and grammar. Any part of the sentence which breaks the rules is highlighted. Suggestions for improvement are shown. The process of correcting grammar is similar to that for spell checking.

Using the thesaurus

This can be used to find a word of **similar meaning** to another word. Words of similar meaning are called **synonyms**.

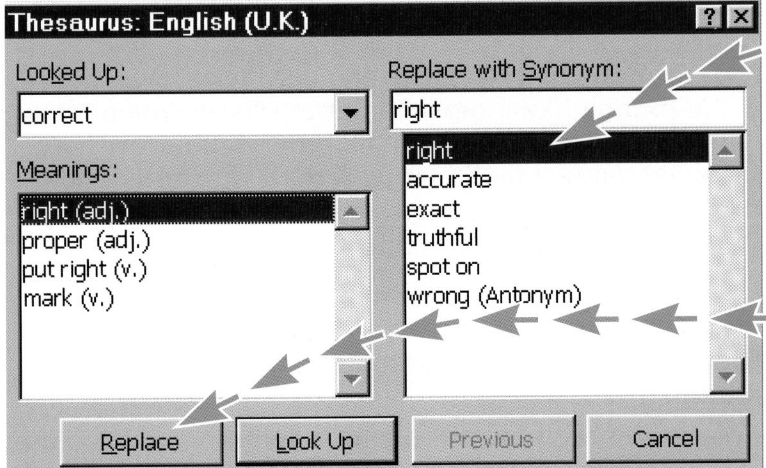

Figure 3.18 *Using a thesaurus*

Word count

It is sometimes useful to know how many words have been typed in a document. For example, you may have been given an essay to complete in no more than 1,500 words.

Some word processors allow you to set a limit on the number of words allowed in a document and when this limit is reached a warning message is given by the software.

Activity

Open the file named 'GREENFINGERS'.

- Use a spell checker to check the spelling.
- Use a thesaurus to find and replace the word 'vivid'.
- Check the number of words.
- Save the file.

Key points

- Always proof read a document before printing.
- A spell checker should be used to check the spelling. Remember that a correctly spelt word used in the wrong context will not be spotted.
- A thesaurus can be used to find a word of a similar meaning to another.
- Word Count can be used to make sure a document is within the maximum number of words allowed.

Mail merge and templates

Mail merge

Companies often need to send standard letters to customers in which the content of the letter is the same and only the name and address need to be changed.

If each letter had to be keyed in individually this would be very time-consuming.

You will find examples of document layouts in the Tutor's File.

Modern word processors can solve this problem by producing multiple copies of the standard letter, adding to the letter the name and address of each person on a **mailing list** stored on a database, spreadsheet or as a text file – known as the **source data file**.

A **personalised letter** is a standard letter which is made to look like a personal letter. The recipient's name and address, and maybe other details, are included using a mail merge. A **mail merge** is the process of producing a personalised letter by merging (putting together) the recipient's personal details stored on the mailing list onto the standard letter.

Steps in creating a personalised letter using mail merge

Creation of the first personalised letter:

1 Word process the standard letter and leave gaps for **markers** to show where personalised data will go. See Figure 3.19.

2 Create a data file of personal data on a **database**.

3 Word processor reads first person's data from data file.

4 Word processor inserts data into gaps in standard letter.

5 Letter printed from word processor.

The above steps are repeated for all people on the mailing list.

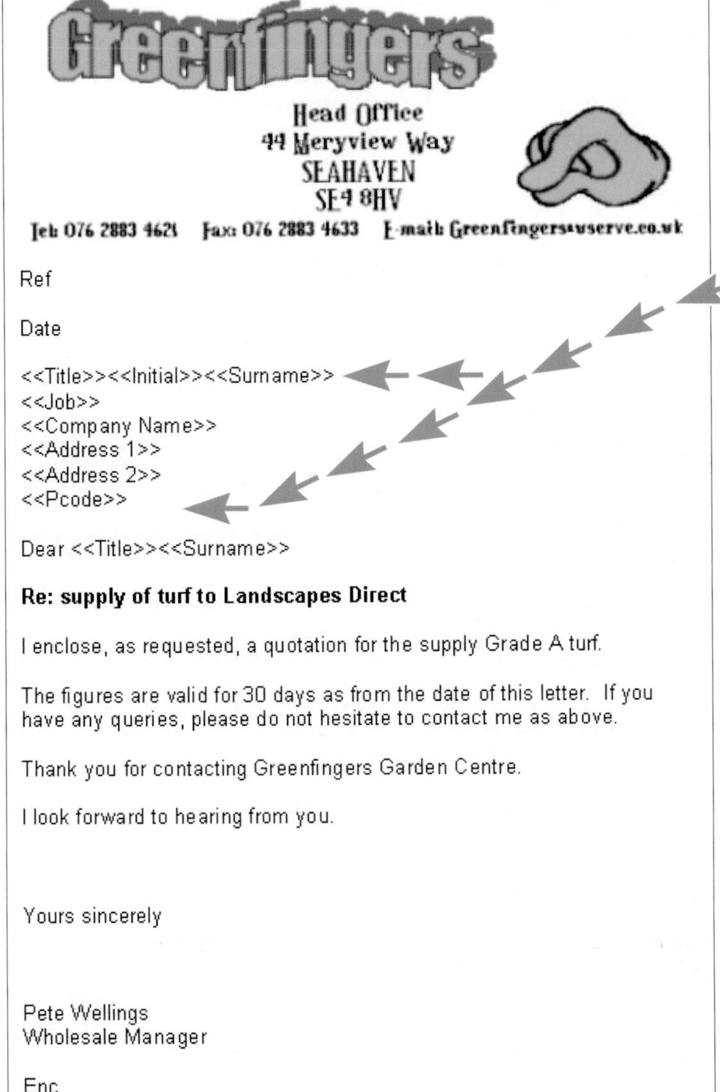

Greenfingers

Head Office
44 Meryview Way
SEAHAVEN
SE4 8HV

Tel: 076 2883 4621 Fax: 076 2883 4633 E-mail: Greenfingers@userve.co.uk

Ref

Date

<<Title>><<Initial>><<Surname>>
<<Job>>
<<Company Name>>
<<Address 1>>
<<Address 2>>
<<Pcode>>

Dear <<Title>><<Surname>>

Re: supply of turf to Landscapes Direct

I enclose, as requested, a quotation for the supply Grade A turf.

The figures are valid for 30 days as from the date of this letter. If you have any queries, please do not hesitate to contact me as above.

Thank you for contacting Greenfingers Garden Centre.

I look forward to hearing from you.

Yours sincerely

Pete Wellings
Wholesale Manager

Enc

Figure 3.19 *Standard letter with markers*

Apart from the Company Name the rest of the standard letter text stays the same for each person's letter

Markers inserted into standard letter. Personalised data items from data file will be inserted for each person's letter

Templates

A **template** is a framework for a document saved as a template file. Templates may be used for letters or memorandums and other commercial documents. A template contains settings that include the font, font size, page layout and any special formatting.

Memos are usually written from a template specially set up for the purpose. All the formats are already set up in the template file so all memos based on that template will look the same.

Key points

- Letters written on behalf of companies and firms are business letters on letterheaded paper.
- The salutation must match the complementary close, e,g. 'Dear Sir' must match with 'Yours faithfully'.
- Enc is used to show that a document is enclosed with the letter.
- Mail merge is used to send a standard letter to a number of people on a mailing list.
- Markers are used in the standard letter for data which changes for each recipient.
- A **template** is a framework for a document saved as a template file such as a business letter or a memorandum.

Activity

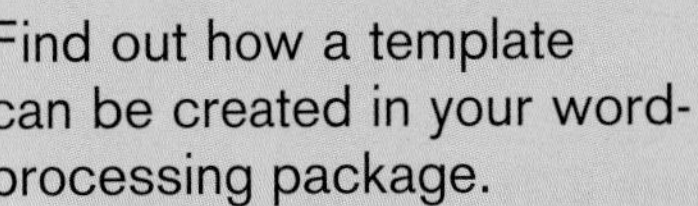

Find out how a template can be created in your word-processing package.

Advanced features

Search and replace

A word processor will allow you to **search** for a word and **replace** it with another one of your choice anywhere it appears in the document. You will have the option to replace or not each time the word is found.

Example:

If Greenfingers changed its name to Greenlands every reference in this textbook to Greenfingers must be changed to Greenlands. In the Find and Replace dialogue box every Greenfingers will be replaced by Greenland.

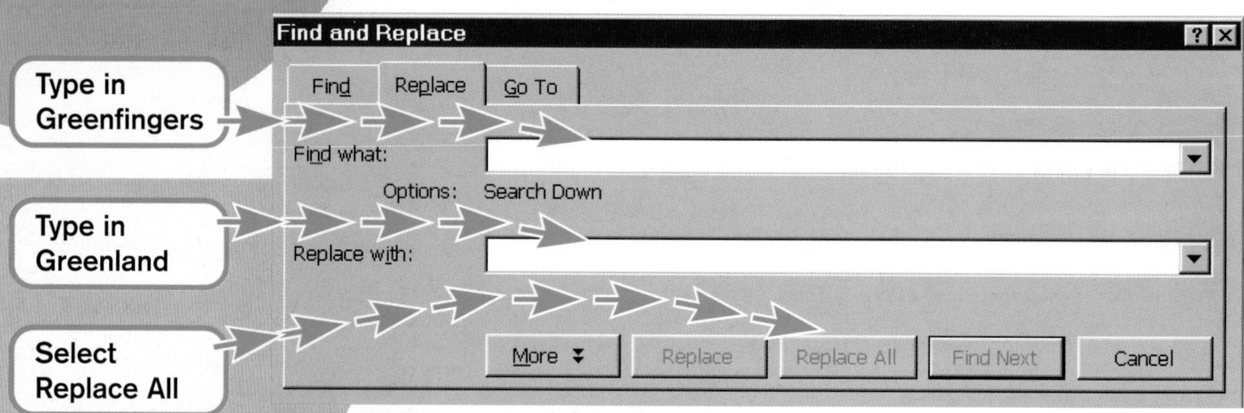

Figure 3.20 *Using Search and Replace*

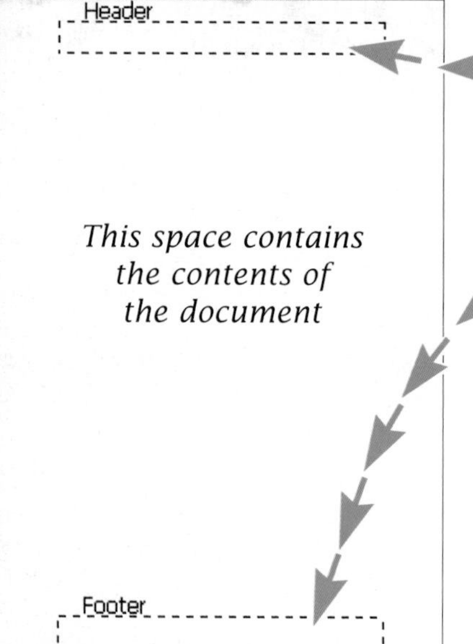

Figure 3.21 *Adding a header or a footer*

Headers and footers

A **header** is text which is repeated on every page of a document in the *top margin* (or head) of each page, e.g. chapter number and chapter title. The page position, style and size of the header can be set within the program.

A **footer** is text which is repeated on every page of a document in the *bottom margin* (or foot) of each page, e.g. a page number which is automatically increased throughout the document.

Headers and footers can include text or graphics, e.g. page numbers, the date, a company logo, the document's title or filename, or the author's name.

Special symbols

To obtain **symbol** characters, such as © or √, the Symbol dialogue box must be used – see Figure 3.22.

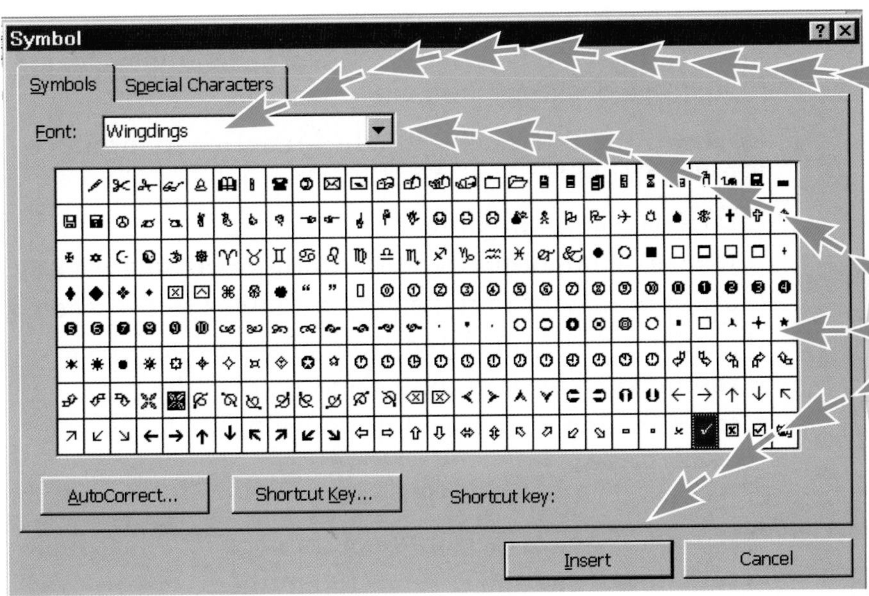

The symbols vary with the font chosen

To obtain a symbol select:
Font
Symbol
Insert
The symbol will now be inserted into the document

Figure 3.22 *Inserting a symbol character*

Integration with other applications

Word processors can 'communicate' with a range of other applications. For example, data from a spreadsheet application in the form of a table or graph, can be **imported** into a word-processed document. This is often used when a business report is being produced.

Similarly, text created in a word processor can be **exported** into a desktop-publishing document. For example, when a newsletter is being created, the text could be created in a word processor and imported into the DTP document.

A document can be created in a word-processing application and sent as an **attachment** to an e-mail message.

Activity

Open the file named 'GREENFINGERS'.

- Replace the word **garden** each time it appears with the word **landscape**.
- Add header: GCSE ICT: Edexcel
- Add footer: © and your name

Key points

- A word can be found and changed using Search and Replace.
- A header is used to place the same piece of text at the top of every page in a document.
- A footer is used to place the same piece of text at the bottom of every page in a document.
- Special symbols such as © are available using the Symbol dialogue box.
- Tables, charts, etc. can be **imported** into a word-processed document.
- Text created using a word processor can be **exported** to a document created using an application such as DTP.
- Word-processed documents can be attached to e-mail messages.

Using desktop publishing tools 1

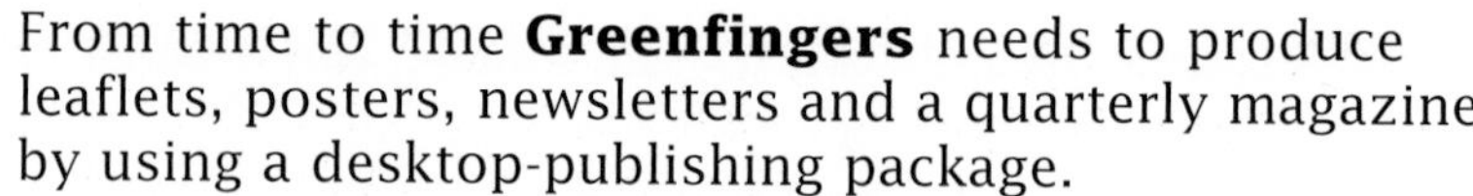

From time to time **Greenfingers** needs to produce leaflets, posters, newsletters and a quarterly magazine by using a desktop-publishing package.

How will the DTP package help Greenfingers produce the documents?

A DTP package will allow:

- text to be imported from the word-processing package
- a wide range of fonts, sizes and styles to be used
- graphics to be imported from graphics packages
- the movement of graphics and text on the page
- the re-sizing of text and graphics to fit the space available
- text flow around graphics
- a page to be divided into columns
- text flow from one column to another
- page layout using guides for accurate positioning of text and graphics.

Some tools and features of a desktop-publishing package

Today's word-processing packages offer many of the features which were only to be found in DTP packages of some years ago. The boundary between word processing and DTP has blurred in recent years, with an overlap of features between the packages.

Fonts

Both word-processing and DTP packages allow the lettering style or font to be changed. This was discussed on page 74.

Kerning

Kerning refers to the space between characters – i.e. the space between letters, punctuation marks, etc. can be adjusted. DTP packages allow changes to be made to character spacing:

This is normal spacing

T h i s i s e x p a n d e d s p a c i n g

This is condensed spacing

Frames

Unlike a word-processing package, a DTP package usually requires text to be entered into a **text frame**, rather than it being keyed in straight onto the page.

Similarly, clip art and pictures are imported into **Clip Art** and **Picture frames**.

DTP packages which require the use of frames are said to be 'frame-based'.

Example:

Greenfingers sends out regular newsletters to customers. Each newsletter is based upon a template or master page similar to the one shown below. The frames are created and the document is then saved. Text and images can then be imported.

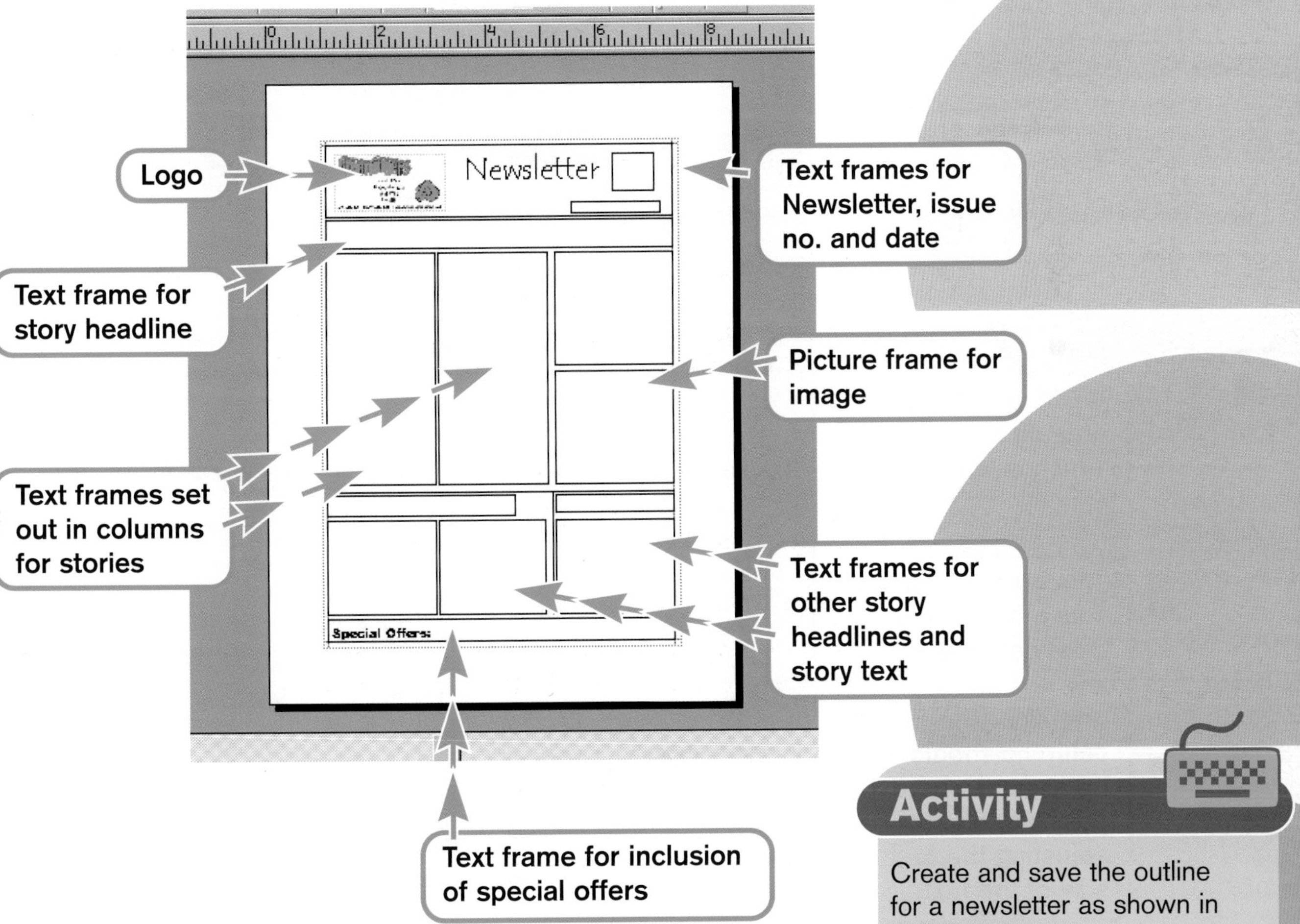

Figure 3.23 *Greenfingers' newsletter template*

Key points

In a DTP package

- text is usually entered into a text frame
- an image is imported into either
  - a Clip Art frame
  - or a Picture frame.

Activity

Create and save the outline for a newsletter as shown in Figure 3.22.

Using desktop publishing tools 2

Frame borders

Frame borders can be made invisible by making the border the same colour as the paper used for printing, e.g. white border on white paper, or by making the line thickness of the border = None.

Borders can be set to be a simple line border or a graphic can be used as the border.

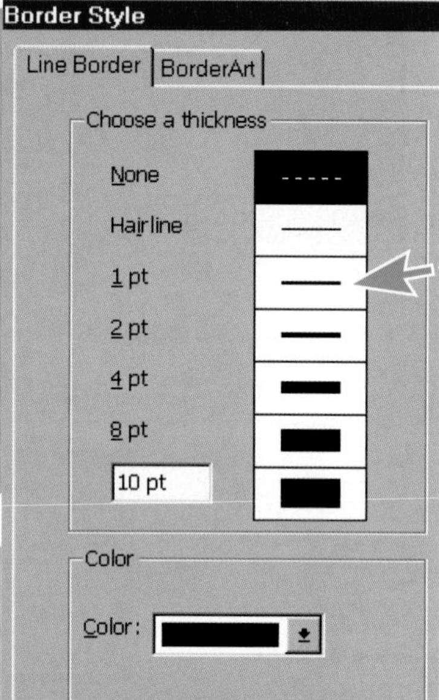

Selecting a Line Border

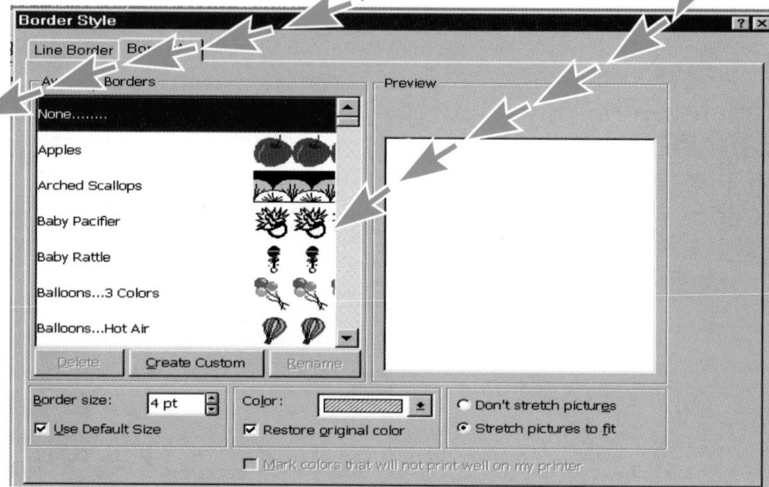

Selecting a border from BorderArt

Figure 3.24 *Types of border*

Text and white space

White space is the area on a page which is 'empty'.

This area is white space because it does not contain any text or graphics. The columns should be aligned where possible, e.g. by adjusting the font size of the text.

This is text arranged on a page in a column. The text can be set out on the page in as many columns as is required, but usually no more than three would be used on a portrait page. The text can be aligned with each column.

This is text arranged on a page in a column. The text can be set out on the page in as many columns as is required, but usually no more than three would be used on a portrait page. The text can be aligned with each column.

This is text arranged on a page in a column. The text can be set out on the page in as many columns as is required, but usually no more than three would be used on a portrait page. The text can be aligned with each column.

This is text arranged on a page in a column. The text can be set out on the page in as many columns as is required, but usually no more than three would be used on a portrait page. The text can be aligned with each column. This is text arranged on a page in a column.

The text can be set out on the page in as many columns as is required, but usually no more than three would be used on a portrait page. The text can be aligned with each column.

This is text arranged on a page in a column. The text can be set out on the page in as many columns as is required, but usually no more than three would be used on a portrait page. The text can be aligned with each column.

This is text arranged on a page in a column. The text can be set out on the page in as many columns as is required, but usually no more than three would be used on a portrait page. The text can be aligned with each column.

This is text arranged on a page in a column. The text can be set out on the page in as many columns as is required, but usually no more than three would be used on a portrait page. The text can be aligned with each column.

Figure 3.25 *White space*

Wizards

Wizards or Design Wizards are often used to provide guided, step-by-step help when creating documents such as newsletters, cards or flyers. The user selects the particular type of publication required from the Wizard list and is then guided through the process of creating the document.

Choices can be made about the colour scheme to be used, the number of columns and whether the document will be printed on one or both sides.

Key points

White space is often used to spread out the contents of a document to make it easier to read.

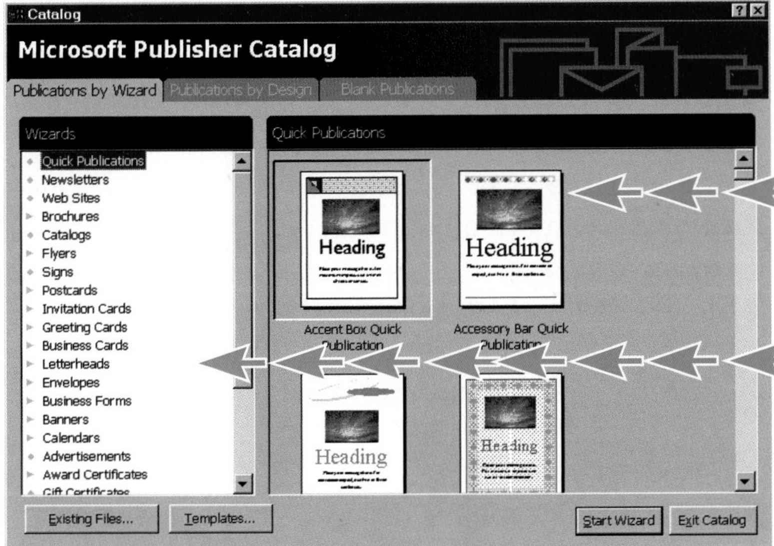

Figure 3.26 *Choosing a Design Wizard in Ms Publisher 2000*

Greenfinger's plant and tree sale is the biggest and best ever! It starts this Saturday with a 10% off offer on all bedding plants.

The sale starts at 9 am and the first 50 customers through the doors will receive an extra 25% on any product purchased.

All customers will receive a voucher for 10% of all bedding plants purchased during the next month.

Even better! Our café is open and will be serving *FREE* tea and coffee throughout the day to all customers.

Don't delay – come straight away to the biggest and best garden product sale!!

Satisfaction guaranteed!

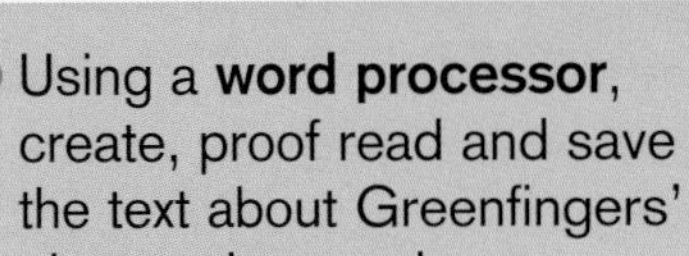

Activity

- Using a **word processor**, create, proof read and save the text about Greenfingers' plant and tree sale.
- Using cut and **paste**, import the text into a text frame in your newsletter and create a border for the frame.
- Save the file as 'PLANT AND TREE SALE'.

Using graphics 1

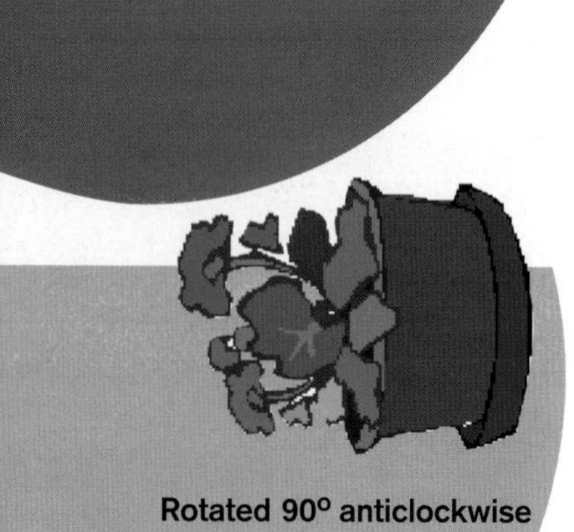

Rotated 90° anticlockwise

Figure 3.27 *Rotating an image*

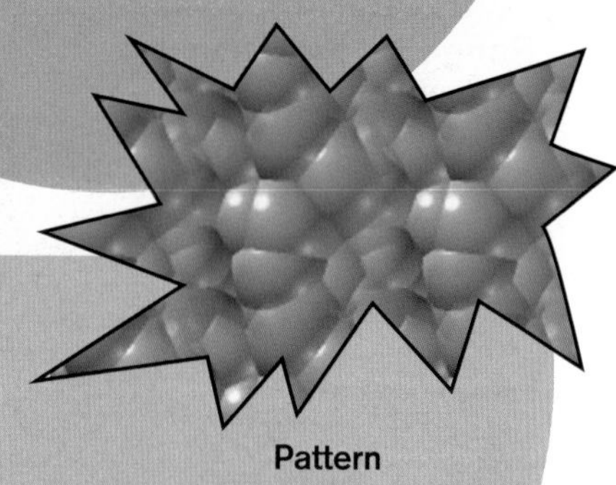

Pattern

Figure 3.28 *Shading and pattern*

DTP documents use a variety of graphics. These can be obtained from:

- a Clip Art library
- a digital camera
- a scanner
- the Internet
- a painting/drawing program.

What can a graphics package be used for?

A graphics package can be used to:

- draw **lines** – lines can be straight or curved.
- draw **pre-defined shapes**
- change the **size** of an image – this is called **scaling**
- **stretch** an image
- cut out part of an image – this is called **cropping**
- **rotate** an image
- **flip** an image
- **adjust** the colour of an image
- **colour** lines and objects
- fill areas with **shading** and **pattern**
- **layer** objects

The Tutor's File includes diagrams of each use.

Text wrap or flow

Where text and a graphic meet, the text can be made to **wrap** or **flow** around the graphic. The text can wrap to the frame or the text can wrap to the object.

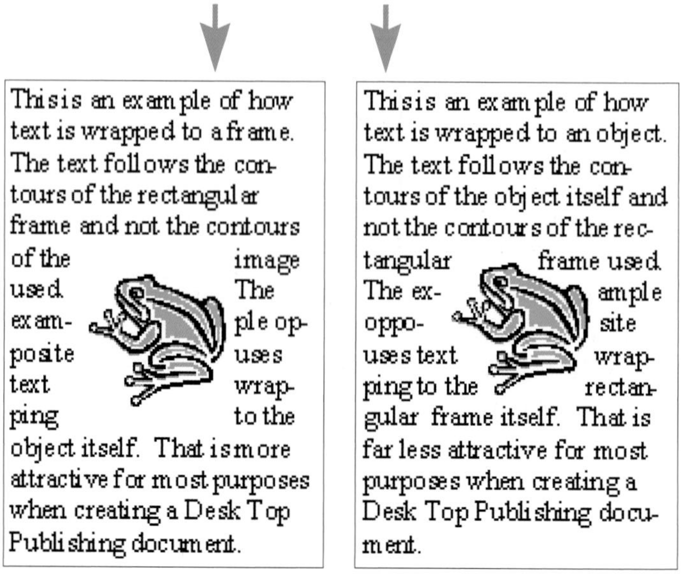

This is an example of how text is wrapped to a frame. The text follows the contours of the rectangular frame and not the contours of the image used. The example opposite uses text wrapping to the object itself. That is more attractive for most purposes when creating a Desk Top Publishing document.

This is an example of how text is wrapped to an object. The text follows the contours of the object itself and not the contours of the rectangular frame used. The example opposite uses text wrapping to the rectangular frame itself. That is far less attractive for most purposes when creating a Desk Top Publishing document.

Figure 3.29 *Text wrapping*

Drawing package

As the name suggests, lines and geometrical shapes such as circles and rectangles can be drawn using a drawing package. Once drawn, the image is saved as a **vector graphics file**.

The image is made up of a collection of independent objects, each of which can be individually selected, moved, resized and edited.

Vector graphics (or **object orientated graphics**) are based upon mathematics – each part of the graphic is given a length, a direction and position. Each object making up the graphic is clearly defined in terms of numbers. As a result, vector graphics are much easier to edit than **bitmapped graphics**.

A vector graphic takes up less storage space than a similar bitmapped graphic. However, vector graphics are not so lifelike, and so are not suitable for storing photographic images.

Painting package

Graphics created within a painting package are called **bitmapped graphics**. A bitmapped graphic is made up of a set of **pixels**.

The main advantage of a bitmapped graphic is that individual pixels can be edited, e.g. a change in colour. However, information must be stored about each pixel in the graphic, so file sizes tend to be very large. Also, unlike a vector graphic, individual parts of a bitmapped image cannot be resized – only the whole image can be resized. This can lead to poor image quality.

Pixel is short for picture element. The VDU screen is divided into rows and columns of tiny squares or cells; each one is a pixel. A pixel is the smallest element that a monitor can display. Bitmapped images are made up of many pixels.

The **resolution** of a picture is defined by the number of pixels in the display. For example, 1024 x 768 will be much sharper than 640 x 480.

Activity

- Open the file saved as 'PLANT AND TREE SALE'.
- Obtain a Clip Art image to match the text and import it into a Picture frame underneath the text.
- Move the image into the middle of the text and make the text 'wrap' around the image.
- Save the file.

Key points

Graphics can be obtained from:

- a Clip Art library
- a digital camera
- a scanner
- the Internet
- a painting/drawing program.

Using graphics 2

Saving graphic files

Once an image has been created in a graphics package it must be **saved** or **exported**.

A **file format** must be specified. There are many different graphic file formats, and they fall into two groups: vector graphics and bitmapped graphics.

Each file format has its individual file format **extension**. You are probably used to seeing the **.doc** extension at the end of a Microsoft Word filename.

Figure 3.30 *A drawing saved as a .gif file*

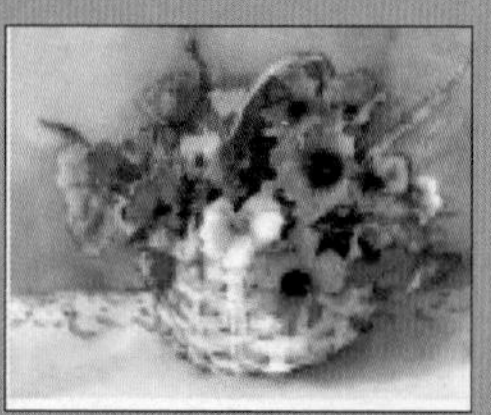

Figure 3.31 *A digital photograph saved as a .jpeg*

File extensions

Vector graphics	
.wmf	Windows MetaFile
.eps	Encapsulated Postscript

Bitmapped graphics	
.jpeg	Joint Photographic Experts Group
.tif	Tagged Image File
.gif	Graphics Interchange File
.bmp	Windows Bitmap

A .bmp file tends to be very large, whereas .tif files are **compressed** and so file size is reduced.

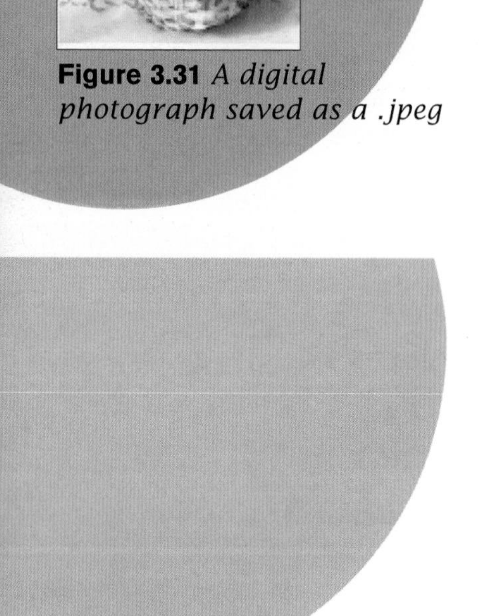

Screen colours

A **.gif** file needs only 256 colours to be displayed. Simple line drawings are usually saved as .gif files.

A **.jpeg** file needs 16 million colours. Photographs taken with a digital camera or scanned images of photographs are usually saved as .jpeg files.

Stages in producing a publication using DTP

Stage 1 The page content is created

At this stage text is prepared in a word-processing package and graphics are collected.

- The text is proof read and corrected for mistakes.
- The document is saved as a text file.

Images can be obtained by:

- designing a new graphic
- capturing using a digital camera or scanner

- importing from Clip Art library
- downloading from the Internet.

The graphic can then be 'edited' in the graphics package. See page 90 for details.

Stage 2 The layout of the page is set out

- The page layout is planned on paper.
- A **template** is set up.

Once this template has been set up it can be used to create as many pages as required. All pages based on the template will have the same layout, but different content. Such a page is called a **master page**.

Stage 3 The text is imported into the page

- Text created in the word-processing package is imported.
- The text can be: – resized and moved
  - – made to flow: from column to column
    - from page to page
    - around graphics.

Stage 4 The graphics are imported into the page

- Graphics created or edited in a graphics package are imported.
- Graphics can be resized and moved.
- Graphics may need to be **cropped** or **scaled** to fit the space available or to achieve the desired image.

Stage 5 Proof reading

- Once the text and graphics are in position, the document is checked for errors. This is called **proof reading** or **proofing** the publication.
- Checks include making sure that:
  - all text is present
  - text does not overlap/overlay a graphic unless required to do so
  - graphics do not cover text.
- Corrections and changes to the layout are made.
- The publication is saved, with a **backup** copy made.
- The publication is printed.

Did you know ?

A template sets out the page layout for the master page. The template defines features such as:

- number of columns
- position of text
- position of graphics
- header and/or footer.

Key points

- Not all applications packages can read all file formats.
- Make sure you know what your packages can read!
- A .bmp file tends to be very large.
- A simple line drawing is best saved as a .gif file.
- A photograph taken with a digital camera or scanned is best saved as a .jpeg file.

So, do I use word processing or DTP?

- Use a word-processing program if the document is mainly text;
- Use a DTP program if the document contains graphics and text, and if the graphics might need to be moved on the page.

Test your understanding

Fill in the gaps

1 The size of a f__________ is measured in p__________.

2 A t__________ is used to find words of similar meaning. Such words are called s__________.

3 The framework for a memo is set up by creating a t__________.

4 Text or graphics at the top of every page in a document is called a h__________.

5 The content of the pages is prepared using a w__________ p__________ for the t__________ and a g__________ package for the p__________, d__________ and other l__________.

6 The space between characters is called k__________.

7 T__________ w__________ is when text is made to f__________ round a graphic.

8 A d__________ package produces v__________ graphic files.
A p__________ package produces b__________ graphic files.

9 V__________ graphics or o__________ o__________ graphics take up less space than b__________ graphics.

10 A line drawing would be saved as a __________, but a photograph would be saved as a __________.

Multiple choice questions

11 Moving text away from a margin is:
a) indenting
b) tabulation
c) justification
d) alignment.

12 Which of the following makes text clearer to read?
a) centring
b) kerning
c) tabbing
d) emboldening.

13 The main purpose of a DTP package is to:
a) design diagrams
b) type in text
c) produce page layouts for printing
d) connect to the Internet.

14 Checking a document for errors is
a) search and replace
b) proof reading
c) justification
d) cropping.

15 The resolution of a picture is defined by:
a) the size of the monitor
b) the number of pixels in the display
c) the speed of the processor
d) the storage capacity of the hard drive.

16 Compression means:
a) to reduce the size of a file
b) to increase the size of a file
c) to backup a file
d) to delete a file.

CHAPTER 4

Spreadsheet

What do we actually mean by a **spreadsheet**? Well, whereas the main purpose of a word processor is to enter, edit and manipulate text, the main purpose of a spreadsheet is to enter, edit and manipulate numerical data, and to make calculations using this data. The spreadsheet screen is divided into rows and columns, creating cells. Each row and column in a spreadsheet is given a unique number or letter, so each cell can be identified rather like a map reference. The data, e.g. a row or column heading, text, a date, or a number, is entered into the cell. (See Figure 4.1.)

Spreadsheet programs make financial tasks, such as calculating staff wages, profit made on goods sold, VAT (value added tax) returns for the government, bank accounts, much easier. A spreadsheet program is an invaluable tool to all kinds of organisations, from small ones such as a neighbourhood baker's shop to your own school or college, or huge companies such as Next, Virgin Megastores, Lloyds TSB or government departments such as the Inland Revenue. On a personal level you might use a spreadsheet to keep track of how much income you receive, what expenses you have and how much is left to save.

Spreadsheet files are known as **workbooks** and may include several **worksheets** all related to the main purpose of that file, rather like chapters in a book. Sophisticated programs can link worksheets or files, so that when you change the numbers on one sheet, the numbers in linked worksheets or files are updated automatically. For example, you might have one sheet showing the money you have earned and spent in January. You could link the balance left over to the next worksheet for February. As you add in the details of your expenses throughout January, the balance shown in February will automatically change.

Let's look at the structure of spreadsheets in more detail.

Cell format

Activity

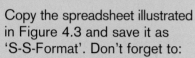

Copy the spreadsheet illustrated in Figure 4.3 and save it as 'S-S-Format'. Don't forget to:

- format the cells with shading and borders as shown
- centre the main headings 'Greenfingers' and 'Invoice' across columns A to D
- use the correct number of decimal places, £ signs, etc.

A typical **spreadsheet** will have row and column headings and textual and numerical data as illustrated in Figure 4.1, but the presentation of Figure 4.1 could be greatly improved. This textbook could have been printed using a very small font without the use of **bold** or *italics* to emphasise headings and sub-headings. The content would be the same, but it would be so much more difficult to read. An interesting, professional presentation is far more appealing to the reader. This is arguably even more important in a spreadsheet, because the majority of the data in it will be numerical. It becomes much easier to read the spreadsheet if attention is given to formatting the cells in an appropriate manner. Just as in word-processing software you can enhance the text in a spreadsheet by:

- using bold, italics or underline
- varying the font size for main or sub-headings
- using different font styles.

	A	B	C	D
1	Greenfingers			
2				
3	Item	Cost Price	Quantity	Total Cost
4	Busy Lizzi	0.06	5000	
5	Begonia	0.07	5000	
6	Geranium	0.23	2000	
7			Total Cost	
8			Vat @ 17.5%	
9			Grand total	
10			3% discount	
11			Amount due	
12			Payment over 3 months	

Figure 4.1 *A very basic spreadsheet layout before formulae have been entered. Notice the problem – text in column A is hidden by data in column B, and text in column C is overlapping into column D.*

In addition, you can improve the appearance of the spreadsheet by:

- centring a heading both horizontally across cells, or vertically within cells
- centring headings across columns
- aligning text to the right to avoid overlapping the next cell

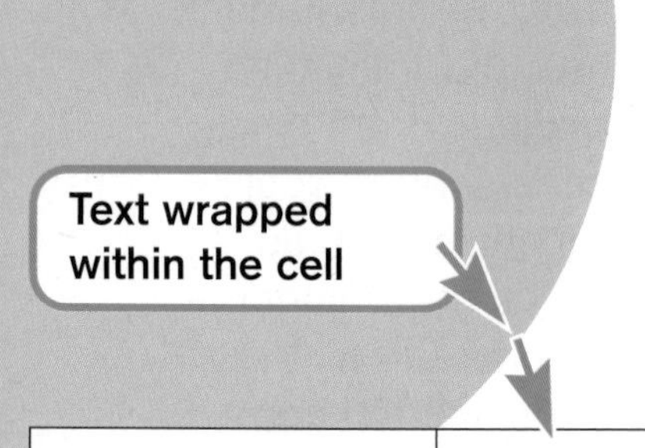

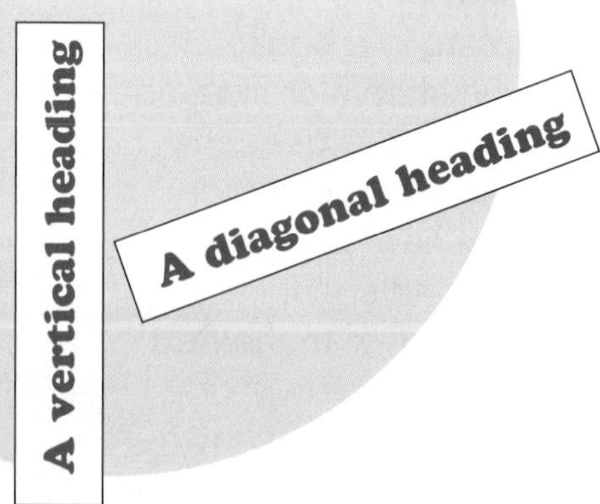

Figure 4.2 *Various heading styles*

- adjusting the cell width or row height
- wrapping text within a cell to avoid having an extremely wide column, or using a vertical heading
- placing borders around or using colour for significant cells – e.g. ones with totals.
- using shading or colour for the background of significant cells.

When designing your spreadsheet you should also pay attention to the following:

- How many decimal places do you need, if any?
- Do you wish to show the currency symbol?
- If yes, is it too cluttered to show the £ sign everywhere, or might it be better to use it just for the totals?
- Do you wish to show negative numbers in red – which can be set automatically.

Figure 4.3 illustrates some of the design features identified. Notice the improvement in the layout of the spreadsheet compared to Figure 4.1.

Key points

- Spreadsheet files are known as workbooks and may include many worksheets.
- Check column width and row height.
- Format important headings so that they stand out.
- Centre main headings across columns.
- Change the orientation of headings or wrap text so that columns are not too wide.
- Use shading and/or borders to emphasise significant cells.
- Choose a suitable number format; e.g. integer (whole number), decimal, currency.
- Show negative numbers in red.

Width of columns adjusted to fit text

	A	B	C	D
1	Greenfingers			
2	Invoice			
3	Item	Cost Price	Quantity	Total Cost
4	Busy Lizzie	0.06	5000	
5	Begonia	0.07	5000	
6	Geranium	0.23	2000	
7			Total Cost	
8			Vat @ 17.5%	
9			Grand total	
10			3% discount	
11			Amount due	
12			Payment over 3 months	

Headings formatted in larger font and centred across columns

Text aligned right

Shaded cells with borders

Text wrapped in cell

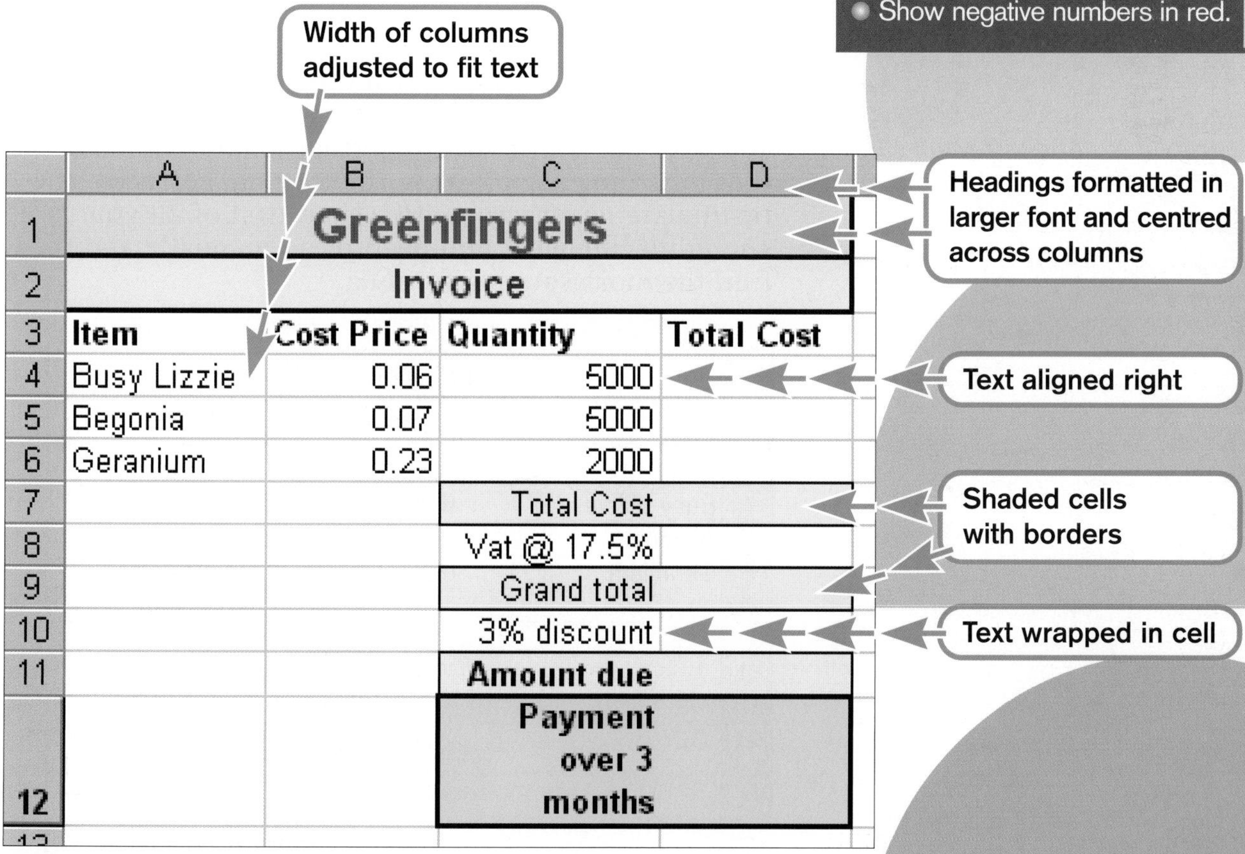

Figure 4.3 *Using formatting facilities to improve the layout*

Formula 1

A formula is a sequence of values (numbers), cell references (e.g. D4), or operators (e.g. addition or multiplication), that produces a new value from existing values. This sounds more complicated than it is. The important point to remember is that in Excel a formula always starts with an equal sign (=). This tells the spreadsheet that a calculation needs to be performed: adding (+), subtracting (-), multiplying (*), dividing (/), finding the average or a percentage. The spreadsheet can do everything a calculator can do – but so much more.

Formulae enable you to make a wide range of automatic calculations that take place instantaneously. The spreadsheet will calculate very simple formula, such as:

Formula	**Result**
=.06*5000	300

But more typically cell references are used in formulae. For example, in cell D4 in Figure 4.1 you would use the formula =B4*C4 to calculate the cost of Bizzie Lizzies.

Formula	**Result**
=B4*C4	300

Although formulae range from the easy to the very complicated, the basic formula types are used over and over again. It is worth getting to know some of these. As long as you write the formula correctly, the results are never wrong. However, first of all you should decide what you need to do manually and then find the most suitable formula.

	A	B	C	D
1	**Greenfingers**			
2	Invoice			
3	**Item**	**Cost Price**	**Quantity**	**Total Cost**
4	Busy Lizzie	0.06	5000	=B4*C4
5	Begonia	0.07	5000	=B5*C5
6	Geranium	0.23	2000	=B6*C6
7			Total Cost	=SUM(D4:D6)
8			Vat @ 17.5%	=D7*17.5%
9			Grand total	=D7+D8
10			3% discount	=D9*3%
11			**Amount due**	**=D9-D10**
12			**Payment over 3 months**	**=D11/3**

Figure 4.4 *This is the Formula View*

The big advantage with formulae is that the spreadsheet will automatically recalculate if any changes are made in the data. For example, if the price of Bizzie Lizzies changes to .07p each, you enter the new price in cell B4 and the total cost will be automatically recalculated in cell D4 – 350.

Arithmetic operators

Formulae use what are called **arithmetic operators** and **comparison operators**. (You will find out more about comparison operators later on.) These terms sound complicated, but are quite straightforward.

Arithmetic operators perform basic mathematical operations such as addition, subtraction, multiplication, division, and so on. Look at Figure 4.4 where the following formulae have now been added:

to	add	Cell D9	=D7+D8
	subtract	Cell D11	=D9–D10
	divide	Cell D12	=D11/3
	multiply	Cell D4	=B4*C4
		Cell D5	=B5*C5
		Cell D6	=B6*C6
	percentage	Cell D8	=D7*17.5%
		Cell D10	=D9*3%
	sum (total)	Cell D7	=sum(D4:D6) (i.e. add all cells in the range D4 to D6)

	A	B	C	D
1	Greenfingers			
2	Invoice			
3	**Item**	**Cost Price**	**Quantity**	**Total Cost**
4	Busy Lizzie	0.06	5000	300.00
5	Begonia	0.07	5000	350.00
6	Geranium	0.23	2000	460.00
7			Total Cost	£ 1,110.00
8			Vat @ 17.5%	£ 194.25
9			Grand total	£ 1,304.25
10			3% discount	£ 39.13
11			**Amount due**	**£ 1,265.12**
12			**Payment over 3 months**	**£ 421.71**

Figure 4.5 *This is the Data View showing the results after the formulae have been entered*

Key points

- Each cell has a unique reference.
- Formulae always start with =.
- Arithmetic operators are: +, -, *, /

Activity

1 Open the spreadsheet saved as 'S-S-Format' and practice the 6 types of arithmetic operators illustrated in Figure 4.4.

2 Change the data as follows and notice the formulae will automatically recalculate. Save it as 'A-operators2'.

Item	Cost Price	Quantity
Busy Lizzie	0.09	4200
Begonia	0.10	3870
Geranium	0.30	1950
Lobelia	0.07	5280

Formula 2

Activity

1. Copy the spreadsheet shown in Figure 4.6, enter the formula shown in cell E3 and then copy it down the rows. Do the same with the formula in cell B8 and copy it across the columns.
2. Copy the spreadsheet shown in Figure 4.7, but *experiment with the formulae.*
   - **a** At first enter the formula in cell D5 as C5*B1. Copy the formula down the 7 rows. You will notice that there are errors in the results.
   - **b** Go back to cell D5 and change the formula to C5*$B$1. (Note: In Excel, a quick way to add the $ signs is to place the cursor in front of the cell reference on the status bar, in this case B1, and press the Function key F4.) Copy the formula down the 7 rows. This time you should find the results match those in Figure 4.7.
   - **c** Imagine that the rate of VAT has been changed to 22%. Change the rate in cell B1 to 22% and you should find the columns for VAT and Retail Price will automatically recalculate.

Relative cell reference

One of the advantages of using a spreadsheet is the facility to replicate or copy formulae across columns or down rows. It is very convenient to be able to replicate the formula, rather than having to keep entering it again and again. If you need to have totals down several rows or across several columns, you can enter the formula into the first cell and then replicate the formula across to the last column or down to the last row. The spreadsheet will automatically change the formula to give the correct cell reference.

Figure 4.6 shows the spreadsheet for Bedding Plant Sales, in Formula View. Notice the formulae in columns F and G. After entering the formulae =SUM(C4:E4) in cell F4 and =F4*B4 in cell G4, they were copied down the column, but the spreadsheet automatically changed the cell references to =SUM(C5:E5) to =SUM(C6:E6) or =F5*B5 to =F6*B6, and so on.

A similar change occurs when formulae are copied across columns. The formula to calculate the total number of bedding plants sold in April was entered in cell C11, i.e. =SUM(C4:C10). As the formula was copied across the columns, the cell reference automatically changed to =SUM(D4:D10) and to =SUM(E4:E10). The spreadsheet assumes that as the formula is copied from cell to cell, the formula should be **relative** to, not the same as, the previous cell.

Try it for yourself – copy the spreadsheet shown in Figure 4.6.

	A	B	C	D	E
1	GREENFINGERS PRICE LIST				
2	Garden Tools - Quarterly Sales				
3	**Item**	**Jan**	**Feb**	**Mar**	**Total**
4	Spade	68	75	49	=SUM(B4:D4)
5	Fork	54	82	76	=SUM(B5:D5)
6	Hoe	12	16	34	=SUM(B6:D6)
7	Rake	12	22	15	=SUM(B7:D7)
8	Total	=SUM(B4:B7)	=SUM(C4:C7)	=SUM(D4:D7)	=SUM(E4:E7)

Figure 4.6 *Notice how the formula references change as they are copied down column E and across row 8*

Absolute cell reference

Sometimes you may wish to refer to one particular cell address many times. Therefore when you replicate the formula, the cell address needs to remain the same, the technical term for which is **absolute**. For example, you might have one cell containing the rate for VAT which is essential for the shopkeeper to know.

Figure 4.7 illustrates this point. The rate for VAT is 17.5% and is entered into cell B1 and the amount of VAT to be paid is calculated in column D. You will notice that the formulae show $ signs before the B and the 1 in the cell reference. These signs are used in Excel to indicate that when replicating the formula, this cell reference must not be changed. Although in the small example shown it would be very quick to key in the formula on each new line, in a commercial spreadsheet you might replicate the formula down hundreds of rows. The other benefit is that if the government changes the rate of VAT, it is a simple matter to enter the new rate in cell B1, and all cells depending on that formula will automatically change.

Key points

- Numbers can be formatted to integer (whole numbers), decimal or currency.
- Relative cell reference – where the cell references change as they are copied down columns or across rows.
- Absolute cell reference – where the cell references remain fixed, as they are copied down columns or across rows.

	A	B	C	D
1	VAT =	17.5%		
2	GREENFINGERS PRICE LIST			
3	Bedding Plants - Boxes of 12 Pot Ready			
4	**Plant**	**Trade Price - excl VAT**	**VAT**	**Retail Price - incl VAT**
5	Busy Lizzie	3.40	0.60	4.00
6	Petunia	5.02	0.88	5.90
7	Geranium	6.51	1.14	7.65
8	Begonia	4.00	0.70	4.70
9	Ageratum	3.40	0.60	
10	Marigolds	4.00	0.70	
11	Lobelia	3.83	0.67	

Note: The formula reference for VAT in cell B1 does not change as it is copied down the rows, because the $ signs before the B and 1 indicate that this reference should remain fixed or absolute.

	A	B	C	D
1	VAT =	17.50%		
2	GREENFINGERS PRICE LIST			
3	Bedding Plants - Boxes of 12 Pot Ready			
4	**Plant**	**Trade Price - excl VAT**	**VAT**	**Retail Price - incl VAT**
5	Busy Lizzie	3.40	=B5*$B$1	=B5+C5
6	Petunia	5.02	=B6*$B$1	=B6+C6
7	Geranium	6.51	=B7*$B$1	=B7+C7
8	Begonia	4.00	=B8*$B$1	=B8+C8
9	Ageratum	3.40	=B9*$B$1	=B9+C9
10	Marigolds	4.00	=B10*$B$1	=B10+C10
11	Lobelia	3.83	=B11*$B$1	=B11+C11

Figure 4.7 *The first view shows the values, and the second the formulae*

Function 1

Spreadsheet functions are simply formulae pre-written into the software, which you can use either on their own, or as part of a more complex formula. The four you are going to use are **Sum**, **Average**, **IF** and **Lookup**.

Sum

If you are using Microsoft Excel at your school or college, you will find the AutoSum icon Σ on the tool bar. If you wish to find the total of a column or row of figures, select the cell at the bottom of the column or to the left of the row, click on the icon and the formula will be written for you. Do be careful when using the AutoSum. It is important to check that Excel has selected the range of cells you require. AutoSum was used to calculate the Total No. Sold in Figure 4.8, but the range selected was not quite right.

Status line showing the formula selected by the AutoSum – notice the error.

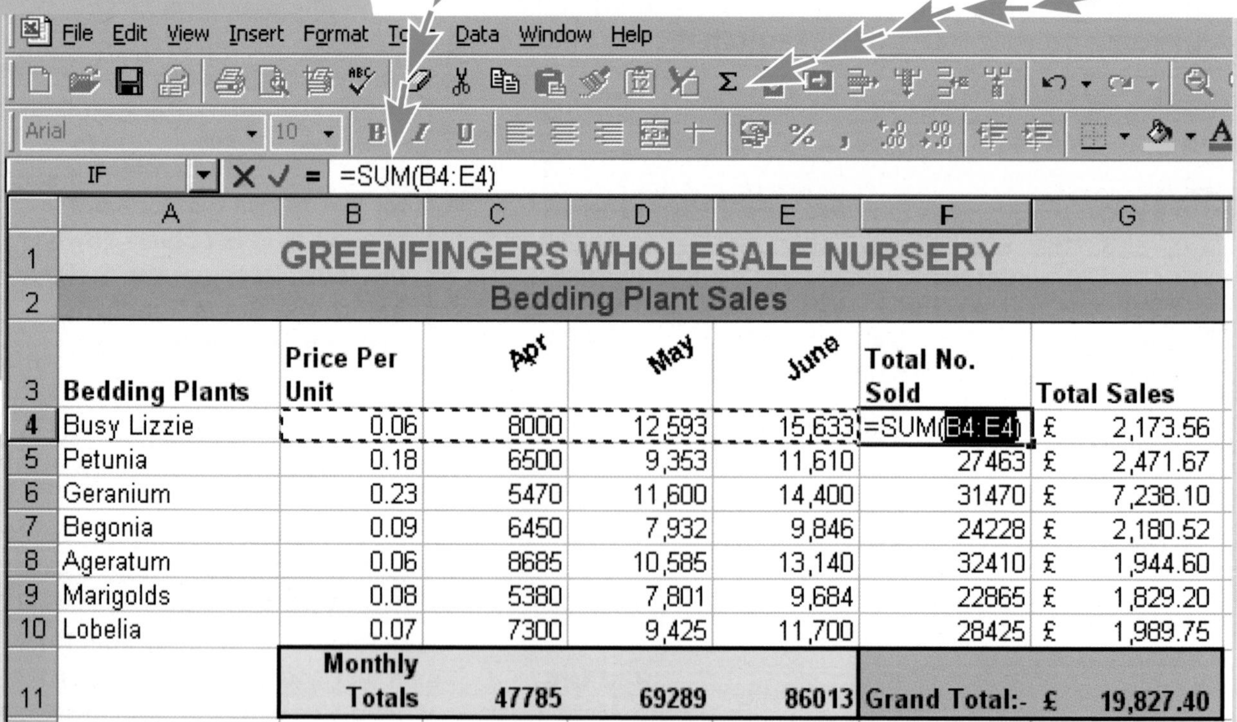

	A	B	C	D	E	F	G
1	GREENFINGERS WHOLESALE NURSERY						
2	Bedding Plant Sales						
3	Bedding Plants	Price Per Unit	Apr	May	June	Total No. Sold	Total Sales
4	Busy Lizzie	0.06	8000	12,593	15,633	=SUM(B4:E4)	£ 2,173.56
5	Petunia	0.18	6500	9,353	11,610	27463	£ 2,471.67
6	Geranium	0.23	5470	11,600	14,400	31470	£ 7,238.10
7	Begonia	0.09	6450	7,932	9,846	24228	£ 2,180.52
8	Ageratum	0.06	8685	10,585	13,140	32410	£ 1,944.60
9	Marigolds	0.08	5380	7,801	9,684	22865	£ 1,829.20
10	Lobelia	0.07	7300	9,425	11,700	28425	£ 1,989.75
11		Monthly Totals	47785	69289	86013	Grand Total:-	£ 19,827.40

Figure 4.8 *The AutoSum function has been used in cell F4, but it has selected the range* B4:E4, *which includes the* price *of the plants. The range* C4:E4 *only is necessary to obtain the total number sold. To correct the error you can either enter C4:E4 yourself, or scroll across cells C4 to E4.*

Average

When you calculate the average, you are not trying to establish the correct number but what is typical of a group or situation. You do this by adding up all the relevant totals, and dividing by the number of totals. For example, if you wish to find out the average number of goals scored by your favourite football team during the season, you add up the scores and divide by the number of matches played. If you want to find the average sales to date, you add up the sales for each month and divide by the number of months. See Figure 4.9. The formula in cell 13 calculates the average score.

C13 = =AVERAGE(C6:C12)

	A	B	C	D	E	F
1		**FINDING THE AVERAGE**				
2						
3		**Seahaven United**			**Greenfingers**	
4		**Weekly Goal Score**			**Monthly Sales**	
5						
6		Week 1	2		January	£ 6,000
7		Week 2	0		February	£ 7,500
8		Week 3	1		March	£ 14,890
9		Week 4	3		April	£ 35,760
10		Week 5	2		May	£ 58,539
11		Week 6	4		June	£ 65,789
12		Week 7	1		July	£ 45,898
13		**Average to date:-**	**1.9**		**Average to date:-**	**£ 33,482.29**

Figure 4.9 *You will notice that the sales were never actually £33,482.29 but this was the average or typical sales, and clearly it is not possible to score nine-tenths of a goal, but on average Seahaven United scored nearly two goals each week.*

The formula for calculating the average is shown in the status line in Figure 4.9. If you were working out the average goal scored by Seahaven United yourself, you would need to add up the total of goals scored – 13 – check how many games have been played – 7 – and then divide the total by the number of games played to get the result – 1.9. The advantage of using the *Average function* available in the spreadsheet is that these various stages are worked out automatically for you.

Key points

- Functions are pre-prepared formulae.
- Use AutoSum to total a column or row *with care.*
- The Average function works out all the stages for you.

Activity

1 Create a spreadsheet as shown in Figure 4.9, using the Average function.

2 Find out the ages and heights of the students in your class or tutor group, and create another spreadsheet to calculate their average age and average height.

Function 2

Activity

Sandra and Pete are trying to estimate how many bedding plants to grow. They have given you the job of preparing a spreadsheet showing the sales for last year.

1 Create a spreadsheet as shown in Figure 4.8. Practice using AutoSum, but check carefully the range selected.

2 Check your totals match those shown. Save the file as 'Bedding Plants'.

3 Sort the spreadsheet in alphabetical order of plants:
   - Highlight cells A3:G10.
   - Select data, sort.
   - Check that you are sorting by 'Bedding Plants' or Column A and in ascending order.
   - Click OK.
   - Save as 'Bedplant'.

4 Insert a column for July totals and include the following data. Make sure you **check that the formulae in column G do include July data.** Save the file.
   July
   7550
   5610
   6960
   4760
   6350
   4685
   5655

5 What simple improvements could you make?
   Which month had the most sales? Why do you think this might be? How could this help them in their future planning?

Comparison operators – If … Then … Else

Comparison operators, as the name suggests, compare two values to determine whether something is true or false. You will be looking for a number greater than, less than or equal to, or combinations of these possibilities. Comparison operators are as follows:

>	Greater than
<	Less than
=	Equal to
>=	Greater than or equal to
<=	Less than or equal to
<>	Not equal to

In a spreadsheet, comparison operators are typically used with the 'IF' function.

We often make statements like '*If* it's fine, *then* we'll have a barbecue'. The implication is that if it's not fine we will do something else. Effectively, we are making a condition, and depending on that condition a certain action will follow. Notice that the words 'If it's not fine, we won't have a barbecue', were not actually said, but the listener would realise the implication. To understand this more clearly, look at the illustration below:

The condition	**True or False**	**Action**
It is fine	True	We'll have a barbecue
It is fine	False – i.e. it is not fine	We won't have a barbecue

Spreadsheets offer this same facility, so that you can ask the spreadsheet to provide answers depending on a certain condition. If that condition is true, then the spreadsheet performs a particular action; if the condition is false then the spreadsheet performs a different action. For example, manufacturers such as JVC, Sony, and British Steel frequently offer discounts to customers who order goods over a certain value. When sales managers are deciding how much discount they can afford to offer, the spreadsheet IF function is a valuable tool in making these calculations.

Sandra and Pete at Greenfingers are trying to promote the wholesale side of the business. They have decided to offer a discount of 1.5% on sales over £5,000: i.e. **If** sales are greater than £5,000, **then** pay a discount of 1.5%, **else** pay nothing. See Figure 4.10.

C4 = =IF(B4>5000,B4*$B$2,0)

	A	B	C	D
1	CUSTOMER DISCOUNT			
2	Sales over £5000 - discount =	1.5%		
3	Customer	Total Sales	Discount	Amount Due
4	Floral Fantasies	£ 5,894	£ 88.41	£ 5,805.59
5	Beech Hill Nursery	9,278	£ 139.17	9,138.83
6	The Red Rose	£ 4,494	£ -	£ 4,494.00
7	Dulton Flower Centre	£ 7,825	£ 117.38	£ 7,707.63
8	Lily of the Valley	£ 2,180	£ -	£ 2,180.00
9	Newford Landscape G[illegible]rdeners	£ 10,678	£ 160.17	£ 1[illegible]517.83
10	Simply Sensational	£ 3,876	£ -	£ 3,876.00
11	Blossoms	£ 5,002	£ 75.03	£ 4,[illegible]6.97
12	Just in Bud	[illegible]	[illegible]	[illegible]

Figure 4.10

If	B4	>	5,000	,	B4	*	B2	,	0
If	(it is ***true***) sales value	is greater than	5,000	then discount is	Total sales	Multiplied by	1.5% (Cell B2)	else (it is ***false***)	discount is zero

In other words, if it is true that the value in cell B4 is more than 5,000, then multiply the value in cell B4 by cell B2 (1.5%) to calculate the discount payable. If it is false, i.e. less than 5,000 (else or otherwise), enter '0' in the cells. In column D the discount is deducted from the sales to give the amount due. Notice what happens if the sales figures are changed, as shown in Figure 4.11.

Notice that the formula has stayed the same, but the values in the Discount and Amount Due columns have changed

C4 = =IF(B4>5000,B4*$B$2,0)

	A	B	C	D
1	CUSTOMER DISCOUNT			
2	Sales over £5000 - discount =	1.5%		
3	Customer	Total Sales	Discount	Amount Due
4	Floral Fantasies	£ 4,987	£ -	£ 4,987.00
5	Beech Hill Nursery	£ 10,346	£ 155.19	£ 10,190.81
6	The Red Rose	£ 2,189	£ -	£ 2,189.00
7	Dulton Flower Centre	£ 9,876	£ 148.14	£ 9,727.86
8	Lily of the Valley	£ 5,467	£ 82.01	£ 5,385.00
9	Newford Landscape Gardeners	£ 12,890	£ 193.35	£ 12,696.65
10	Simply Sensational	£ 2,378	£ -	£ 2,378.00
11	Blossoms	£ 8,765	£ 131.48	£ 8,633.53
12	Just in Bud	£ 2,389	£ -	£ 2,389.00

Figure 4.11 *Illustrating the IF function*

Key points

- Comparison operators compare two values.
- The IF function gives a result depending on the *condition* set.

Function 3

It is also possible to use the IF function, to display text rather than make a calculation, as shown in Figure 4.12.

Example 1

	A	B	C	D
1	PETTY CASH - DAILY EXPENDITURE			
2	DATE	RECEIPTS	EXPENDITURE	BALANCE
3	06/03/00	150.00		150.00
4	07/03/00		45.00	105.00
5	08/03/00		25.78	79.22
6	09/03/00		14.89	64.33
7	10/03/00		34.21	30.12
8	Balance at the end of the week:-			30.12
9				
10	YOU NEED TO DRAW MONEY FROM THE BANK			

Example 2

	A	B	C	D
1	PETTY CASH - DAILY EXPENDITURE			
2	DATE	RECEIPTS	EXPENDITURE	BALANCE
3	13/03/00	150.00		150.00
4	14/03/00		5.00	145.00
5	15/03/00		16.23	128.77
6	16/03/00		4.05	124.72
7	17/03/00		12.00	112.72
8	Balance at the end of the week:-			112.72
9				
10	Enough Money in the Account			

Figure 4.12

You will notice that the two examples show different statements in cell A10. The formula in cell A10 is:

=IF(D8<100,"YOU NEED TO DRAW MONEY FROM THE BANK","Enough Money in the Account")

The formula is saying that, ***If*** the balance at the end of the week is less than £100, ***then*** the statement "YOU NEED TO DRAW MORE FROM THE BANK", will appear on the screen. The implication is that if the balance is more than £100 (***else*** or otherwise), the statement "Enough Money in the Account", will appear.

C5 = =IF(B5>8000,B5*$B$3,IF(B5>4000,B5*$B$2,0))

	A	B	C	D
1	CUSTOMER DISCOUNT			
2	Sales over £4,000 - discount =	1.5%		
3	Sales over £8,000 - discount =	2%		
4	Customer	Total Sales	Discount	Amount Due
5	Floral Fantasies	£ 4,987	£ 74.81	£ 4,912.20
6	Beech Hill Nursery	£ 10,346	£ 206.92	£ 10,139.08
7	The Red Rose	£ 2,189	£ -	£ 2,189.00
8	Dulton Flower Centre	£ 9,876	£ 197.52	£ 9,678.48
9	Lily of the Valley	£ 5,467	£ 82.01	£ 5,385.00
10	Newford Landscape Gardeners	£ 12,890	£ 257.80	£ 12,632.20
11	Simply Sensational	£ 2,378	£ -	£ 2,378.00
12	Blossoms	£ 8,765	£ 175.30	£ 8,589.70
13	Just in Bud	£ 2,389	£ -	£ 2,389.00

Figure 4.13 *This shows two IF formulae, which is known as 'nesting'. Up to 7 'IF' functions can be nested in Excel 97 or 2000.*

Activity

Task A

1 Copy the spreadsheet shown in Figure 4.10, to practice the 'IF' function and absolute cell references. Use the following formula in cell C4:

=IF(B4>5000,B4*$B$2,0)

Make sure you copy the formula *exactly*, including commas and brackets as shown.

The formula in D4 should be =B4-C4.

Copy the formulae down the rows and compare your results with Figure 4.10.

Save the file as 'GF-Discount'.

2 Change the sales data in column B as shown in Figure 4.11 and notice the Discount and Amount Due columns recalculate automatically.

3 See what happens if the discount is applied to sales greater than £4,000. Change the formula in cell C4 and copy it down the rows.

Task B

1 Copy the spreadsheet shown in Figure 4.12, Example 1, using the following formula in cell A10:

=IF(D8<100, "YOU NEED TO DRAW MONEY FROM THE BANK", "Enough Money in the Account")

Again copy the formula *exactly*, including commas, inverted commas and brackets as shown. Save the files as 'Money'.

2 Alter the expenditure as shown in Example 2 and notice that the statement in cell A10 will automatically change.

3 You decide you only need to keep £30 in petty cash. Change the formula accordingly.

Task C

Sandra and Pete are so pleased with the increase in business as a result of the discount scheme, they have decided to offer different levels of discount. Sales over £8,000 will now attract a 2% discount, and sales over £4,000 will attract 1.5% discount.

1 Open the file saved as GF-Discount and **resave** as **GF-Discount-new**.

2 Insert a new row above row 3. In **cell A3** enter the heading **Sales over £8,000 – discount =** and in cell B3 enter the discount **2%**.

3 Amend the formula in cell C5 as follows and notice the Discount and Amount Due columns will automatically recalculate. The formula should be:

=IF(B5>8000,B5*$B$3, IF(B5>4000,B5*$B$2,0))

It is important to give the larger discount first. If you 'ask' Excel to search for sales over £4,000 first, it will include all sales over this amount and apply the 1.5% discount. It will not then look for amounts over £8,000. If you ask for amounts over £8,000 first, the spreadsheet will find those amounts, and apply the discount, and then search again for the second 'IF' function, i.e. amounts over £4,000, and apply the 1.5% discount to those values. Everything else will show zero discount. See Figure 4.13 opposite.

Function 4

	A	B
1	GREENFINGERS LOOKUP	
2	Product Ref	Bedding Plants - boxes of 12
3	BP001	Ageratum
4	BP005	Begonia
5	BP010	Busy Lizzie
6	BP015	Geranium
7	BP020	Lobelia
8	BP025	Marigold
9	BP030	Petunia
10		**Shrubs**
11	SH001	Azalea
12	SH005	Clematis
13	SH010	Fuchsia
14	SH015	Hebe
15	SH020	Jasmine
16	SH025	Lavender
17	SH030	Pyracantha
18	SH035	Rhododendron
19	SH040	Rose
20	SH045	Standard Rose
21		Pots
22	PO001	Glazed - small
23	PO005	Glazed - medium
24	PO010	Glazed - large
25	PO015	Terracotta - small
26	PO020	Terracotta - medium
27	PO025	Terracotta - large
28		Miscellaneous
29	MI001	Compost
30	MI005	Gro-bag
31	MI010	Manure

Figure 4.14 *The worksheet 'Products', which is the Lookup table*

Lookup

The **Lookup** function allows you to search for an item in a linked worksheet and then copy data related to that item into the original worksheet. For example, Greenfingers could have a Lookup table listing prices for the various products sold, linked to a template for an invoice. (An invoice is a statement of how much is owed for goods or services that customers have already received.) **Templates** in a spreadsheet are just like those described in the chapter on word processing, i.e. a framework for a standardised document, which can be used every time a new invoice is raised.

When the product name is entered into the 'Description' column in the invoice, the price of the item is automatically copied from the Lookup table into the 'Unit Price' column in the invoice. This saves time as the administrator preparing invoices does not have to look up a long price list, and reduces the risk of errors when he or she copies the data from the price list. If Greenfingers changes the price of any of its products, the Lookup table can easily be amended.

Figure 4.14 shows a worksheet called 'Products' which contains the list of products and the trade prices. Remember this list is quite short and is a sample of the products Greenfingers sell. The data in the Lookup table can be arranged down a column – i.e. vertically – or across rows – i.e. horizontally.

A second worksheet called 'Invoice' is the invoice template. When the quantity ordered and the product description are entered, the price of the product is automatically entered into the 'Unit Price' column and the totals and VAT are calculated as shown in Fig 4.15.

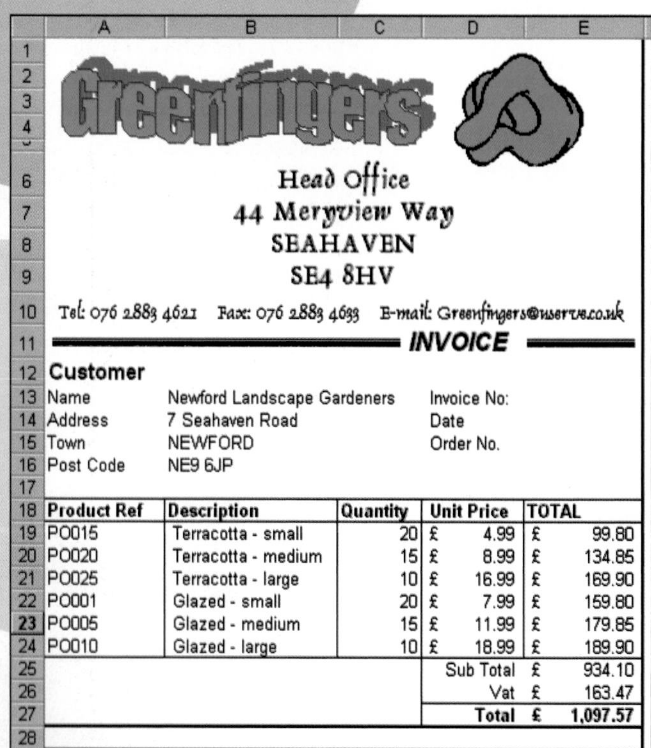

Greenfingers

Head Office
44 Meryview Way
SEAHAVEN
SE4 8HV

Tel: 076 2883 4621 Fax: 076 2883 4633 E-mail: Greenfingers@userve.co.uk

INVOICE

Customer

Name	Newford Landscape Gardeners	Invoice No:
Address	7 Seahaven Road	Date
Town	NEWFORD	Order No.
Post Code	NE9 6JP	

Product Ref	Description	Quantity	Unit Price	TOTAL
PO015	Terracotta - small	20	£ 4.99	£ 99.80
PO020	Terracotta - medium	15	£ 8.99	£ 134.85
PO025	Terracotta - large	10	£ 16.99	£ 169.90
PO001	Glazed - small	20	£ 7.99	£ 159.80
PO005	Glazed - medium	15	£ 11.99	£ 179.85
PO010	Glazed - large	10	£ 18.99	£ 189.90
			Sub Total	£ 934.10
			Vat	£ 163.47
			Total	**£ 1,097.57**

Figure 4.15 *A completed invoice using the Lookup table*

Activity

1 Open a new file and save it as a template named 'Look up'.

2 Rename the first worksheet as 'Products' and copy the data shown in Figure 4.14.

3 Rename the second worksheet as 'Invoice' and copy the invoice layout shown in Figure 4.15. You can choose your own logo and font style for Greenfingers. The example shown used WordArt for the company name.

4 Enter suitable formulae for the totals and VAT.

5 The formula for Lookup in cells B19 to B24 is:

=VLOOKUP

A19Products!

$A$3:$C$31,2,0)

The formula is saying look up the data from the Products worksheet range from A3:C31, and if you find an entry which matches cell A19, then enter the price of the product from column 2.

Notice the reference to the range shows the absolute cell reference, so that the range stays the same when the formula is copied down the column. The reference to the cell – i.e. A19 – is relative, because it must change as the formula is copied.

6 Test it out for yourself, but be very careful to enter the product name exactly as it appears in the Lookup table; e.g. if you use 'Rose' in the table, don't enter 'Roses' in the invoice.

There is a problem however. If no match is found the error message #N/A appears. To overcome this, so that nothing appears in the cell, it is necessary to combine an IF function with the Lookup function as follows:

=IF(ISERROR(VLOOKUP

(A19,Products!$A$3:$C$3

1,2,0))," ", VLOOKUP

(A19,Products!

$A$3:$C$31,2,0))

Edit the formula as shown and you should find that the error message no longer appears in the template.

7 If you enter =C19*D19 in the total column, a similar problem occurs and another error message appears when the template is blank – #VALUE! This can also be overcome by combining an IF function with the formula:

=IF(ISERROR(C19*D19)

," ",(C19*D19))

In both cases the IF statement is effectively saying that, if one of the Excel error messages appears, enter nothing in the cell – the blank is indicated by the inverted commas " ", with no data between.

8 Delete any test data so that you have a blank form and save the file as 'Lookup template'.

9 Print a copy of each sheet and the Formula view for the invoice. Close the template file.

10 Open a **new** file using the template you have created. This is very important, so that your blank template is retained for the next order.

11 Copy the data shown in Figure 4.15 and check your results.

Macros

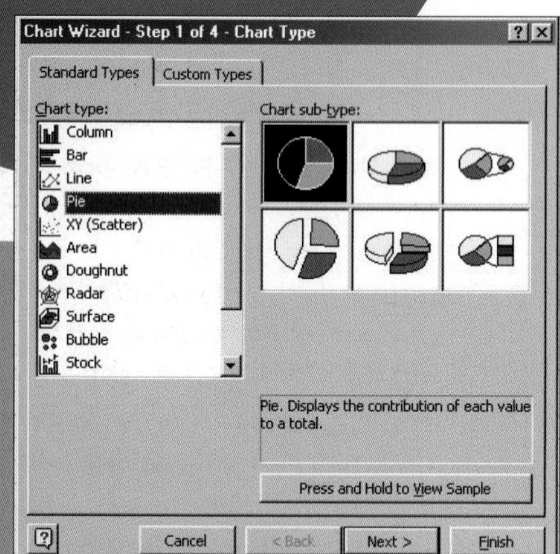

Figure 4.16 *An example of a Chart Wizard dialogue box in Microsoft Excel*

What is a macro?

Have you ever used a cassette recorder to record a favourite song from the radio or a video recorder to record a football match or film? The purpose of recording it was so that you could play it back whenever you wanted to.

A **macro** is very similar – only this time you are recording a series of keystrokes or mouse clicks you regularly perform using the computer so you can 'play them back' automatically. It is a sequence of commands that is activated by a special key combination, a click of the mouse on an icon or through the drop-down menus.

For example, everytime you click on [print icon] you are activating a macro which automatically goes through the process of selecting File, Print, OK – one click instead of three. Alternatively, you could select CTRL + P.

Purpose

The general purpose of macros is to make the use of software applications convenient, easier and more effective. They do this in three specific ways:

- by reducing input errors
- by speeding up processing
- by standardising routine procedures.

All three save time by replacing often-used, sometimes lengthy series of keystrokes with shorter versions. This eliminates frequent retyping, and reduces typing errors. It also enables users who are unfamiliar with a program to replay sets of instructions pre-recorded by someone more adept with the application.

There are numerous macros pre-prepared in the software, and if you consider the icons on the toolbars, such as [spellcheck icon] which activates the spellchecker, or [drawing icon] which activates the drawing toolbar, you will realise that you are using macros all the time. Whenever you click the AutoSum button Σ to add up a column of numbers in a spreadsheet, you are using a calculation macro.
When you use [chart icon] to create a chart you are using a macro called a **wizard**. Wizards take you step by step through a sequence of actions and help you to carry out automated routines. Macros also exist in word-processing and database applications.

Activity

Check out the difference in the number of keystrokes when you click an icon on the toolbars compared to using the drop-down menus to follow the same procedure, for the following:

- font colour
- the fill tool
- sorting data in order lowest to highest
- printing the spreadsheet

Default macros

A default macro is the choice made by a program if the user does not specify an alternative. Default macros are built into programs. Each time you open a new document or worksheet you are presented with default values. For example, a spreadsheet program might default to portrait layout, with margins of 2.5 cm top and bottom and 1.9 cm left and right. The font style might be Arial in size 10. This provides a recognisable format, a starting point, until the user specifies otherwise.

If the user wants to regularly adopt a different style, he or she could record a macro to change the default settings. For example, landscape layout is often a better choice for printing spreadsheets. However, rather than recording a macro there is an alternative solution. You might decide to create a template just as we have done for the Lookup table and invoice.

Clicking the icon is usually quicker than using the menus, but sometimes there are advantages to using the 'longer route', such as when you wish to print part of a document, or more than one copy.

Custom macros

You can also design your own personal macros for tasks which you need to repeat often. For example, it is very useful to include a footer in your documents giving your name, the name of the file and the date it was created.

This takes about 20–25 keystrokes depending on the length of your name. Assign the block to a macro and it could be run with only one keystroke each time it was needed. Try it for yourself.

All these examples demonstrate how the use of macros can save time and make everyday tasks easier. Creating macros in most applications software is easy. Although the way macros are recorded varies in different applications, the general procedure is the same. You start the macro recorder, record a sequence of actions and stop the recording. You can then run (play back) the macro whenever you need to perform that same sequence.

Did you know ?

Macros can help organisations to process enquiries efficiently and collect valuable research by standardising enquiry procedures. For example, if you want a quote for car insurance you might telephone the insurance company and talk to an operator in the call centre. The operator will ask you a series of questions. He or she will be following screen prompts to request information, which will then be entered into a form on the screen. This is to ensure that all relevant information is gathered.

When all the data has been entered, a macro will automatically calculate an insurance premium based on the information you have given. At the same time the company can collect useful information to help them monitor their service and again macros can be used to total the number of times specific requests have been made.

Key points

- A macro is a recording of a computer task you use frequently.
- A macro is activated by an icon, a shortcut key, or by selecting the macro file.
- Default macros are prepared for you, but you can design your own macros.
- Using a macro is much quicker than repeating the task every time you need it.

CHAPTER 4

Graphs and charts

A textbook such as this will almost certainly include pictures, illustrations and diagrams, which help to clarify the information given in the text. **Graphs** or **charts** can be very helpful tools to illustrate numerical information, and spreadsheet programs provide easy-to-use facilities to create the graphs/charts. However, it is important to check that the type of graph/chart chosen is appropriate for the data and that it is clearly labelled. The 'reader' must be able to understand the graph/chart easily and find it beneficial to have the information presented in this way, otherwise it is a waste of time producing the chart.

Probably the most frequently used examples of graphs and charts are:

- Column charts
- Pie charts 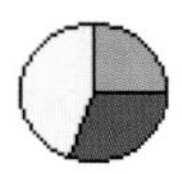
- Bar charts 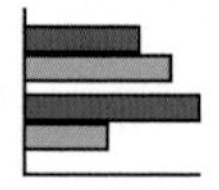
- Line graphs 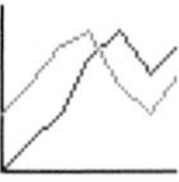

A well-presented graph or chart might include:

- A main title
- Axis titles
- Axis scale labels
- Data or series labels
- A legend where appropriate.

Let's experiment with creating charts and a graph using the Bedding Plants spreadsheet shown in Figure 4.8 on page 102. The aim is to compare the sales value of the different types of bedding plant. Cells A3 to H10 were highlighted to use as the basis for the chart, column style was selected, a legend included and main and axes titles added. Figure 4.17 shows the chart produced.

Unfortunately, the chart is not very helpful, the problem being that too many cells were selected from the spreadsheet. Before selecting the cells from which to create a chart, it is essential to decide what information you are trying to present. Given the aim of the chart mentioned above, it would have been more appropriate to select cells A3:A10 and H3:H10. See Figure 4.18 for the result.

You will notice that this time there is no legend. Since there is only one set of data for each type of plant, there is no need for a legend. Neither is there a title for

Activity

1. Open the spreadsheet Bedplant and create a column chart by selecting cells A3 to H10. Make sure you have included the data for July sales. Include main and axes titles, data labels and a legend. You should produce a chart similar to the one in Figure 4.17.
2. Create a second chart like the example in Figure 4.18. If you are using Excel, highlight the cells A3:A10, press the Ctrl key, then move the cursor and highlight cells H3:H10. (Pressing the Ctrl key before moving the cursor to the next block you wish to highlight allows you to select non-adjacent cells.)
3. Experiment with creating different chart styles to compare the sales for the four months as illustrated in Figures 4.19 and 4.20.
4. Create further charts showing:
   - the total *number* of plants sold
   - the *average* number sold
   - a comparison of the total number sold and the total value of the sales.

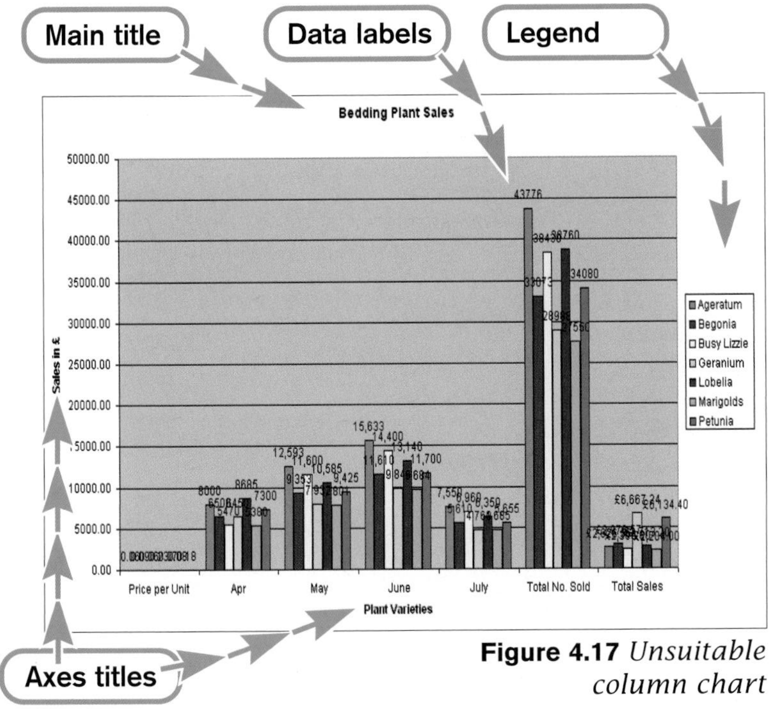

Figure 4.17 *Unsuitable column chart*

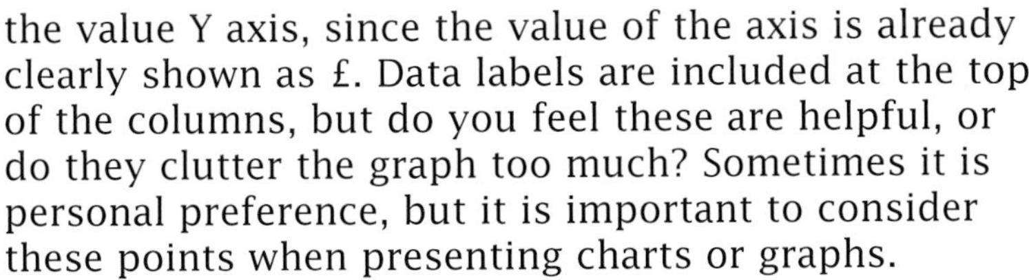

the value Y axis, since the value of the axis is already clearly shown as £. Data labels are included at the top of the columns, but do you feel these are helpful, or do they clutter the graph too much? Sometimes it is personal preference, but it is important to consider these points when presenting charts or graphs.

Using the same selection of cells, Figure 4.19 shows a pie chart with percentages rather than values. This time the legend has a purpose, to identify which segment represents which plant. Figure 4.20 shows a line graph. Which of these options do you prefer? Which represents the information most clearly?

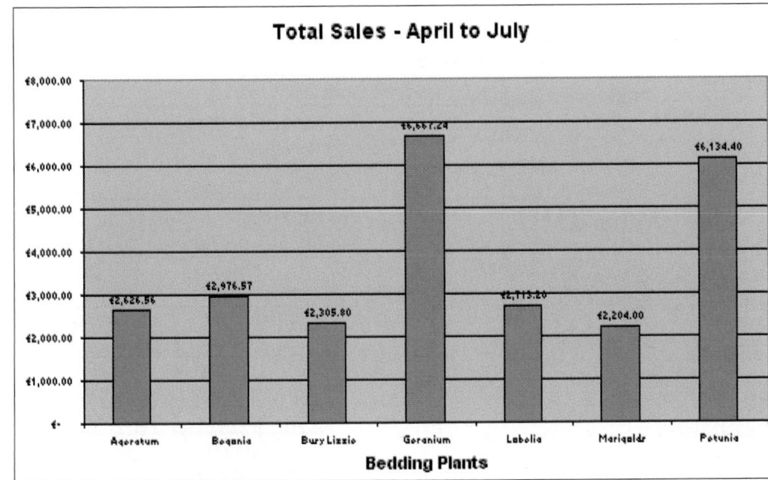

Figure 4.18 *Column chart*

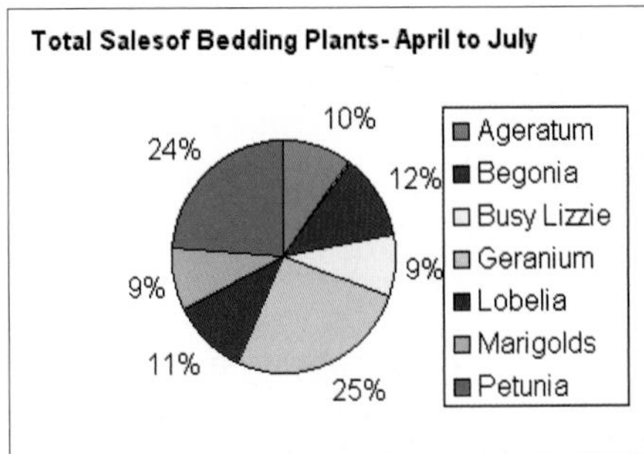

Figure 4.19 *Pie chart*

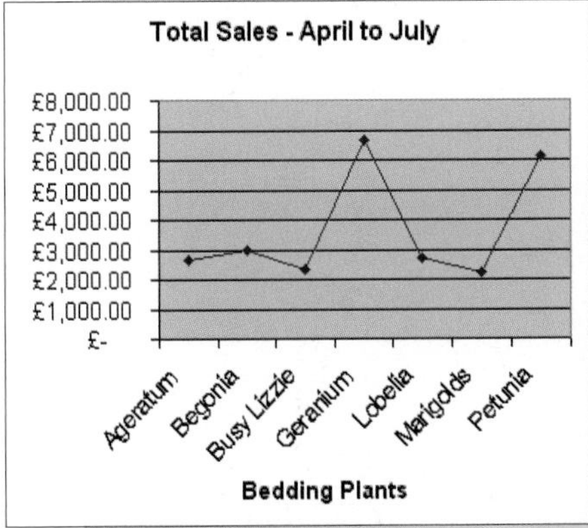

Figure 4.20 *Line graph*

Key points

- Graphs and charts illustrate the numerical data.
- Think about what you want the graph/chart to show before selecting the cells.
- Check if a legend is necessary.
- Choose a suitable title and axes titles.
- Select the style of graph/chart which best illustrates the data.

Test your understanding

Fill in the gaps

1 Numbers can be formatted as i__________, d__________ or c__________ . The number of decimal places can vary, but is often set to two.

2 When copying a formula using r__________ cell reference, the spreadsheet changes the reference automatically as you scroll down the rows or across the columns.

3 When copying a formula using a__________ cell reference, the reference stays fixed. To keep the reference fixed you must use d__________ signs before the letter and the number, e.g. $D$4.

4 Spreadsheet fu__________ are formulae already prepared for you. You have learned about 4 spreadsheet fu__________, S__________, A__________, I__________ and L__________.

5 Identify the following signs:
> g__________ t__________,
< l__________ t__________,
= e__________ t__________
>= g__________ t__________
or e__________ t__________,
<= l__________ t__________
or e__________ t__________,
<> n__________ e__________ t__________
These are known as c__________ operators.

6 Identify the following signs: + p__________, – m__________, * m__________, / d__________ . These are known as a__________ operators.

7 A t__________ is a ready-prepared blank form such as an invoice.

8 M__________ are 'recordings' of keystrokes or mouse clicks and are used for frequently used actions.

9 G__________ and ch__________ illustrate the numerical data in the spreadsheet. Common examples are c__________, b__________ or p__________ ch__________ and l__________ g__________.

10 What formula has been used in Figure 4.21 to calculate the values shown in the following cells:
a) D4 __________
b) D7 __________
c) D8 __________
d) D9 __________
e) D10 __________
f) D11 __________
g) D12 __________

Multiple choice questions

Questions 11–13 refer to Figure 4.21

11 The heading 'Item' has been:
a) aligned left
b) centred
c) aligned right
d) justified.

12 The heading 'Greenfingers' has been:
a) centred
b) aligned left
c) aligned right
d) centred across cells A1 to D1.

13 Which of these is shown in cell C3?
a) a row title
b) a main title
c) a column title
d) a total title.

	A	B	C	D
1	Greenfingers			
2	Invoice			
3	Item	Cost Price	Quantity	Total Cost
4	Busy Lizzie	0.06	5000	300.00
5	Begonia	0.07	5000	350.00
6	Geranium	0.23	2000	460.00
7			Total Cost	£ 1,110.00
8			Vat @ 17.5%	£ 194.25
9			Grand total	£ 1,304.25
10			3% discount	£ 39.13
11			Amount due	£ 1,265.12
12			Payment over 3 months	£ 421.71

Figure 4.21

CHAPTER 5

Database

Do you have a **database**? You may not think so, but you probably do. A database is any organised collection of data or information. It might not be very well organised, but your personal address or telephone book is a database. The more phone numbers or other information you add to your database, the more space you need and the harder it is to find the precise piece of information you want. Imagine the amount of information kept by government agencies such as MI5, the CIA or the Inland Revenue. Even small businesses will need to store and access databases of information; for example, Heinemann, the publisher of this book, will have information on authors such as us and customers, such as your own school or college, who purchase the book. A computer-based system can store vast amounts of data, organised for easy, flexible access.

In today's world, more databases than we are even aware of will hold information about us, because it is so much easier to store and transfer data held on a computer, than it was when all databases were hand-written. Have you ever done any of the following:

- subscribed to a magazine
- opened a bank or building society account
- applied for a driving licence
- paid for goods or services with a debit or credit card
- applied to a college.

If you have ticked any of the items in this list, then details about you will be stored in a database file.

The important point to remember is that a database is a store of related data. An address book will contain the same types of data for each person, such as:

- last name
- first name
- address
- telephone number
- and possibly date of birth.

A computerised database

These days we tend to think of a database as existing only in computers, but databases have always existed. It used to be commonplace in offices to have card index boxes. Each card would be written out with the same kind of details, just like the address book, and most often filed in alphabetical order. This too is a database.

If you can simply flick through a set of cards in a small box sitting conveniently on your desk, why bother with a computerised database? What has changed? See Table 5.1.

Computerised Database – Advantages	**Card Index – Disadvantages**
A vast amount of data can be stored on one disk.	You would need many, many boxes to store the same quantity of data.
Records are entered once – but can be searched in all kinds of ways – e.g. alphabetically, numerically, selectively, by date.	If the index cards are stored alphabetically but you would also like them in date order, you would have to write out a second set of cards. You would then have the problem of making sure both sets were kept up-to-date.
Searching for information is fast – even in a huge database.	Searching for information can be very slow.
Data can be lost – but should be able to be retrieved if backups are kept.	Cards are easily lost, filed in the wrong place or mislaid.
Can perform calculations – e.g. you could ask the database to calculate the VAT on a price and give the cost price, VAT and total price.	The calculations would have to be written out manually.
If the rate of VAT changes, this is easy and quick to update.	Difficult and slow to update.

Table 5.1 *The advantages of a computerised database and the disadvantages of a paper-based card index system*

Data and information

You will notice that Table 5.1 refers to data and information. So what is the difference?

Data is small, individual details such as the cost price and selling price of items sold. *Information* is what can be discovered from *the data*. For example, if Greenfingers wanted to find out how much profit was being made from various items, the difference between cost price and selling price – the data – would be the profit – *the information*. The percentage profit could also be calculated, to provide further information on the most profitable lines. See Table 5.2. Notice that there isn't much difference between the selling price of the two items, but there is a 10% difference in the profit. This kind of information is invaluable to businesses and very quick to obtain from a computerised system.

Data			Information	
Item	Cost Price	Selling Price	Profit	Percentage Profit
Spade	£18.23	£23.70	£4.47	30%
Rake	£15	£21	£6	40%

Table 5.2 *Data and information*

Figure 5.1 *A paper-based card index system*

Key points

- A database is a store of related data.
- Data is entered into the database.
- Information is what you find out from the data.
- A computerised database:
  - can store vast quantities of data
  - makes searching quick and flexible
  - can perform calculations.

Activity

Think about Greenfingers. What details about its wholesale customers do you think the company might need? A list has been started below, but what other details would be useful? Make a list of all the details you think will be necessary and keep it for future reference.

- Contact person
- Company name
- Street
- Town.

Database structure

A database consists of a **file**, containing many **records**. Each record will include the **fields**, into which will be entered the appropriate **data**. Each record will contain the same fields, but sometimes a field is left blank in a particular record; e.g. if there is no e-mail address the field for e-mail will be left blank.

Records

A database file is a collection of records.

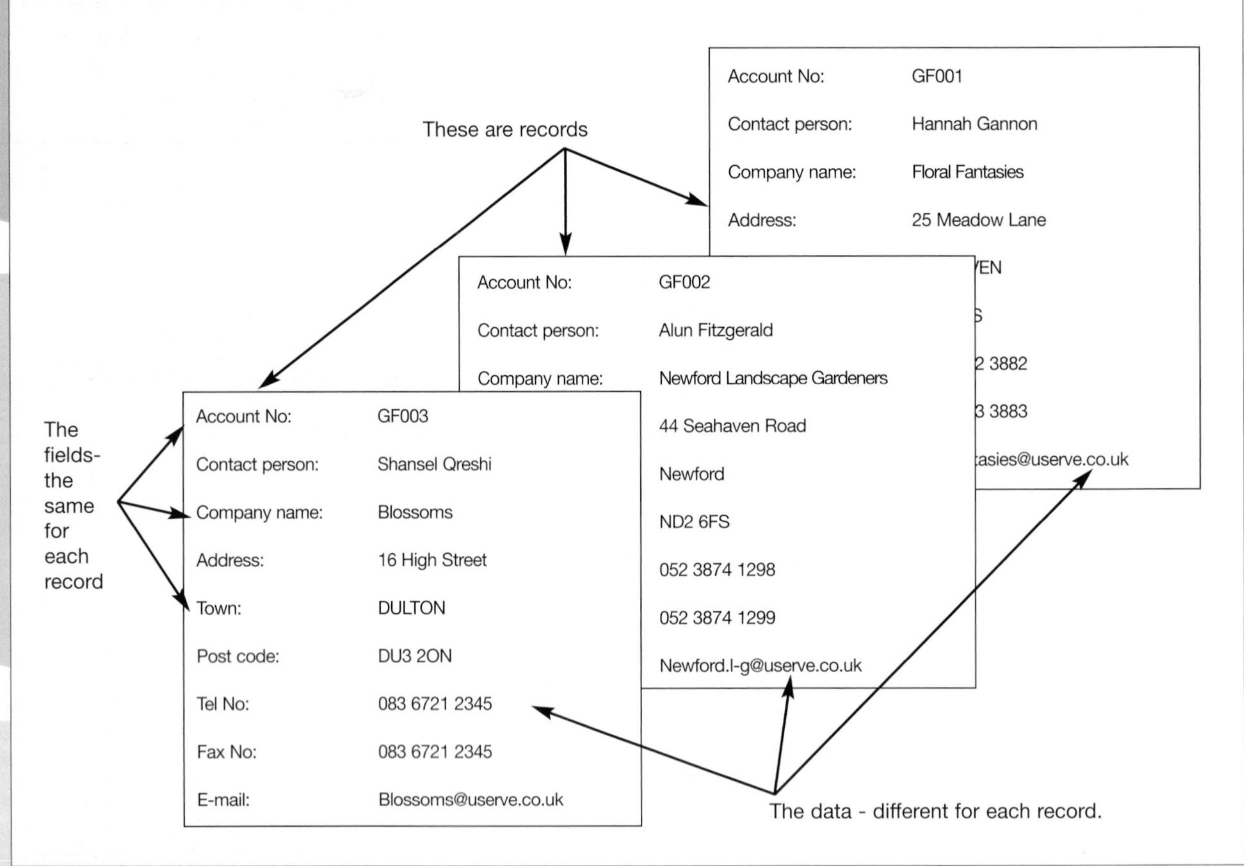

Figure 5.2 *Database records*

Tables and forms

A database is usually designed through a Table. Once the Table design is complete, the Form View is created. The data entry clerk will use the Form View to enter new data or look at existing data on screen. The layout on screen can be designed in a variety of styles, just as forms for different purposes are laid out differently. You may wish to view one record at a time on screen or you might want to see all records listed under the different field names. A computerised database provides great flexibility in the way you look at the data and it is easy to switch between looking at one record on screen or a list of all records. Figure 5.3 illustrates the Datasheet View for the three records shown in Figure 5.2. Figure 5.4 shows just one record, in Form View.

Did you know?

If you have a field for Cost Price and you wish to know how much the VAT is, in Access you can create a calculated control, which will automatically work out the answer for you. You might then create another calculated control to find the Total Price. If the Cost Price changes, then the VAT and Total Price will immediately be adjusted.

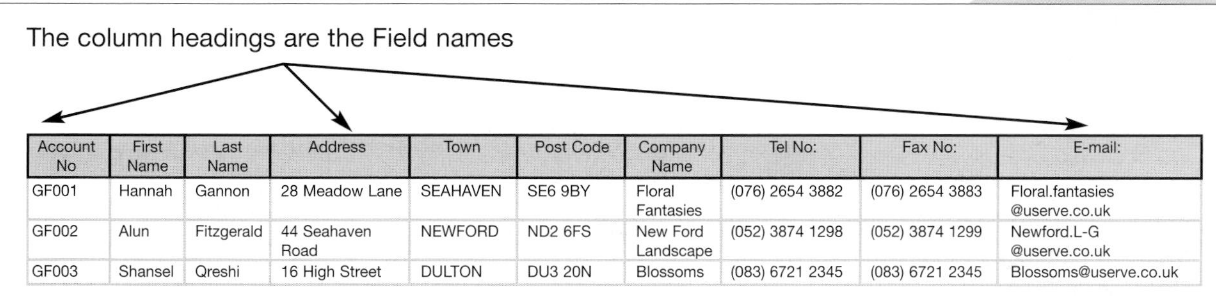

Account No	First Name	Last Name	Address	Town	Post Code	Company Name	Tel No:	Fax No:	E-mail:
GF001	Hannah	Gannon	28 Meadow Lane	SEAHAVEN	SE6 9BY	Floral Fantasies	(076) 2654 3882	(076) 2654 3883	Floral.fantasies @userve.co.uk
GF002	Alun	Fitzgerald	44 Seahaven Road	NEWFORD	ND2 6FS	New Ford Landscape	(052) 3874 1298	(052) 3874 1299	Newford.L-G @userve.co.uk
GF003	Shansel	Qreshi	16 High Street	DULTON	DU3 20N	Blossoms	(083) 6721 2345	(083) 6721 2345	Blossoms@userve.co.uk

Figure 5.3 *Database records shown in Datasheet View*

Figure 5.4 *One database record shown in Form View*

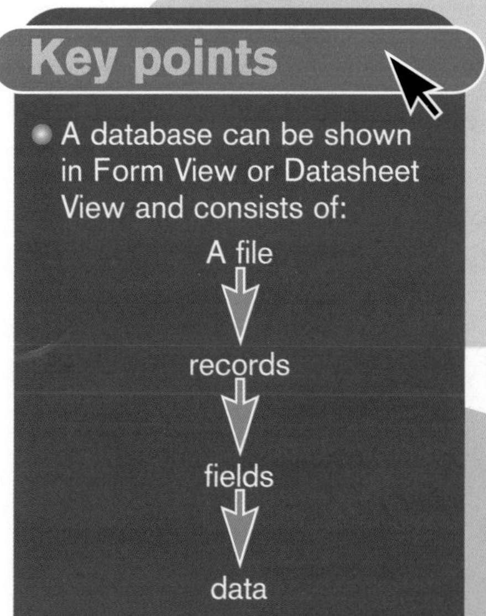

Key points
A database can be shown in Form View or Datasheet View and consists of:
A file
records
fields
data

Database design 1

Did you know

Combo boxes and **check boxes** are facilities provided by the database program to make data entry easier and more accurate. *Combo boxes* are used where the data is limited to a particular selection; e.g. BP/SH/PO/MI (Greenfingers uses codes for the product description: BP – bedding plants, SH – shrubs, PO – pots, MI – miscellaneous)

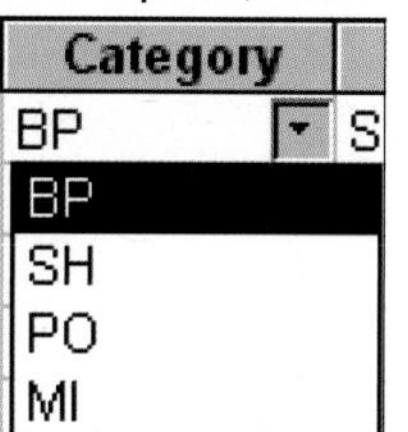

Figure 5.5

Check boxes are used where there is a yes/no option. A ✓ in the box indicates 'yes' and the box is left blank to indicate 'no'.

Figure 5.6

Activity

Refer to the list of fields you identified for Greenfingers' database of wholesale customers, and decide the appropriate type of field and a suitable length. Plan this out on paper – a form to assist you is available in the Tutor's File. Your database will be much more effective and less likely to require changes if you take this planning stage seriously.

Understandably students on an ICT course like to get their fingers on the keyboard/mouse. They don't really want to *write* anything! However, when planning a computerised database, it is very important to *think carefully* about the design, *before* you actually start creating the fields in the database. It would be perfectly possible to create every field as text, because text allows you to enter letters and/or numbers into the field. However, if you did use all text fields, you would not be able to:

- make calculations, such as finding out the VAT on the price of an item
- use the order date to search for orders placed in a specific month, or before or after a particular date
- search easily for a particular category, such as bedding plants or shrubs.

To facilitate these tasks, the field for the price of the item would have to be numerical, the field for the date of order would have to be a date field, and it will be much easier to find a category if they are specified in a choice field. Let's look at this in more detail.

Setting up a computerised database – field names, field length, field data type

Decide the purpose of your database, and then plan:

1. **The fields you need**. In other words, the *names* of the fields; e.g. Account No., date of order.
2. **The data type for each field**. Should you use text, number, date, time, choice?
3. **Encoding the data**. Greenfingers might encode the colours available for the plants; B – blue, R – red, Y – yellow, P – purple, M – mixed, keeping the length of the field to 1 digit, which reduces the space required for storage and display.
4. **The length of the fields**. How many characters do you need in a particular field? For example, you would not design a field with decimal places for the price of a house. House prices are not quoted as £56,789.58, but a price field for items in the garden centre would be quite different and decimal places would be necessary. It is good practice to allow just enough room for the data so that you don't waste the computer's memory or the display area on screen.

Field data types

Table 5.3 lists some typical data types for fields which are useful in a database.

Type of field	Purpose	Advantages/Possible uses
Text/character – sometimes called alphanumeric	Any data – letters, numbers or symbols on the keyboard – can be entered into a text field	• Names/addresses • Where you might include extra detail/description
Numerical Integer Select the number of digits required, e.g. 3	A whole number Allows space for a maximum of three digits, e.g. 156	• Restricts data entry to whole • Cannot enter 4 or more digits • Reduces the risk of errors • Can be listed in numerical order • Reduces space for storage and display
Decimal	A number with decimal places – you can usually decide on how many to the right and left of the decimal point, e.g. 15.67	• Suitable for money where prices include pence – 15.67 • Measurements – 4.25 km
Currency	Can be set as an integer or with decimal places	• Suitable for money and would show the currency specified, e.g. £5.67
Counter or AutoNumber	A numeric value – as each new record is entered the counter automatically selects the sequence	• Suitable for a member ID, student ID, account no., etc. • Ensures that each member ID, account no., etc. remains unique
Date	A typical date format will be prepared, e.g. --/--/--	• Restricts data entry to 1–31 for the day, and 1–12 for the month Can search for: • birthdays in a given month • those older or younger than a given age • orders placed before, after or on a given date
Time	A typical time format will be prepared, e.g. --:--:--	• Can be used where employees are paid by the hour • Hours worked can be calculated from time clocked on and off
Choice • Male/female • True/false • Colours red blue green	Data entry is limited to the selection that has been pre-determined. Choice fields can also be encoded, e.g.: M – for male, F – for female, R – red	• Speeds up data entry • Can search for specific entries, such as 'male', 'true' or 'green' • Reduces space for storage and display

Table 5.3 *Fields used in databases*

Database design 2

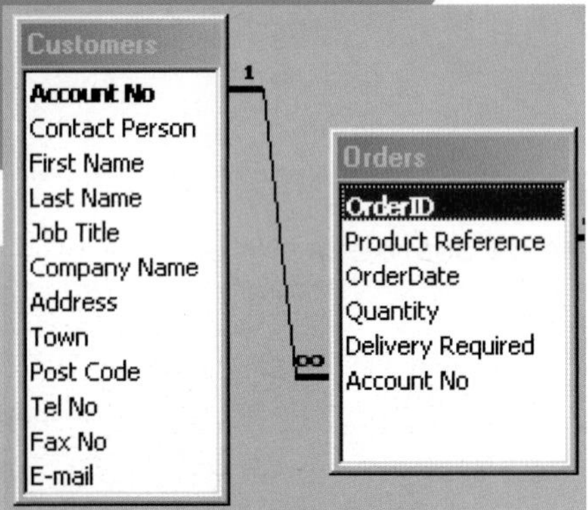

Figure 5.7 *The relationship between two tables in Greenfingers' database*

Did you know

For purposes of understanding database relationships, this explanation has been limited to two tables, but most commercial databases would have more complex relationships including three, four or more tables.

Did you know

The sophisticated facilities of the modern database assist the police in fighting crime. The system has the facility to capture an image, so the arresting officer can easily check the prisoner's identity, and check whether s/he is a known criminal. Details on known criminals can be immediately e-mailed to other police officers who may have a special interest in the prisoner. (Source: *IT Training*, 14 July 1999.)

Relationships

Just as a book is divided into chapters, a database is designed into two or more sections known as tables, which are related or connected to each other, rather than having several separate files or one huge file. Let's consider just two tables: Customer and Order.

The Customer table would include the fields:

- Account No. (a unique reference)
- Contact Person
- Company Name
- Address
- Town
- Post Code
- Telephone No.
- Fax
- E-mail

The Order table would include the fields:

- Order No. (another unique reference)
- Account No.
- Date of Order
- Product Reference (also a unique reference)
- Description
- Price
- Quantity

To build the relationship it is essential that one unique field is repeated in each of the linked tables. Look at the examples above and you will see that the fields for Account No. link the tables. See also Figure 5.7. When tables are linked in this way, it is possible to search each table separately or to select fields from all linked tables. From the **data** above, it would be possible to find out **information**, such as:

1. The contact person for a given customer.
2. Who placed a particular order.
3. The items ordered by a particular customer over a period of, say, 6 months.
4. The items included in a particular order.

Key fields – primary and foreign

You have already seen that each record in a database usually has one unique field, which identifies that record as different from every other record in the file. This field is the **primary key**. No doubt when you enrolled at school/college you were given a student ID number, which is different from every other student in the school/college. It is essential that the primary key is unique, otherwise the computer will not be able to identify the record required if two students have the same name. Records are automatically sorted in order of the primary key.

When this unique field is used in another table, it is known as a **foreign key**. Let's look at Greenfingers' database and identify the primary and foreign keys (see Table 5.4).

Manufacturer Database		
Table	**Primary key**	**Foreign key**
Customer	Account No.	
Order	Order No.	Account No. Product Reference

Table 5.4 *Greenfingers' database*

Wizards

As you can see, designing a database is a complex procedure. You can design the table yourself, but modern database programs include **wizards** to make it easier. A wizard takes you step by step through the process, giving you choices at each stage. Figure 5.8 shows a wizard where a form is being created from the Customer table. You can select which fields you want to use, but you can customise the table to suit your particular purpose.

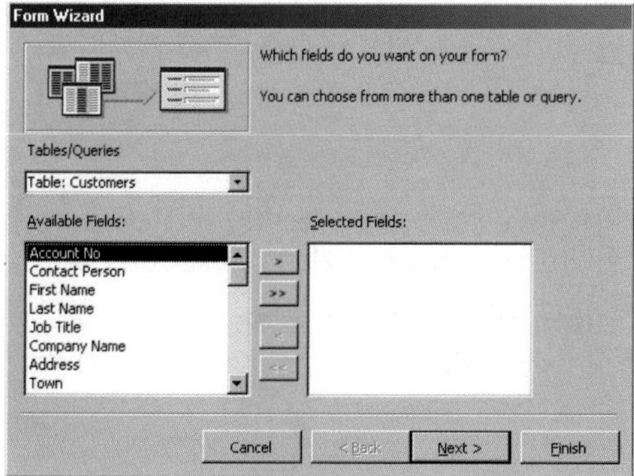

Figure 5.8 *Form Wizard dialogue box*

Key points

It is essential to consider carefully:

- the tables required
- the field names, length and type
- the unique primary key for each table
- the key field which links the tables
- wizards to make designing the database easier
- modifying the wizard design to suit your needs.

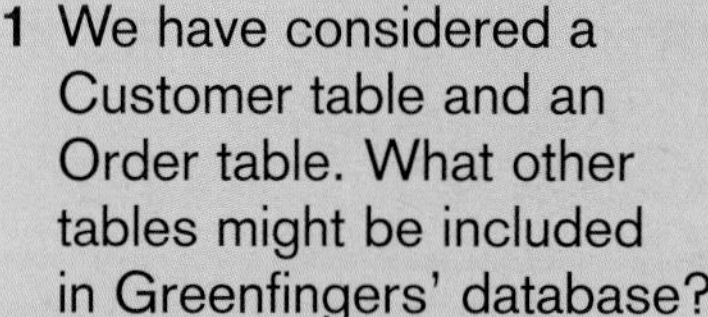

Activity

1. We have considered a Customer table and an Order table. What other tables might be included in Greenfingers' database?
2. Using the form provided in the Tutor's File, identify the fields required in these tables and decide:
   - the field data type and length
   - the field length
   - the primary key for each table
   - the key field which would link the tables together
   - the foreign keys in the tables, if any.

Accuracy checks

Did you know ?

A gentleman in America suddenly discovered he was listed as dead in one computer, because cheques were returned marked 'deceased' across his signature. He spoke to his bank who reassured him that the error would be rectified, but his troubles had just begun. The rumours of his death spread through the computer systems much faster than he could hope to correct the information! As a result his social security was stopped, his Medicare was stopped and he felt helpless against the power of the computer. It took over a year to rectify all the errors. You might think this is an isolated incident, but thousands of lives are disrupted each year by faulty data in computer systems.

(From a video, *The Dream Machine*, of a series by BBC2 called *The Passing of Remoteness*.)

The most sophisticated data-handling system in the world is completely useless if the data entered into the system is not accurate in the first place. Manual systems rely on the operator to proof read for accuracy whereas a computerised system can build in accuracy checks to reduce the risk of errors.

Validation

The word valid means suitable. If you have fantastic audio equipment for a mobile disco, but try to play CDs on a tape deck, you will not have any music! A silly example, but the tape deck was not suitable or valid for playing CDs. Computers use three very important validation checks – type, range and check digits. If invalid data is entered the computer will indicate an error.

Type check

Table 5.5 illustrates the various data types, which may be used in a database. If a field has been designed for numbers, the computer will not accept letters in that field. If a field has been designed to accept a choice of colours – red, blue, green, yellow – it will not accept any other colour in that field.

Range check

A number field may include a further check as well as the type check. The field can be limited within a set range, by giving a minimum or maximum figure or both.

Data to be entered	Data actually entered	Data correct
25	25	√
25	52	**X** – but is accepted because it is of the correct *type*.
25	q5	**X** – computer immediately signals an error, because 'q' is not a number.
red	red	√
red	blue	**X** but the choice of blue is accepted because it is included in the list of options – i.e. the correct *type*.
red	purple	**X** – computer immediately signals an error, because none of the colours listed in the choice above starts with a 'p'.

Table 5.5 *A type check*

Check digit

It is very easy to make an error when keying in a lengthy account number. To prevent such errors a **check digit** is often added to the end of the account number. The check digit is calculated from the other digits of the account through a specific formula as an accuracy check. Therefore, if an error has been made, the check digit will not calculate correctly.

Verification

To verify means to check. The operator may verify the entries visually on screen and check them again against the original document. Sometimes a second operator will read the data out loud to the first operator, who checks on screen that the entries match. This is particularly useful for numerical data, as errors cannot easily be spotted by proof reading.

Verification can also be undertaken by one operator keying in the data, and another operator keying it again. The computer indicates any differences and a check can be made against the original document to establish whether the first or second entry is the correct one. It is an excellent method of ensuring accuracy, but time-consuming and expensive.

An example of verification by entering data twice, which you may well have used, is setting a password. As the original entry is encoded, usually as asterisks, you are always asked to enter the password again, just in case you made an error the first time.

Electronic verification can be made where a unique field has been used for a product reference. A list of all unique codes used by the company are stored in the computer, and if the code entered does not match one in the list, then an error is indicated. This works on the same basis as a spell checker, using a '*custom dictionary*' of the product references. It will, of course, still be possible to enter one of the listed codes, but *not* the correct one. To prevent errors on the unit price, the product reference could be set to generate the relevant price automatically. The total cost and VAT would also be automatically calculated from the number of items and the unit price. If the code for the correct item has been entered, then these fields will also be correct.

Other useful methods of verification are control or hash totals (see batch processing on page 134).

Key points

- Examples of accuracy checks are validation and verification.
- Validation checks include type checks, range checks and check digits.
- Verification checks may be manual, usually through a visual check on screen, or electronic through the use of unique fields.

Activity

Refer once again to the design of Greenfingers' database.

1 Did you include any validation techniques or any unique fields? If not, could you amend your design to include some?
2 Would you be able to verify electronically any fields?
3 Create a table similar to Table 5.5 to establish which errors would be detected, if a field is set with a lower limit of 500 and an upper limit of 3,000.
4 Test a date field to find out if the computer will accept 13 for the month, or 31 for the day for the months of February, April, June, September and November.

Testing the database

Did you know

Although spell checking is more typically associated with word processing, the facility is also available in database applications and can be useful as a means of verification.

Once you have created the fields and built the relationships, it is important to check that it is working as you intended. You will need to consider testing the following:

- Entry of data by type (e.g. will the field accept text when it should only accept number?).
- Entry of minimum and maximum range (e.g. the price range for products is between £10 and £99 – will the field accept £9 or £101?)
- Entry of data out of range (e.g. there are no more than 31 days in a month – will the field accept 32 as the day in a date field?).
- Is it easy to enter, add, delete or change data? If not, does the layout need changing? Is the field format unsuitable?
- Can you create suitable queries or reports? Decide on the information you require, and check whether it is possible to obtain it.
- Is it easy to progress between different screens in the database you have set up? If not, what can you do to simplify it? Do the command buttons open the right form or table?

Log of testing

It is good practice to prepare a log of testing on paper, in which you decide on data to enter into each field, the result you expect and then compare it with what actually happens. Let's look at some examples of test data, which might be used for Greenfingers' Order table.

Activity

Refer to the tables you have already planned for Greenfingers' database.

- Prepare a log of testing as shown in Table 5.6.
- Enter the data you have selected in your log and check if the results match what you expected.
- Plan some queries and reports, and check if the results are as expected.
- If necessary amend the field design
- Ask someone else to use your database to ensure it is user-friendly.

Field name	Field type	Data to enter	Expected result	Actual result
Price	Currency	4.99	Accepted	Accepted
Price	Currency	Four pounds ninety-nine pence	Rejected	Rejected
Price	Currency	Four pounds ninety-nine pence	Rejected	Accepted – field type probably set as text and not currency
Order Date	--/--/-- (date format)	12/01/00	Accepted	Accepted
Order Date	--/--/-- (date format)	12/13/00	Rejected	Rejected
Order Date	--/--/-- (date format)	12/13/00	Rejected	Accepted – field type probably set as text and not date format
Quantity	Integer	5	Accepted	Accepted
Quantity	Integer	5	Rejected	Rejected
Quantity	Integer	5	Rejected	Accepted – field type probably set as text and not number
Category	Choice of: bedding plants, shrubs, pots, miscellaneous	Shrubs	Accepted	Accepted
Category	Choice of: bedding plants, shrubs, pots, miscellaneous	Tools	Rejected	Rejected, but perhaps you need to consider adding this category to the list

Table 5.6 *Log of testing*

It is very important *not* to assume the database will work as you intend. If the result of your testing is not as expected, you need to revise the design. Once you have tested the database, the data from your information sources can be entered.

Key points

- *Do not* assume the database is working correctly.
- Prepare a log of testing.
- *Follow* the log and amend the design if necessary.

Using the database 1

Data capture

Having tested the database you are now ready to enter the data. This may be by keying in the data from a paper-based form, or by direct data capture, such as hand-held terminals for meter readings (see page 135). Direct data capture removes the necessity of keying in data from source documents and is becoming more and more common. Examples of direct data capture include:

- Bar codes *read* by light pens or scanners.
- Magnetic ink character recognition used on bank cheques to input the unique branch sort code, customer account number and amount.
- OMR – optical mark readers – often used for attendance registers in schools and colleges and for 'marking' multiple-choice examination papers.
- OCR – optical character recognition – which identifies the *shape* of the character, often used to scan text into a word processor, which can then be edited as required.

Any kind of form can be used as a paper-based source of data capture. Typical examples include application forms for college, university, driving licence, car, house, health insurance, TV licence. Such data may be given over the telephone and entered directly into the computer. Where a paper-based source is used, it is very important that the data-capture form and the computer screen follow a similar pattern so that it is easy and quick to copy the data into the computer.

Bar codes are not just used for identifying tins of beans on supermarket shelves; they are used for many reasons, not just items that are sold. For example, when blood is donated, the same bar code is put on the bag of plasma, the platelet bag and the blood sample from one particular individual, to identify the exact source and data such as the blood group.

Thousands of cheques per minute can be processed using magnetic ink character recognition.

The new European Union passports use OCR for the holder's details on the back page of the passport.

Editing the database

Editing a computerised database is usually much easier than with a manual system. From time to time you may need to:

- add new fields or change existing ones
- amend (change or alter) a record – e.g. if an address changes
- append (add) a new record – e.g. a new customer
- delete (remove) a record – e.g. a product item is discontinued.

If you need to amend or delete a record, the computer will quickly locate the correct record for you. New records are automatically filed in correct order of the primary key. Any indexed fields (see page 131) will also be updated automatically.

Database queries

Searching the database to find specific information is known as a query. The query defines the parameters – i.e. what do you need to know. The result of your search/query may be presented on screen or printed on paper. A well-designed database file, with appropriately linked tables, allows the user to search for – to *query* – information by selecting **fields** from *any* of the tables.

Let's imagine that Pete Wellings wants a list of the contact people and telephone numbers of the customers. It would be possible to ask the database for this information. Table 5.7 might be the result of this query, although in practice Greenfingers would have many more than 3 customers. Now let's look in more detail at the different ways we can search the database.

Key points

- Data capture may be manual or electronic.
- Searching for specific information is known as a query.

Contact Person	Company Name	Telephone Number
Hannah Gannon	Floral Fantasies	076 2654 3882
Alun Fitzgerald	Newford Landscape Gardeners	052 3874 1298
Shansel Qreshi	Blossoms	083 6721 2345

Table 5.7 *The result of a query*

Using sort, search, logic and comparison conditions

Sorting by selected key field means presenting a query in a particular order – e.g. alphabetical, numerical, order of date. The order can be ascending (lowest to highest), i.e. A–Z or 1–100, or descending (highest to lowest), i.e. Z–A or 100–1. The query illustrated in Table 5.7 might have been requested in alphabetical order of company name – the selected key field – in which case the report would have looked like Table 5.8.

List the steps necessary to obtain this information from a manual system where the customer details were filed in order of account number.

Contact Person	Company Name	Telephone Number
Shansel Qreshi	Blossoms	083 6721 2345
Hannah Gannon	Floral Fantasies	076 2654 3882
Alun Fitzgerald	Newford Landscape Gardeners	052 3874 1298

Table 5.8 *Database sorted in alphabetical order of Company Name*

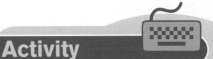

Using the database 2

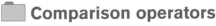

Comparison operators

As with spreadsheets, if you search a database using **comparison operators**, you will be looking for a number greater than, less than or equal to.

- > Greater than
- < Less than
- = Equal to
- <> Not equal to
- >= Greater than or equal to
- <= Less than or equal to

(If, like me, you confuse the signs for *greater than* and *less than*, try to remember that *less than* < points to the left.)

Pete Wellings has a problem – an order from Floral Fantasies has gone astray. They say the order was placed in the early part of May, so Pete searches the database to check whether the order was received. The criteria for the search used comparison operators, i.e. order dates after or greater than 01/05/01 and before or less than 31/05/01. By using comparison operators the selection is limited by the particular relational operator used. See Figure 5.9.

	Description	Trade Price	Supplier Name	Email Address
▶	Ageratum	£3.40	Suffolk Seeds	SuffolkSeeds@userve.co.uk
	Begonia	£4.00	Suffolk Seeds	SuffolkSeeds@userve.co.uk

Figure 5.9 *Results of a search using comparison operators*

Logical operators

When you search a database using **logical operators**, the criteria for selection is *and, or, not*. The computer checks to establish whether it is *true* or *false* that any records match the criteria. If a true match is found, then the records will be displayed. Again the search illustrated in Figure 5.9 required orders placed in May *and* those placed by Floral Fantasies. By including *and, or,* or *not* in the search criteria, the selection is limited by the particular logical operator used.

Activity

Once again look back at the fields in Greenfingers' database. Which of the fields would be suitable to index?

Indexing fields

When you read a novel, you generally start at the first page and carry on until the end (unless you like to cheat!), but, as you well know, a textbook is different and the reader often wants to look something up without reading all the previous pages. At the back of this book you will find an alphabetical list of the topics covered in the book and the page number where that topic can be found – the index. Without an index it would be very difficult to find that topic. Basically, the index makes it much quicker to search the book for the particular information required.

An index in a database is much the same. A given field in a database can be indexed by categories; e.g. 'Products' would be a suitable field to index. Although indexing can speed up searching the database, it is not wise to index too many fields, as each index will be updated automatically when records are added to or removed from the database, which might slow down the process. Choose fields to index that are likely to be used frequently in searches.

Key points

- Comparison operators find information *greater than, less than* or *equal to.*
- Logical operators *–and, or, not* – look for a *true* match to the criteria.
- Index fields make it quicker to search the database.
- A report will customise the layout for the result of a query.

Database reports

The result of a query is presented in table format. If you wish to present the results with a specific layout, you can design a report. Figure 5.10 illustrates the difference.

You have the opportunity of choosing various options in the design report, and once again wizards are available to help you design the report layout quickly and easily.

Table View

Account No	Company Name	Order ID	Product Reference	Order Date	Quantity
GF001	Floral Fantasies	3	BP020	03/05/01	300

Report View

Products

Description	Ageratum
Trade Price	£3.40
Supplier Name	Suffolk Seeds
Email Address	SuffolkSeeds@userve.co.uk
Description	Begonia
Trade Price	£4.00
Supplier Name	Suffolk Seeds
Email Address	SuffolkSeeds@userve.co.uk

Figure 5.10 *The difference between Table View and Report View*

The user interface

One of the benefits of a modern database is the ease with which user-friendly screens can be developed. You need to know how to design and create effective data-entry screens, both in content and layout, and also simple methods of moving from screen to screen. You also need to consider how to present your queries. Queries are automatically presented in table format, or you can design a report and customise the layout (see Figure 5.10).

Layout of screen

Although the Form Wizard makes it very easy to create a Form View from the Table View, the result will probably be in columnar format, where all fields are listed one under the other (as shown in the Report View of Figure 5.10). All the right-hand side of the window is wasted, and the form may not fit in the screen window. Another common ready-prepared format is tabular, where all the field names are listed across the screen with the data in rows underneath. This is not much different from Table View. It may be convenient to use the wizard so that all the fields are *transferred* from the table into the form, but rearrange them into a more appropriate layout.

Do try to fit all the fields into the screens if possible, and do think about the position of the fields – they should be presented in a logical order and follow, where applicable, any data capture form the data entry clerk is following. As already explained, combo or check boxes also make the interface more user-friendly as it is easier to enter the data.

It is also important to consider the following points. In fact, the first three apply to any work you are doing on the computer!

- Font style – **whilst fancy fonts may look attractive, they are not necessarily easy to read.**
- Font *size* – are main headings in a larger size? Are the field labels big enough to read easily, but not so big they take up too much space?
- Use of colour – different colours can improve the appearance, but do not vary the colour too much and make sure it is easy to read (e.g. yellow for the font is not easily visible on a white background, and dark backgrounds do not print well).

- Use of coded data – as already suggested Greenfingers' database might use BP for Bedding Plants, PO for Pots, SH for Shrubs and MI for Miscellaneous.
- Validation of data on entry – is the data valid or suitable for its purpose? If all the fields have been designed as text, any data will be accepted, but if careful consideration has been given to the format of the field (see Table 5.3), invalid or unsuitable data will not be accepted. Has a primary key been set? If so, it will not be possible to use the same account number or reference for a new record. If the data-entry clerk makes a mistake and tries to enter invalid data in the field, an error message will occur.

Key points

- The user interface must be easy to use.
- Choose font style, size and colour carefully to enhance the screen design.
- Use validation techniques to ensure accuracy.
- Ensure ease of access between tables and forms.

Moving between screens

A complex database is likely to include several forms. It is much easier for the user to access the form required if an opening screen has been designed with command buttons to open each part of the database. It is also possible to include command buttons on a form to switch back to the opening screen. See Figure 5.11.

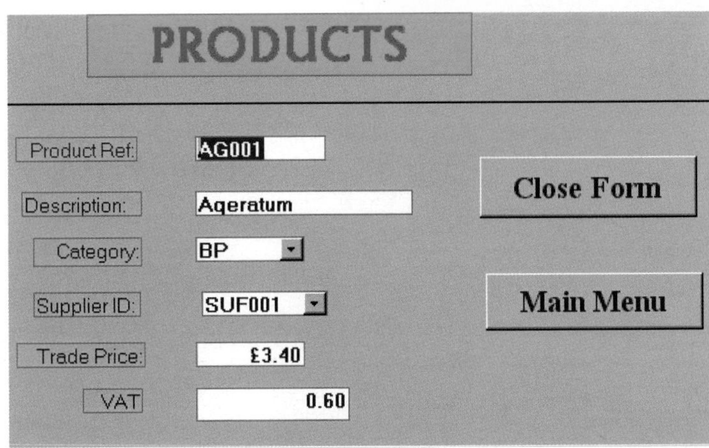

Figure 5.11 *An opening screen with buttons. If you click on the relevant button it will take you to the form named, e.g. Products. The button 'Exit Database' closes right out of the programme. On the Products form, buttons will close the form or take you back to the Main Menu.*

Methods of processing 1

Every day businesses are dealing with millions of transactions, which need to be recorded into their computer system. A transaction could be paying a bill, enrolling at college, booking a holiday. In some cases it is essential that the transaction is recorded into the computer immediately, and in others it can wait for a few hours, a day or even longer. There are two basic methods used to process the data: **batch** and **transaction**.

Batch processing

Batch processing is used for large quantities of similar transactions which are processed regularly, e.g. at the end of the day, weekly, monthly, quarterly, but are *not required urgently*. The transactions are collected over a period of time, e.g. gas, electricity or water meter readings, and when all the relevant data is ready, the batch is processed all together. The main advantage of batch processing is that the operator can load the batch in one go rather than entering each item individually. The computer automatically processes the data without the operator having any further involvement.

The *permanent* records of all the customers are kept on the **customer master file**. When the meters are read the details of the customer account reference and the number of units of gas used are entered into a temporary file – the **transaction file**, which contains only the information that has changed.

To try to ensure the accuracy of the data, **control** or **hash** totals are used as verification techniques. Control totals are *meaningful* numbers, such as:

- the total number of entries calculated
- the total amount due by all customers
- the total number of gas units used by all customers.

Hash totals are *meaningless* numbers, such as:

- adding up all the account numbers
- the total of the meter readings.

The computer records control or hash totals when the data is entered into the meter reader's hand-held terminal. After the data is transferred into the customer master file, the control or hash totals are compared electronically and if they differ an error report is produced. The operator can then check where the error occurs. For example, if the original

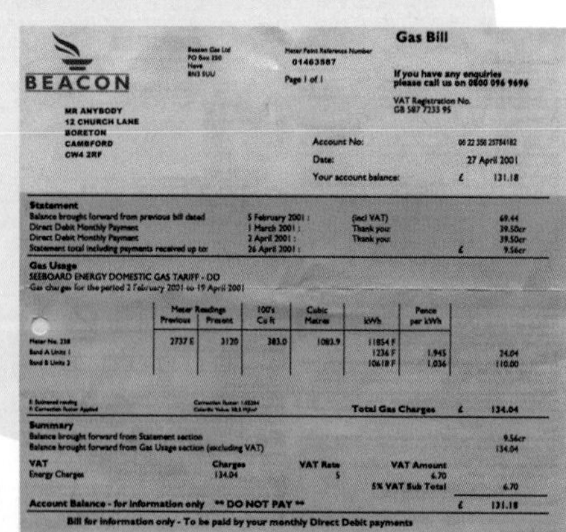

BEACON

Gas Bill

Meter Point Reference Number
01463587
Page 1 of 1

If you have any enquiries please call us on 0800 096 9696

VAT Registration No.
GB 587 7233 95

MR ANYBODY
12 CHURCH LANE
BORETON
CAMBFORD
CW4 2RF

Account No: 00 22 356 23784182
Date: 27 April 2001
Your account balance: £ 131.18

Statement

Balance brought forward from previous bill dated	5 February 2001 :	(incl VAT)	69.44
Direct Debit Monthly Payment	1 March 2001 :	Thank you	39.50cr
Direct Debit Monthly Payment	2 April 2001 :	Thank you	39.50cr
Statement total including payments received up to:	26 April 2001 :	£	9.56cr

Gas Usage
SEEBOARD ENERGY DOMESTIC GAS TARIFF - DD
Gas charges for the period 2 February 2001 to 19 April 2001

	Meter Readings Previous	Meter Readings Present	100's Cu ft	Cubic Metres	kWh	Pence per kWh	
Meter No. 238	2737 E	3120	383.0	1083.9	11854 F		
Band A Units 1					1236 F	1.945	24.04
Band B Units 2					10618 F	1.036	110.00

Total Gas Charges £ 134.04

Summary

Balance brought forward from Statement section			9.56cr
Balance brought forward from Gas Usage section (excluding VAT)			134.04
VAT	**Charges**	**VAT Rate**	**VAT Amount**
Energy Charges	134.04	5	6.70
		5% VAT Sub Total	6.70

Account Balance - for information only ** DO NOT PAY ** £ 131.18

Bill for information only - To be paid by your monthly Direct Debit payments

Figure 5.12 *A gas bill*

number of entries was 858, but after the master file is updated only 857 entries are recorded, clearly one has been missed and must be identified.

Let's consider preparation of gas bills.

1 The names, addresses and account numbers of customers to visit are downloaded into the meter reader's hand-held terminal via a modem.
2 The meters are read and the new meter reading is logged into the hand-held terminal against the customer's account number.
3 The new readings are uploaded using the modem and telephone line into the gas board's database and stored in a temporary *transaction* file.
4 The control or hash totals are verified.
5 The transaction file is sorted into the same order as the customer master file. This is important if the master file is stored on tape, as tapes use serial access, i.e. working from start to finish, and the tape would have to be wound back and forward if the transaction and master files were not in the same order. This transaction file is then processed with the master file.
6 The computer calculates the difference between the old and new readings, i.e. the number of units used.
7 A new updated master file is created.
8 The control and/or hash totals are automatically verified.
9 Any error report is produced.
10 Customer bills are printed.

Key points

Main characteristics of batch processing:

- used for *large* amounts of *similar* data, e.g. gas, electricity, water, telephone bills, payroll
- not urgent to be up-to-date right *now*
- data which is processed regularly – daily, weekly, monthly or quarterly
- *all* the data is available *before* the batch is processed
- no operator required whilst the program is being run
- file generations are frequently used for added security.

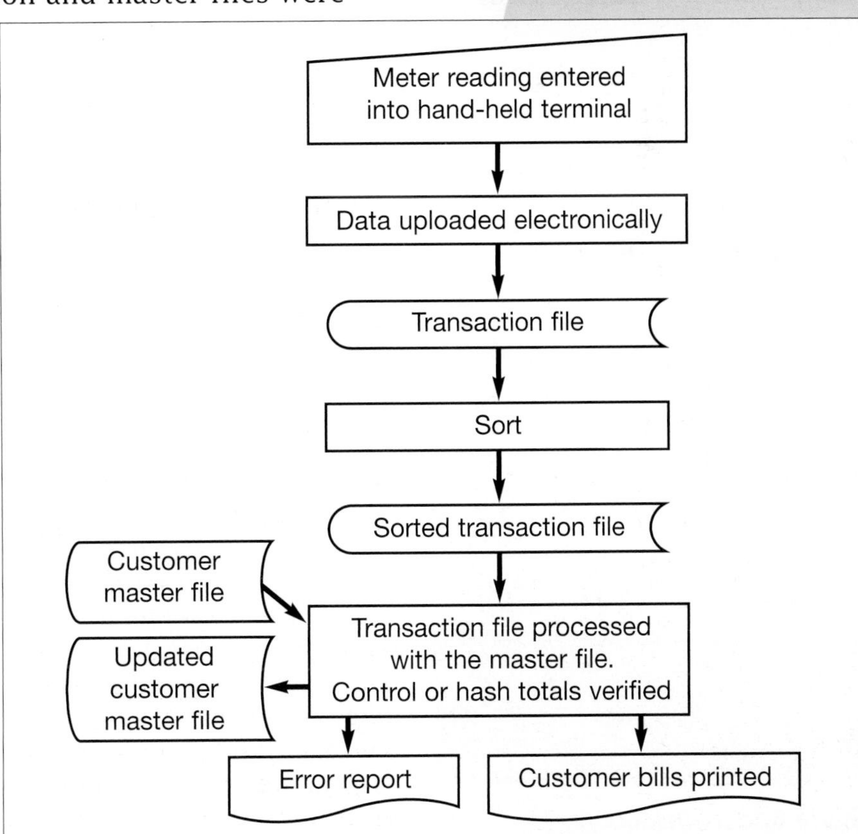

Figure 5.13 *Flow diagram illustrating the process from data collection – meter read at customer's home – to producing gas bills*

Methods of processing 2

File generations

There is always a small risk that data on a master file can be lost or damaged, so three versions, or **generations**, of the master file are retained. The oldest master file is known as the *grandfather* file, which is kept with its transaction file. These two files are used to create a new master file, the *father*. The father file is kept with its transaction file, and they are used to create the most up-to-date master file, the son. When the next batch of data is received, the father file replaces the grandfather, the son replaces the father, and a new son file is created. It is always possible to re-create the master file if any data is lost or corrupted. This system is usually used with tapes but could also be used with disks.

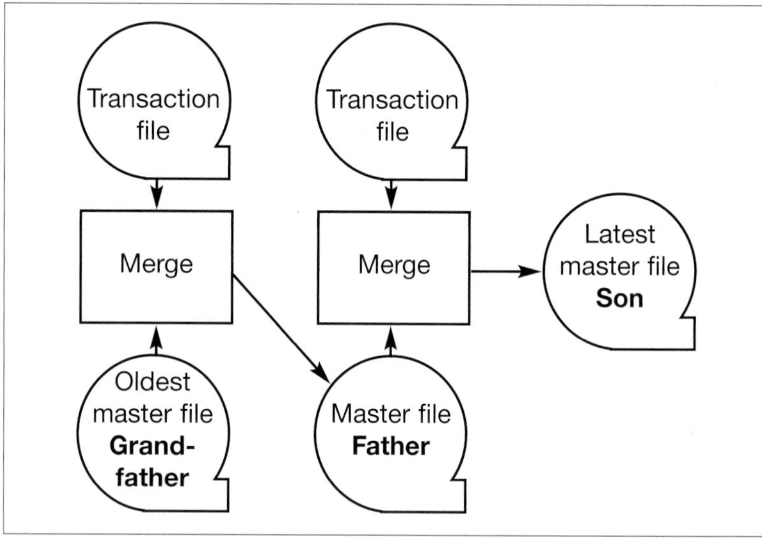

Figure 5.14 *File security using grandfather-father-son file generations*

Transaction processing

Transaction processing is a method of processing where each transaction is carried out as soon as necessary, often *immediately*, and by direct interaction between the operator and the system. It is used when it is important that information held on computer is up-to-date. For example, your family has decided to book a package holiday to Spain, which includes flight and accommodation. You do not want to arrive at the airport to find too many people have been booked and there are not enough seats on the plane, or that two families have been booked into the same rooms at the hotel.

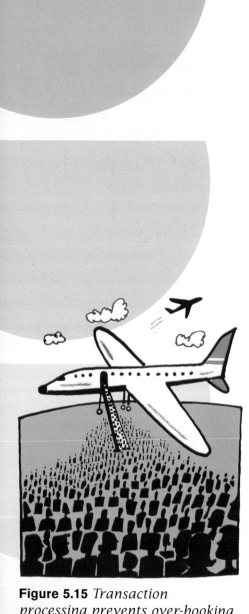

Figure 5.15 *Transaction processing prevents over-booking*

When you go to the travel agent to book a holiday, the clerk searches the Computerised Reservation Service and checks for availability. If you decide to make a reservation, it is recorded *immediately*. Obviously, it would be foolish to wait until the end of the day to enter all the bookings into the computer as a batch, as inevitably there would be frequent instances of double bookings. On arrival at the airport or hotel, customers would become very irate to find other people booked in the same seats or rooms.

This type of interactive processing, where the operator enters all the data for one transaction and the computer is updated immediately, is known as a **pseudo real-time** system because it is updated *continually* and *more or less immediately*. This type of real-time system often involves very large databases held on a mainframe computer, and is used by companies such as Thomas Cook for reservations and Tesco's for updating stock. (An example of an *actual* real-time system would be a computer in an aeroplane, where a delay of even a few seconds is clearly unacceptable.)

Key access methods

There are two main methods of accessing files – **direct access** and **serial access**.

When using direct access the computer can go straight to the record required, which is fast and is therefore suitable when transaction processing is undertaken.

When using serial access the computer has to 'look at' each record in turn from the beginning of the file until the required record is reached. This is clearly slower than direct access and is suitable for batch processing. It is important that the transaction file is sorted in the same order as the master file, so that the computer does not have to keep returning to the beginning of the file to find the next record to be updated.

Key points

Main characteristic of file generations:

- frequently used for added security.

Main characteristics of transaction processing:

- used for small amounts of data
- important to be up-to-date right now
- each item of data is keyed in as it 'arrives'
- operator sits at a terminal and interacts directly with the computer.

Main characteristics of file access:

- **direct access** is suitable for transaction processing
- **serial access** necessitates the file being read from the beginning and is suitable for batch processing.

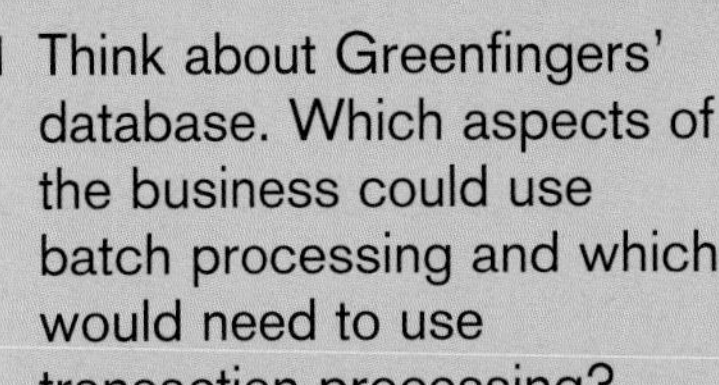

Activity

1 Think about Greenfingers' database. Which aspects of the business could use batch processing and which would need to use transaction processing?

2 Find three examples where batch processing would be suitable for businesses, and three where transaction processing would be required.

Test your understanding

True or False?

1 Numerical data would be a suitable type to enter in a character field.

2 Searching the database is easier if you use all text fields.

3 A range check could be used for the months of the year.

4 The data can be presented in Table View or Form View.

5 A flat file database is more effective than linking tables in a relational database.

6 A field designed in a time format will not allow a number greater than 60 for the seconds and minutes.

Fill in the gaps

7 D__________ is small, individual details such as the cost price and selling price of items sold. I__________ is what can be discovered from the data.

8 A database consists of a f__________, containing many r__________ . Each r__________ will include the f__________, into which will be entered the appropriate d__________.

9 When designing a database it is important to think about the names of the f__________ required, the d__________ t__________ for each f__________ and the length of the f__________ .

10 Examples of accuracy checks are ve__________ and va__________.

11 A t__________ check ensures that the right kind of data is entered in the field.

12 A r__________ check ensures that data is within certain limits.

13 A c__________ digit is added to the end of a number as an accuracy check.

14 A database query can be presented as a table or customised using a r__________.

Multiple choice questions

15 A field for male or female might use:
a) a check box
b) a lookup box
c) a combo box
d) a selection box.

16 A field for yes or no might use:
a) a check box
b) a list box
c) a combo box
d) a selection box.

17 Searching the database is known as:
a) a question
b) a query
c) asking
d) lookup.

18 'and', 'or' , 'not' are examples of:
a) logical operators
b) mathematical signs
c) indexes
d) comparison operators.

19 Wizards:
a) make searching easier
b) are used for accuracy
c) make designing the database easier
d) are used for data capture.

20 Indexes:
a) make searching easier
b) are used for accuracy
c) make designing the database easier
d) are used for data capture.

CHAPTER 6

Communication

Figure 6.1

In this chapter we will be looking at how a computer network will help Pete and Sandra of Greenfingers when they move to their new premises. You will learn how they will be able to link their computers in the main office and communicate between the new garden centres in Dulton and Newford.

At present Pete and Sandra have their own separate computers bought several years ago and which are now outdated. As their computers are not linked together they are known as 'stand-alone systems'. Each computer system has its own operating system and application software. There is an individual set of data on each machine. Data has to be transferred between machines and Pete and Sandra cannot share peripherals such as a printer. Only Sandra's computer is linked to a printer, so when Pete wants to print his work, he has to save his work on disk and use Sandra's machine to print. This can cause Pete problems as Sandra's PC has an earlier version of word-processing software – Word 2.0 – but Pete uses Word 6.0 on his machine. In addition, they both have a copy of the customer database on their individual machines and sometimes there is confusion over who has the latest version of the file.

A **network** is several computer systems linked together so that facilities such as printers, storage, computer programs, etc. can be shared. When computers are linked together like this, it is very easy to exchange information between them, which overcomes the kinds of problems Pete and Sandra are experiencing. When Pete and Sandra move they intend to upgrade their computers and are considering installing a computer network. Your home computer is probably a stand-alone system, whereas your school or college will probably have a network.

Types of network 1

Local area networks (LANs)

A **local area network** (**LAN**) is a group of computers linked together over one small geographical area, usually one building, an office in a building, or across a several buildings on one site. Your school or college will probably have a local area network. The LAN can consist of just two machines connected together (you could do this at home if two members of your family both have home computers: this is not so uncommon as you may think!). Alternatively, it may consist of a large number of computers located in several buildings. Usually if the distances involved are less than two kilometres, the network is a LAN. The system will be connected together using the organisation's own cabling. Most LANs are connected to a powerful machine called a server. There are a number of ways in which the LAN can be linked, but each different network configuration (layout) is known as a *topology*. You will learn more about servers and common network topologies later on in this chapter.

Did you know

Did you know that Microsoft Windows Millennium edition (Me) has a Home Networking Wizard to allow two or more computers to be linked together. (See Figure 6.3.)

Dumb terminals

Sometimes in very large organisations a LAN will consist of a mini or mainframe computer, a very powerful computer, with a number of '**dumb**' **terminals** (a dumb terminal has no processor or hard drive) connected to it. However, as computers have become more and more powerful, most LANs consist of a number of PCs connected to a *server*. The server is not used by any one person, but contains one or more hard drives, which can be accessed very quickly by the other PCs on the network.

Did you know

Not all LANs are server-based networks; there is another type called peer-to-peer networks. These are very simple networks that do not have a machine which is used only as a server, but have several computers linked together to share resources such as files, printers and scanners. This type of network needs to be in one general location, such as a room or several rooms on one floor of a building, and can be difficult to manage. It is not generally recommended to install a peer-to-peer network when there are more than 10 machines.

Servers

The most common servers are **file servers**, but larger networks may have servers that have different uses. A network may have a **print server** (sometimes the file server and print server will be the same), and a **web server**, for example. The file server provides central disk storage for the users of a network. It identifies each user's files separately, and will not allow another user to access them. Files are *downloaded* from the file server to the workstation, and *uploaded* from the workstation to the file server. Users will be able to access their files from any workstation on the network. You have probably experienced this at school or college – although you may like to sit at the same workstation in a classroom, it is not necessary as you can access your files from any machine. A file server may also have a shared drive (sometimes referred to as the pool drive) where all users can access files.

Your school or college may have a shared drive, where teachers can save files that they want all the students to have access to.

A web server is a computer connected to the Internet. Browsers can access the web server to find and display different pages of a web site. You will use a web server to publish a web site in Chapter 7.

The print server is responsible for controlling requests for printing. As each print request is received, it is placed in a print queue and once the previous request has been completed, it commences the next one.

This is quite a difficult and complex topic, so let's look at a simple diagram to represent printing. In Figure 6.2 the arrows represent the flow of information between the network components.

Key points

- LANs consist of a group of PCs connected to a powerful computer, usually a server.
- LANs are connected using an organisation's own media.

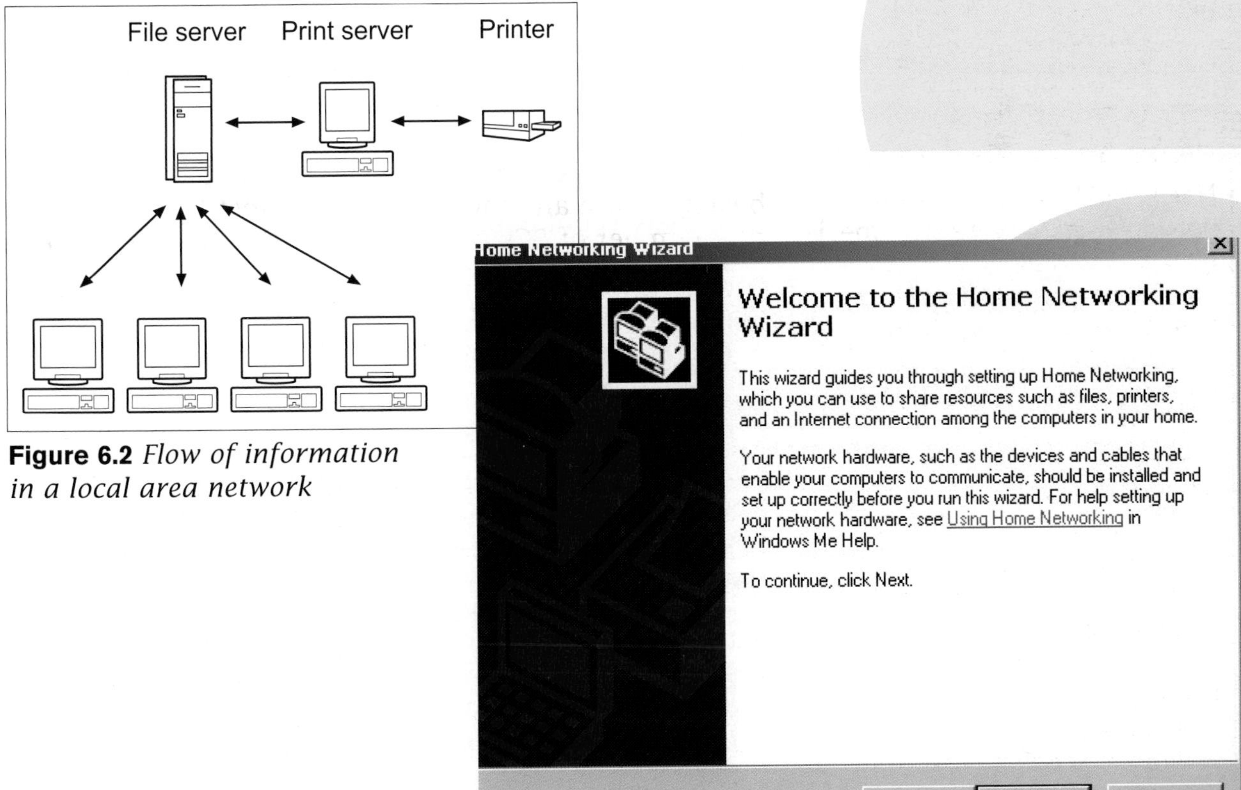

Figure 6.2 *Flow of information in a local area network*

Figure 6.3 *The Windows Me Networking Wizard*

Types of network 2

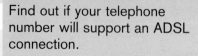

Activity

It is very likely that the computers you use at school or college are linked together in a LAN. Find out:

- Whether the PCs you use are connected in a LAN.
- If so, how many computers are linked.
- How many servers are used in the system.
- If there is more than one server, what types are used.

Do you think Greenfingers needs to install a LAN or a WAN? Perhaps you feel they need both. Remember Pete and Sandra's problem regarding printing. Do you think that a network will help them?

Activity

Find out if your telephone number will support an ADSL connection.

Wide area networks (WANs)

A **wide area network (WAN)** consists of computers connected together over a wide geographical area, usually over two kilometres and even worldwide. Communication over a WAN can be by telephone lines, satellite or microwaves. Many organisations such as banks and companies, such as Virgin Megastore, will have their main computers situated in one place, usually the head office, and will connect with their branches by means of telephone wires. A company will have to use links for a WAN provided by telecommunication companies such as British Telecom or Mercury, and pay charges for these services.

The original telephone link – the **public switched telephone network** (**PSTN**) – operated at low speeds, but more recently high-speed networks have been built. **Public data networks** (**PDNs**) are specifically for data transmission, whereas the **integrated services digital network** (**ISDN**) carries voice, data, images and video through a single *digital* line. With the PDN and ISDN systems it is no longer necessary to convert the signal into *analogue* forms for transmission. We will be looking at the difference between 'digital' and 'analogue' transmission later in this chapter.

Asymmetric digital subscriber line (**ADSL**) is the latest telecommunications technology that allows extremely rapid data transmission along a normal telephone line. ADSL gives a continuously-available, 'always on' connection. This service, which is much faster than an ISDN system, is available to more and more telephone exchanges in the UK.

Types of WANs

There are two types of WANs – **public wide area networks** and **private wide area networks**. Public WANs are available to most of the public, usually through telephone and cable TV networks, whereas private WANs use privately owned or rented lines and may be accessed only if you are a subscriber to the system. The best known examples of public WANs are the Internet and cable television. You will learn more about the Internet later in this chapter.

Many large commercial organisations have their own private WAN which links shops or branches throughout the world or country. An example of an organisation with its own private WAN is Reed Executive plc, a recruitment agency. Reed has 250 branches throughout the UK and Ireland and has a private WAN connecting them via their own leased telephone lines. Their IT department is able to provide support to solve IT problems which their branches may have, without leaving the office. The single network holds details of tens of thousands of employers seeking staff, as well as current job seekers. Their 2,000 or so recruitment consultants have access to the network through the PC on their desks. Branches are able to exchange information regarding vacancies and possible people to fill them. Reed have their own web site which we will look at later in this chapter.

Key points

There are two types of network:

- Local area networks (LANs) – a group of computers linked over one small geographical area, usually one building or one site.
- Wide area networks (WANs) – a group of computers connected over a wide geographical area, even worldwide.
- WANs can be public or private.

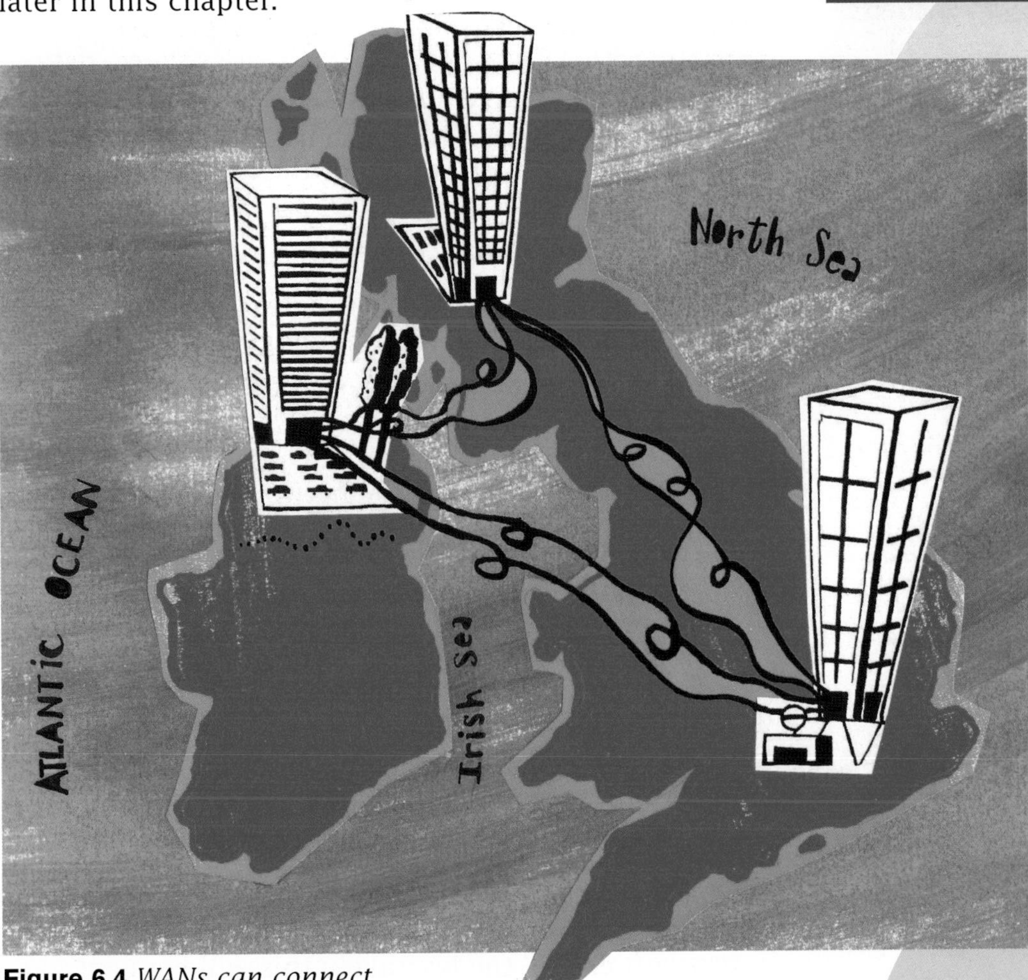

Figure 6.4 *WANs can connect organisations throughout the country*

Advantages and disadvantages of a networked ICT system

Figure 6.5 *Network manager*

Advantages

- Expensive peripherals, such as printers and scanners, can be shared among several users.
- Software can be shared – it is cheaper to purchase a 'network software licence' for the number of machines using the software, than buying individual licences for stand-alone machines.
- It is convenient to store data and software on one machine, the *server*, and for all users to access the data through the server. Files can be accessed from any PC without having to pass disks. This also avoids having to duplicate information. It is very difficult to ensure that each stand-alone PC holds up-to-date, accurate information, and the data is updated once only.

  Pete and Sandra both have a copy of a customer's database file and have to enter or change a record on both machines. They have often made typing errors when inputting the data, which has meant that integrity (correctness of information) of the database has been affected.

- Messages can be sent almost instantly to users on the network, whether the network is a LAN or a WAN, and even if the message is being sent across the world. This facility is referred to as e-mail – we will be looking at *e-mail* later in this chapter.
- It is possible to control users' access rights. Users are issued a login name and a password (usually by the person in charge of the network – the network manager) before they can access the network. This ensures that only people who are allowed to can access data, which helps to ensure that neither the copyright nor data protection laws are infringed. The network manager can limit the data and software which individual users or departments can access by setting read/write privileges on files.
- It is easier to manage backing up of data on a network. The network manager will be responsible for regular backing up of data. Also, all the data is stored in one place – on the file server. Have you ever lost an important file because you forgot to make a backup? The more closely monitored backup procedures are, the less likely this will happen.

- Software is consistent throughout the network and can be loaded centrally on the server. If Pete and Sandra install a LAN and use it to deliver software and data files the difficulties experienced by having two different versions of Word will be resolved. Also, the network manager can make sure that no illegal software is being used if software is installed on the server.
- The network can be maintained and supported centrally. Software is installed once on the server rather than having to be done on each separate stand-alone computer. Also, the network manager can often solve problems centrally, without even leaving his desk to go to the user's machine.

Disadvantages

- The equipment needed to run a network – cables, network cards, servers and the rental of telecommunication links – can be expensive. A stand-alone system may be cheaper.
- Only certain designated people should have access to the nuts and bolts of the system. Therefore, in order for a network to be maintained properly, one or more specialists will probably need to be employed to manage the system. This is usually a network manager and his or her assistant/s, depending on the size of the network. A cheaper alternative for a small business may be to pay for a specialist company to provide network support when it is required.
- A network relies totally on the file server working properly. If there is a problem with the server and data cannot be transmitted, this can have a disastrous impact on an organisation. Important information will not be able to be accessed and tasks may have to be done manually. Have you ever experienced problems because 'the network is down'? This could be because there is a problem with the server.
- Security can be a problem, especially when the network is connected to the Internet. Viruses can be introduced onto the network from a user's floppy disk, by downloading a file from the Internet, or from receiving and opening an infected e-mail. If a virus gets onto a network it can affect all the machines on it. There is also a danger of hacking, a topic which you learnt about in Chapter 1. A security policy needs to be implemented and closely monitored on a network to ensure that everything is done to make the system as secure as possible.

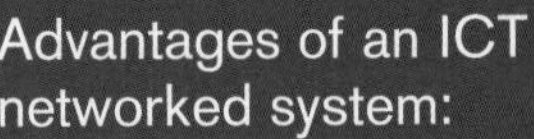

Key points

Advantages of an ICT networked system:

- Access to the system from any workstation.
- Central storage of data and software.
- Sharing of expensive peripherals.
- Control of users' access rights.

Disadvantages of an ICT networked system:

- Cost of installation.
- Reliance on a server.
- Need for security.
- Need to employ a network manager.

Activity

Find out who has responsibility for your school or college network. Is there a public drive where staff can save files, but students can access them as 'read only'? Find out who is responsible for controlling access to the network and issuing passwords. How frequently is the network backed up?

Network components

As you have learnt, a network links together a series of PCs to share facilities such as software and printing. Communication across the network can be achieved by microwave or satellite link, which is necessary to send signals over long distances for a WAN, or by some type of cable, which would be typical in a LAN.

Networking is not just connecting computers together with cables, although cables usually play an important part. A network also requires such components as network connectors, network interface cards (NICs), special software, PCs (known as clients) and of course in a server-based network, at least one server.

Did you know ?

New technologies are being developed all the time. Systems are being developed to use radio signals and infra-red for networking without cables, however cabling will still be around for quite some time!

Cables

The type of cable used to connect a network has a major impact on the speed and accuracy with which it operates, and the ease of installation. Table 6.1 compares popular types of cable:

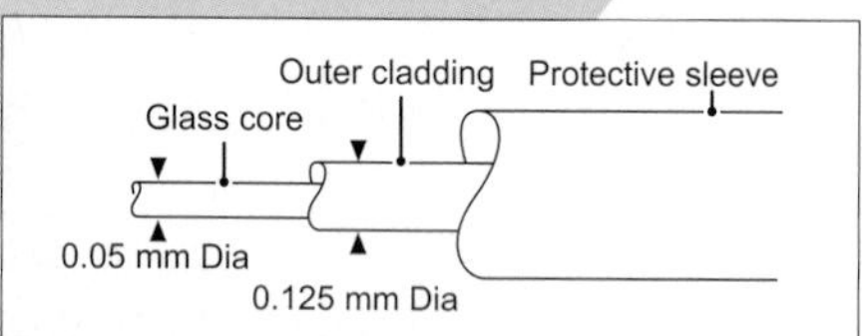

Figure 6.6 *Fibre optic cable*

Fibre optic cable	Unshielded twisted pair	Coaxial cable
• Expensive to install. • Extremely fast achieving data transmission speeds greater than l gigabit per second or 1000 million bits per second over great distances. • Communicates the data with pulses of light instead of electricity and is less susceptible to distortion (see Figure 6.6).	• Very popular, similar to telephone wire. • Cheap and has high transmission rates. • Small in size so cables are easily sunk into cabling ducts. • Comes in different categories with different transmission speeds. The latest has speeds of 1 gigabit per second (very expensive).	• Same type of cable that is used for connecting a television aerial to a television set. • Was the most widely used network cabling as it was inexpensive, light, flexible and easy to work with. • Unshielded twisted pair is now far more popular than coaxial cable due to its considerably faster transmission rates.

Table 6.1 *Types of cable*

Servers

As already explained, most LANs are server-based, the server being a powerful computer used for the storage and distribution of data around the network. Although nowadays many of the PCs are capable of acting as a server, it is better to use one that is designed specifically for the job. A server can have multiple CPUs (central processing units), large banks of hard disks and the capability to cope with hardware failures without the end-user even noticing. For example, some servers are equipped with two power supplies so that if one goes down, the server can switch to the other. Most servers allow an external tape drive or optical disk drive to be connected for backing up the system.

Workstations

A workstation is a single-user PC connected to the network. Workstations are sometimes referred to as a client. A workstation can be an ordinary PC, with a disk drive and a processor connected to the network, or a semi-dumb terminal with a less powerful processor and perhaps no disk drive.

Network interface cards

In order to access the network, each PC, including the server, must be fitted with a **network interface card**. This is a printed circuit board which slots into the motherboard, and contains all the necessary electronics and connections to allow the PC to link into the network.

Connectors

These are used to connect network cables to PCs or other devices. A network card will have connectors on it for network cables.

Operating system

As you learnt in Chapter 2, in addition to application software computers also require an operating system. Many networks in business use Windows NT or the newer Windows 2000 as their operating system. Other examples of network operating systems would be Novell, Unix or Linux.

A network operating system can:

- produce a log of the programs as they are run, recording who has used the computer, for how long and what they did
- charge the appropriate account if the user is paying
- organise the use of hardware and software facilities, ensuring that everyone has a fair share, but giving precedence to those users with a *high* priority over those with *low* priority
- maintain network security.

Did you know

You can buy a server with several hard disks that are known as 'hot pluggable'. This means that the server has a bank of hard disks on the front that can be removed and swapped over without turning the machine off.

Key points

Cabling is an important component of LANs. The type of cable used can vary in terms of performance and cost.

The hardware and software requirements for the formation of a LAN include:

- appropriate cabling
- workstations
- network interface cards
- at least one server
- a network operating system.

Activity

Find out what operating system your school or college has installed on their network.

Network topologies

> **Did you know**
>
> Some networks can be a combination of both the star and bus topologies and are called star bus networks! In a star bus topology several star topology networks are linked together with one main cable.

The **network topology** is the way in which the nodes in a network are arranged – a node may be a computer or another device such as a printer. The way in which the network is arranged affects the way in which it operates. Let's look at two common topologies in use – the bus and star networks.

Bus network

In a **bus network** (see Figure 6.7) all the nodes (devices) share a single cable (see Figure 6.6) with the ends *terminated* using a *terminator*. The messages are transmitted in either direction from one point along a single bus from any PC to any other. Problems arise when more than one user wishes to send a message at the same time. To overcome this, the workstation checks first whether the bus is busy. If it is, then the station has to wait.

A bus network is cheap and easy to install. Extra workstations can be added without disrupting the network, and it is also fairly easy to locate faults in the cable. However, if there is a problem with the cable the whole network fails, and if too many workstations are attached to the network, performance is slow.

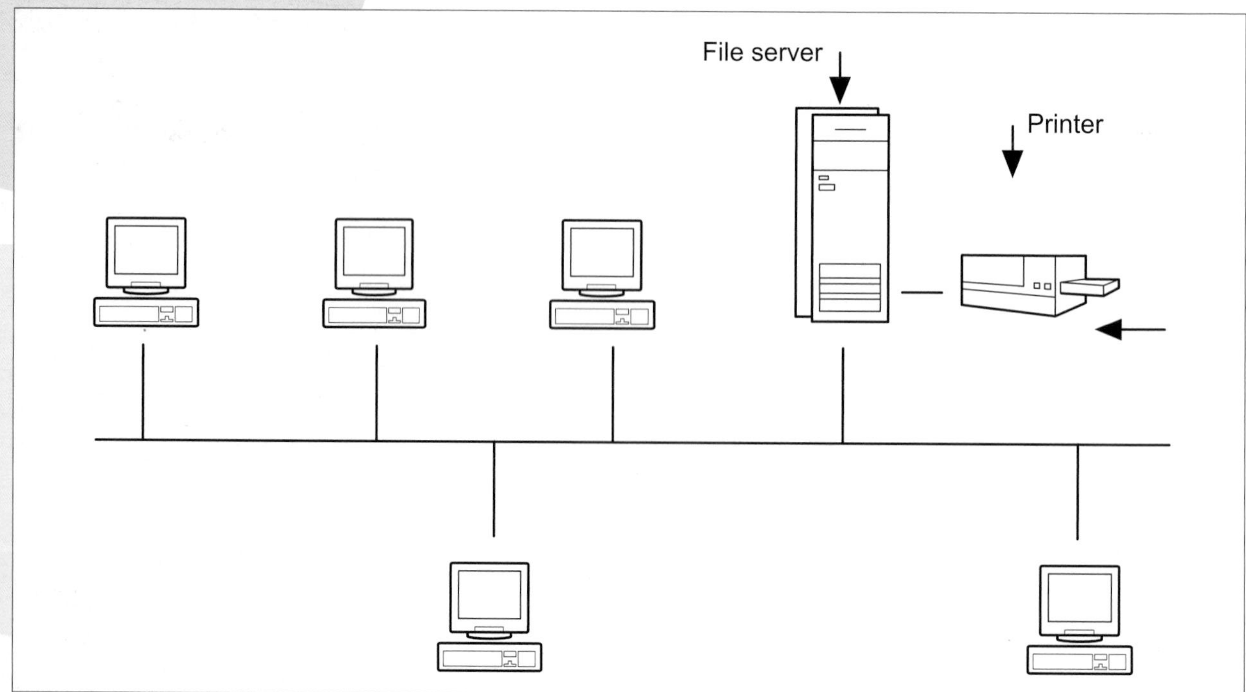

Figure 6.7 *A bus network*

Star network

The main difference in a **star network** compared to a bus network is that each node is connected individually to a central point, usually a hub to which the server would be connected (see Figure 6.8). When this topology was first used, computers were connected to a centralised mainframe computer or file server. Nowadays most star networks are connected to a hub, which is a small device for transmitting signals. Signals received by the hub from a sending computer are transmitted to all computers on the network.

A star topology has a good, reliable performance even when the network is busy and has greater fault tolerance than other topologies. This is because each workstation is served by its own cable. A breakdown in one cable does not affect the other stations, and it is simple to add workstations without interfering with the network.

However, as cable can be a significant cost of a network, a star topology may be expensive to install. Also, if the hub or server breaks down, then the whole network is affected.

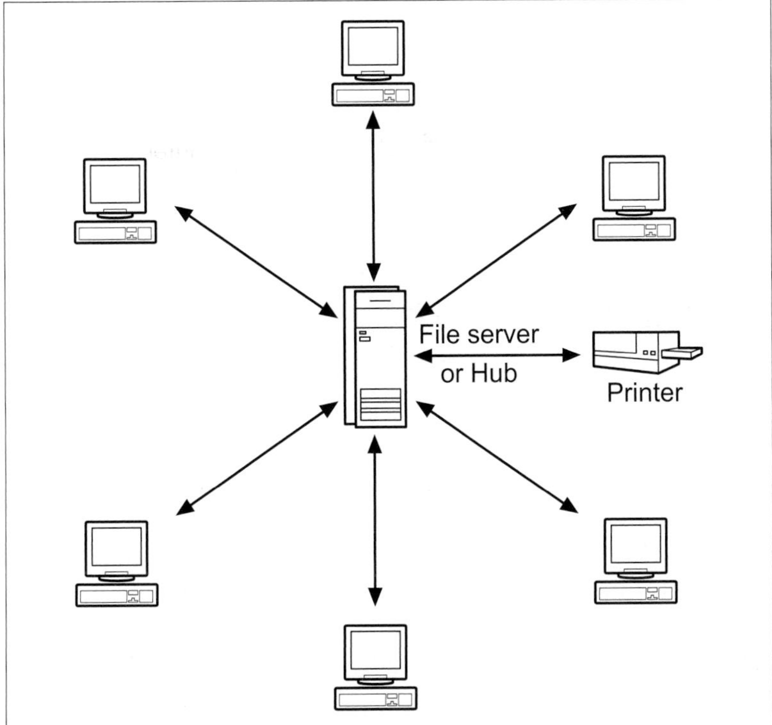

Figure 6.8 *A star network*

Key points

- A bus network is simple to install, easy to extend and is economic in its use of cable. However, it can be slow, and if the cable breaks it can affect many users.
- A star network allows extra computers to be added easily, and the failure of a computer does not affect the rest of the network. However, if the hub or central point fails, the whole network will go down.

Activity

- Find out what network topology is used at your school or college.
- What network topology would you recommend to Pete and Sandra?
- Draw a diagram to show the network you feel Greenfingers needs to install to meet the needs of the expanding business.
- What hardware and software will they need to purchase?
- Are there any other considerations they should take into account, e.g. will they need to employ a network manager?

Methods of communicating information 1

Figure 6.9 *The post is a slower way of communicating than the computer*

Over the last 20 years or so, technology has played an increasingly important part in the way we communicate. Let's look at the advantages and disadvantages of the various methods of communication.

Post

Despite the advent of new technologies we still use the postal service for many purposes. Post will probably still be around even after all homes and businesses have access to e-mail.

Did you know ?

The postal service is sometimes referred to as 'snail mail'.

Telephone

The telephone is still an essential part of business and home life, whether it is a traditional landline or a mobile phone.

Advantages of post	Disadvantages of post
• You are not dependent on technology. • Parcels and bulky items need to be sent by post. An order placed over the phone or through the Internet still has to be sent by post. • Some people consider a hand-written letter to be more *personal* than a fax, or e-mail. • It is still considered more acceptable to send an invitation to an event such as an important business function, e.g. an annual general meeting (AGM), or to a wedding or party, by post.	• It is slow. • Items can be lost in the post. • The recipient can deny receiving an item – it may be necessary to send a letter by *recorded delivery* or *registered post* to ensure that it reaches its destination. • It can be expensive to send a mail shot to a large number of people.

Table 6.2 *Advantages and disadvantages of the post*

Advantages of telephone	Disadvantages of telephone
• It is interactive – you can receive instant feedback. • It is more personal than sending a letter, fax or e-mail.	• Increased telephone costs as people are inclined to chat more. • The phone number being called may be engaged. This is frustrating and timewasting. • Unless the call is recorded, there is no record of any agreement that may have been reached. • Any formal outcomes need to be confirmed in writing, whether by letter, fax or e-mail. • Time differences when phoning abroad.

Table 6.3 *Advantages and disadvantages of the telephone*

 Fax

A facsimile message – known as fax – is used to send the contents of a document, including text and/or pictures, via a telephone line. The image is converted into electronic form so that it can be transmitted via the telephone line, and an exact copy of the document is printed by the receiving fax machine.

If the PC has a fax/modem you do not even need the document to be fed into the machine as hard copy. The fax software creates your header sheet for you and you just type in your message. The computer communicates directly with the receiving fax machine. Similarly, a fax received by a computer will be stored electronically and printed as hard copy as desired.

Advantages of fax	Disadvantages of fax
• Hand-written documents, drawings and documents containing signatures can be faxed. • It is almost instantaneous, and therefore much quicker than using the post. • You can fax a document anywhere in the world, as long as the recipient has a fax machine. • If you are working on the computer with a fax/modem when a fax arrives, you do not have to break off to read it. The fax/modem will automatically answer the telephone (as long as you have remembered to set the software to do this!) and store the fax on the hard drive. Faxes can therefore be stored on your PC rather than filing a paper copy.	• It can be time-consuming to send several pages of fax. Each page has to be scanned and converted into electronic signals one at a time. • The phone line cannot be used whilst you are sending faxes. Many businesses have a separate fax number to prevent this being a problem. • The recipient must have a fax machine, and the machine must be turned on. • Most fax machines will not allow you to fax in colour. Some modern fax machines do allow this, but generally you can only fax in colour between machines of the same model. • If you have a PC with a fax/modem and you wish to fax a document that is not stored on the PC, you have to scan it in first. • You can receive 'junk' faxes, rather like the junk mail most people receive.

Table 6.4 *Advantages and disadvantages of the fax*

Methods of communicating information 2

Did you know ?

An Intranet is the name give to an internal communications system for a particular organisation or company providing similar services to the Internet. An Intranet is only accessed by authorised users and allows secure e-mail communication and distribution of data. Many schools and colleges now have their own Intranet.

Videoconferencing (sometimes referred to as teleconferencing)

Sometimes from time to time Pete and Sandra have to go to meetings with their wholesale customers or suppliers. This is time-consuming, especially when the suppliers are some distance away. Videoconferencing would enable them to have a meeting without leaving the office. It allows them to talk to each other, and see each other as they do so.

You learnt about a piece of hardware called a web cam in Chapter 2. As long as each person has a web cam attached to their computer, and the necessary software, they can hold a meeting without stepping out of the office.

Advantages of videoconferencing	Disadvantages of videoconferencing
• Reduced travel costs. • Meetings can take place without leaving the office. • No time wasted travelling to meetings. • Meetings can be arranged at short notice. • Participants can still attend a meeting even if they are physically unable to, for example due to bad weather preventing them travelling.	• Not all the people with whom you wish to have an electronic meeting may have the necessary equipment. • It may be necessary for confidential documents, for example a contract, to be viewed and signed in person. • It may not be as productive as a face-to-face discussion round a table. • Meetings may be disrupted due to a technical failure.

Table 6.5 *Advantages and disadvantages of videoconferencing*

Figure 6.10 *The Amstrad Em@ailer*

E-mail

At home and in business, e-mail now plays an important role. E-mail is like an electronic letter, sent in most instances via the computer instead of the postal service. It is a very sophisticated method of electronic transfer, where messages and documents can be sent from one computer to another using a communications link such as a modem and a telephone line. You can receive and send the electronic equivalent of letters, pictures and even sound. Documents prepared on a word processor or other software package, or a document scanned into the computer can be transferred either immediately if it is urgent, or can be stored along with the e-mail address of the receiving computer, and can be sent later. If you have a web cam attached to your PC, you can even send a video e-mail. You can now send e-mails, often referred to as text messages, from devices such as mobile phones and Internet TVs.

In order to send an e-mail you have to know the e-mail address of the person you wish to e-mail. This is usually a short code, often made up of the user's name followed by the Internet service provider's code, but this can vary. If Greenfingers' ISP is a fictitious company called 'Userve', their address could be:

greenfingers@userve.co.uk

If you are sending an e-mail via the Internet you have to connect to the Internet service provider's (ISP) server. The e-mail is stored on the server in a mail box until the person you have e-mailed logs on to check if they have received any messages. Many companies have internal e-mail systems via LANs, private WANs or an Intranet so that all their employees can communicate easily with each other.

Did you know

- At the time of writing more than 6 million people in the UK now have digital television set-top boxes which are capable of sending and receiving e-mail.
- There are 37 million mobile phones in circulation, many of them with e-mail capabilities.
- The Amstrad Em@iler (see Figure 6.10) is a small device that plugs into a phone socket. It looks like a telephone with a small LCD on the top from which you can send e-mails, faxes or use as a normal phone. (Source: *PC Active*, 21 February 2001, pages 58–61.)

Advantages of e-mail	Disadvantages of e-mail
• A message can be sent almost instantaneously to someone, and at a time when you choose. • You can send an e-mail to several people at once. • You can forward an e-mail on to someone else. • You will usually be notified if the message fails to reach its destination. • Some e-mail systems will notify you when an e-mail has been read by the recipient. • The cost is much cheaper than using the post – just the cost of a local phone call – irrespective of where in the world you are e-mailing. • You can attach files and graphics saved using other software applications. • E-mail messages, and any attached files, can be saved and edited by the recipient. • You can e-mail or send text messages from a variety of devices, including many mobile phones.	• There are still businesses and homes without the equipment to send e-mails, although the numbers are declining rapidly. • Junk mail is a problem. Pete and Sandra would have to consider buying special software to filter it out. • Viruses can be transmitted via an e-mail. • Unless you have a new e-mail alert, you have to remember to check your mail box. • You can be overloaded with e-mails – all marked urgent.

Table 6.6 *Advantages and disadvantages of e-mail*

The Internet

Figure 6.11 *Information overload*

Did you know

The World Wide Web was developed in 1991 by Tim Berners-Lee at the European Laboratory for Particle Physics, known as CERN. CERN calls itself 'where the web was born'. Try visiting their web site at www.cern.ch/public. In June 1993 there were only 130 web sites, whereas now there are millions!

Did you know

Many organisations check their employees' e-mails to ensure that they are not abusing the system for their own personal use.

Junk e-mail is often referred to as spam, and 'spam control' is the name given to filters used to trap unwanted e-mails.

The **Internet** is the world's largest wide area network and is often referred to as the network of networks. The Internet was created by the US Department of Defence in the late 1960s as a way of enabling government researchers working on military projects to share files. This original Internet was called ARPANET. Even as recently as 1995, many people would not have heard of the Internet, and certainly not have used it. Terms such as the World Wide Web, e-mail, e-commerce, chat rooms, bulletin boards, newsgroups would have drawn blank faces. Information can be passed between different countries across the globe at the press of a key. Via the Internet a company can advertise its services, give customer support, distribute software and participate in e-commerce. E-commerce is the name given to any business activity, such as placing an order, booking a holiday, or even managing a bank account that is undertaken online by electronic means. At the time of writing, the number of adult Internet users is estimated by the research firm Gartner to be 16.4 million and is expected to rise to around 25 million by 2005. (Source: *The Sunday Times*, 11 March 2001.)

World Wide Web

I am sure you are familiar with the term **World Wide Web**, but what is it? The WWW is a part of the Internet where a set of multimedia documents (documents that can consist of words, sound, video, images or animation) are connected by way of **hyperlinks** so you can move from one document to another with a mouse click. Each document is called a web page and a set of web pages make up a web site. The WWW therefore is a huge collection of web pages stored on Internet servers throughout the world.

A web page is written using **HTML** (**hypertext markup language**). Hyperlinks are the connections that let you jump from one web page to another either within a web site or to someone else's web site. A web page will have its own unique identification or address. This is known as a **universal resource locator** (**URL**) and usually starts with http:// or www. The http stands for hypertext transfer protocol. Every address is constructed in the same manner (see Figure 6.12). An example of a well-known web address is http://www.bbc.co.uk, which is the web site of the British Broadcasting Corporation.

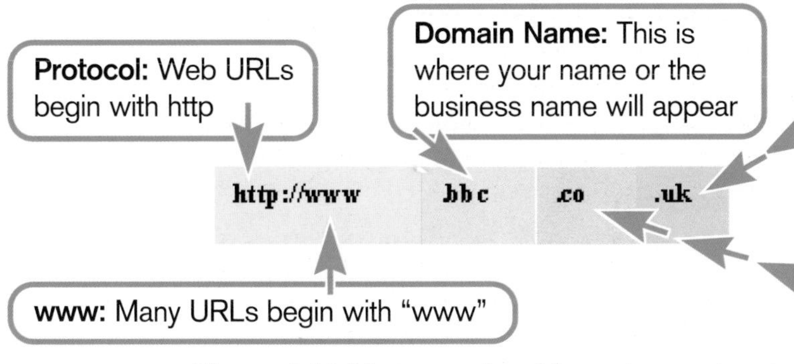

Protocol: Web URLs begin with http
Domain Name: This is where your name or the business name will appear
Country: This national TLD indicates the country, e.g. ".uk" indicates the United Kingdom, "ca" indicates Canada
http://www bbc .co .uk
Top Level Domain (TLD): The combination of letters indicates the type of site, e.g. ".ac" indicates a university, college or academic body, "co" indicates a company
www: Many URLs begin with "www"

Figure 6.12 *How a web address is constructed*

Chat rooms

In a **chat room** you can hold typed conversations with people throughout the world in real time. Unlike e-mail where you have to wait for a person to log on, check their mail box and then send a reply, chat rooms are where several people meet online to discuss a common interest. Web sites will often provide lists of chat rooms available, and also provide the opportunity to create a new chat room and invite other like-minded people to join.

There has been a great deal of controversy about chat rooms. At the time of writing a report from the Internet Crime Forum recommends the creation of a kitemarking program for chat rooms by the end of 2001. It is hoped that this will prevent chat rooms being used by inappropriate people. However, if used sensibly they can provide an ideal way of chatting to people throughout the world. Many businesses with representatives in different locations sometimes use chat rooms to hold meetings. Some universities and colleges put teachers in rooms, where they are available to support students with their studies online.

Newsgroups

These are similar to chat rooms, but whereas chat rooms are 'real time', **newsgroups** are discussion areas on the Internet, where you can post a message and read replies from other people. Some colleges have created newsgroups for students studying on a particular course, where students can post a message and obtain support from other students. Newsgroups are ideal places to share common interests, debate issues, or to help you solve a particular technical problem. Newsgroups are accessed through your ISP.

Did you know ?

Users of chat rooms rarely use their own name, but use a nickname. Remember, it is always important when using a chat room never to disclose your personal details. Observe common sense and take safety and security precautions at all times when using chat rooms.

Activity

Visit the BBC's education pages on their web site at www.bbc.co.uk/education/schools/revision . You will find excellent resources to help with your revision for your GCSE subjects.

Connecting to the Internet 1

To connect to the Internet you will need a computer (in most instances), a telephone line, a modem, an Internet service provider (ISP), a web-browser and e-mail software. Let's look at these individually.

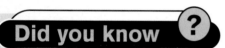

Modem

This is a device that converts the digital signals from a computer into analogue signals that can be sent down a phone line. These analogue signals are then converted back to digital signals by a modem at the receiving end. The name modem is short for **mod**ulator-**dem**odulator. An analogue signal is a continuous signal, representing an output which can travel along a telephone line. For example, speech is a form of analogue transmission; whereas, a digital signal conveys information in the form of digital 'on' and 'off' pulses. The 'on' and 'off' pulses of digital transmission represents the binary digits (0s and 1s) that a computer can process. Modems can be internal or external. Your home computer probably has an internal modem that slots into the motherboard.

The most important aspect of a modem is the speed. The faster the modem, the quicker you will receive information. The speed with which the modem transfers data is measured in bits per second (bps). Currently, the fastest modems transfer data at a maximum speed of 56 kbps (56 kilobits per second). This is an important consideration if you are paying for the telephone call whilst you are online. Some modems can reduce the cost of transmission by compressing the data before it is sent.

If you can receive cable TV you may be able to connect to the Internet using a cable modem at far greater speeds than using a traditional modem.

If your computer or LAN is using an ISDN line, a traditional modem is not required. However you will need a special device called an ISDN terminal adaptor. An ADSL connection will need a special modem with a splitter. The splitter will not be used if you are not using the Internet. Its purpose is to just sit there looking for the high-frequency messages that tell it that you are using the Internet.

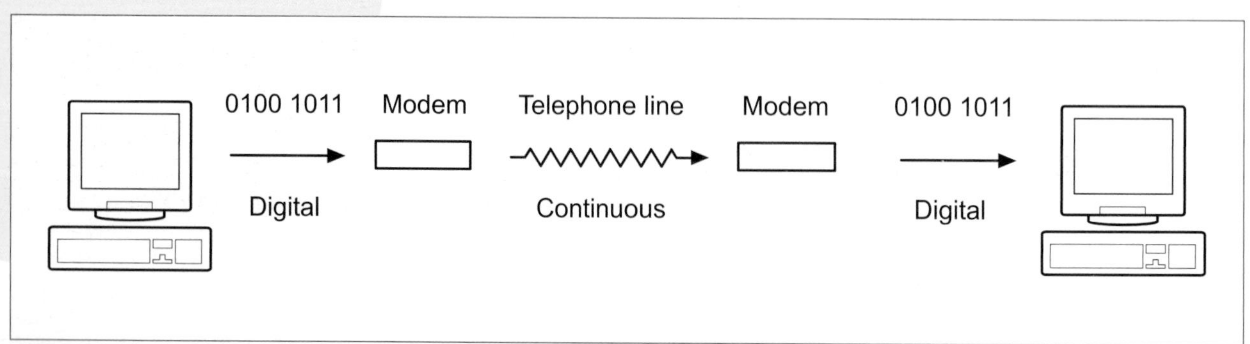

Figure 6.13 *An analogue signal*

Internet service provider

All homes and business users will need an **Internet service provider**. Examples of ISPs are, Demon, Freeserve and BT Internet. Large organisations will probably have a communications server permanently connected to the Internet and will rent a high-speed connection (e.g. digital leased line) direct to their ISP.

Originally, all subscribers had to pay to be connected to an ISP, now many ISPs do not charge for this facility although you will often be charged for the time spent on the Internet. This is the cost of a local telephone call. Increasingly, more ISPs are offering unlimited access online for a standard monthly charge. Examples of these are BT Internet or AOL. Most of the ISPs offering this service penalise heavy users by cutting them off if they have been on line for more than two hours. Users who reconnect repeatedly may be deemed to be abusing the system and barred from the service. (Source: *The Sunday Times*, 4 February 2001, Money section, page 5.)

If you are lucky enough to have an ADSL connection at home, for a monthly fee you have very fast continuous access, day or night, without the worry of being cut off!

Web browser

I am sure you have used the term 'surf the net'. Well, a **web browser** is the special software which lets you do this as it enables you to view web pages and to click on the hyperlinks. The most common web browsers are Microsoft Internet Explorer and Netscape Navigator.

When you double click on your browser to start it up, you can access web pages only if you are connected, via your ISP, to the Internet. However, some computers are configured so that launching the browser will cause the modem to dial up and connect to the Internet. When you connect to a web browser, the default web page, called the home page, will be loaded. This is often the web site of the company whose computer you are using, the web site of your ISP, or it can be any web site you have chosen.

Did you know?

Demon Internet was the first ISP and was developed by Cliff Stanford. The date the first user logged on was l June 1992. (Source: *Internet Active*, October 2000, page 46.)

Key points

To connect to the Internet you need:

- a modem
- a web browser such as Microsoft Internet Explorer
- an e-mail communications package
- an Internet service provider
- a computer or other device such as an Internet PC.

Connecting to the Internet 2

Activity

- Investigate which web browsers are available at your school or college? If there is more than one, try them and note the differences between them.
- Which e-mail software package does your school or college use? If you have a home computer, do you use the same e-mail package?

E-mail

We have discussed the advantages and disadvantages of e-mail earlier in this chapter. In order to send e-mail you need special e-mail communications software. Examples of popular e-mail software are Microsoft Outlook, or Microsoft Outlook Express, and Netscape Messenger. Many businesses also use business-orientated e-mail programs such as Lotus Notes. Some ISPs, such as AOL (America on Line), provide their own e-mail programs, which you must use if you have subscribed to that service.

Sending an e-mail

In order to send an e-mail using software such as Outlook Express, you would:

1 Prepare your message offline to save telephone charges and click the **Send** button to store it in the **Outbox**.
2 Connect to the Internet via your ISP.
3 Click on the **Send and Receive** option.
4 You may have to enter a password to access your mailbox at your ISP. In Outlook Express and most other programs you can configure it to automatically enter the password.
5 Your e-mail will be sent, and your mailbox at your ISP will be checked for incoming mail.

Click on the Send button to store the e-mail in the Outbox

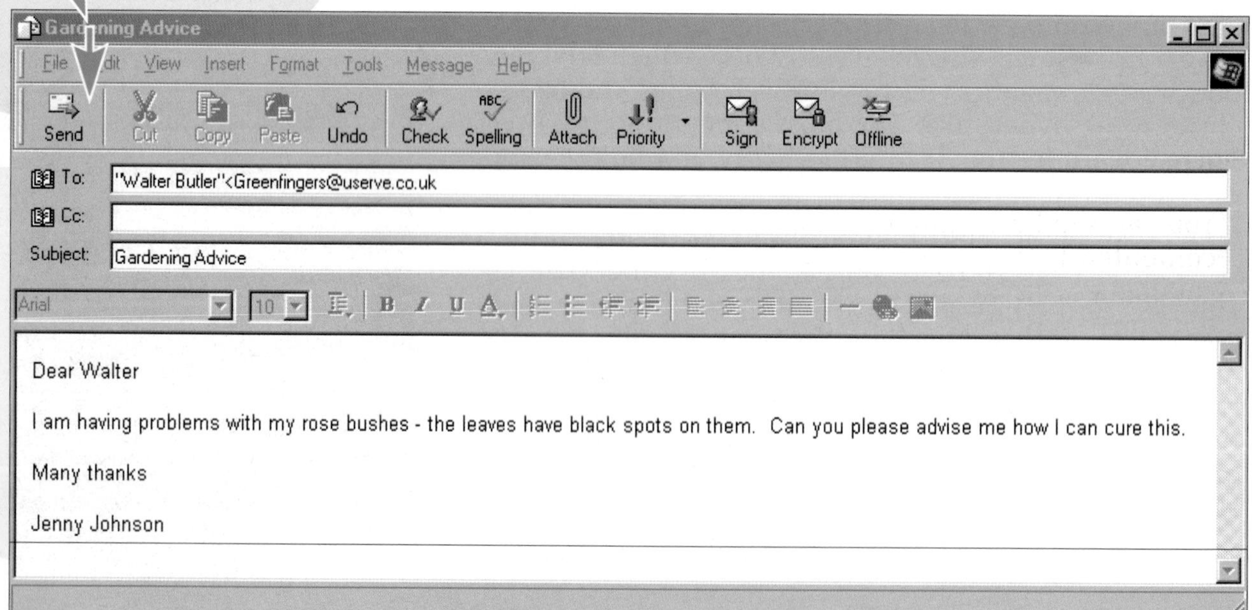

Figure 6.14 *An example e-mail prepared in Outlook Express*

Common features of e-mail communications software

- You can work offline, save a message and send it whenever you wish.
- You can create an address book of the e-mail addresses of all your friends. Pete and Sandra will be able to create an address book of all their customers.
- You can create a distribution list. Pete and Sandra can divide their address book into different categories, e.g. business customers and domestic customers, in the same way you would organise your files on your hard disk (see Figure 6.15).

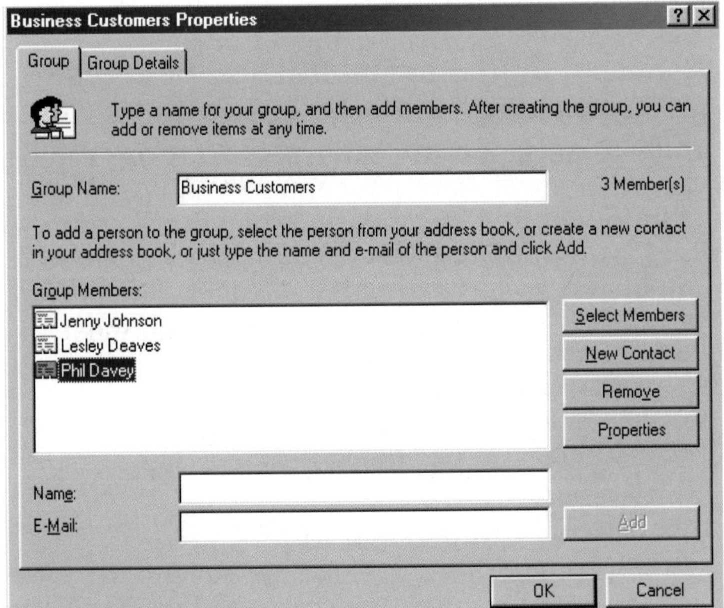

Figure 6.15 *Example of setting up a Group using Outlook Express*

- You can send attachments of any file on your computer. Pete and Sandra will be able to attach catalogues, price lists, graphics and other documents to their customers.
- If you want to attach a confidential file, you can add a password to the file for security.
- You can send copies of a message to many people.
- You can forward e-mails you have received to other users.
- Messages are automatically date and time stamped.
- You can add a different *signature* to an e-mail, depending on the recipient. For example, Greenfingers' garden advisor, Walter Butler, uses his official signature when sending e-mails to customers or suppliers.

Did you know?

If you have been receiving unwanted e-mail (spam) from one particular e-mail address it is possible using Outlook Express to divert any messages straight into the Deleted folder. The e-mail will still be downloaded but will not be put in your Inbox as it will be deleted automatically.

Did you know?

Many people now have their own web-based e-mail address through companies such as Hotmail. By logging on to the Hotmail web site and entering a user name and password, you can access your e-mail wherever you are in the world.

Key points

Features of e-mail:

- the user can work online or offline
- the user can reply to e-mails or forward them on to another person
- it allows the user to create an address book and mailing lists
- it allows the user to add attachments.

Alternative ways of accessing the Internet

There are ways of accessing the Internet other than with a PC. The following are examples.

Mobile phones

Some newer mobile phones can be used as a modem, which can be connected to a notebook computer, personal digital assistant or handheld device in order to access the net. Wireless application protocol (WAP) mobile phones can be used to access a stripped down, text only, version of web sites. However, access speeds are slower than traditional modems and actually typing in the web site addresses (URL) is far slower than with a keyboard.

Personal digital assistants (sometimes referred to as a palmtop computer)

A traditional **personal digital assistant** (**PDA**) can be used as a diary, will store phone numbers, postal and e-mail addresses and include other functions, including games, to-do lists and calculators. Some are very sophisticated, are rather like a pocket PC, and can include such things as mini-versions of Word, Excel and Internet Explorer. They can be used to send e-mails or search the WWW using a suitable mobile phone. Most have an infra-red light facility to connect them to a PC and transfer data.

Internet TVs or set top boxes

You can buy an Internet TV. These are easy-to-use TVs, which also have the ability to access the WWW and send e-mails – all while you are watching your favourite television programme! From this a new term has evolved –'t-commerce' – i.e. e-commerce on television. Also, special boxes can be purchased which sit on top of a normal television and will adapt the television into an Internet TV. Users can navigate round the Internet using either an infra-red remote control or a keyboard. Keyboards are usually optional, but are useful for composing e-mails.

Internet TVs and set-top boxes do not contain the large amount of memory found in a PC, therefore access to complex web sites, with sound and moving picture files, can be restricted. On page 164 you will learn about how a PC can store recently used web pages. As Internet TVs generally do not have hard disks or any form of backing store, this may not be possible.

Activity

Do a survey amongst your classmates to find out how many people have used an alternative way to the PC of accessing the Internet.

Did you know ?

In December 1997, 5% of UK individuals were using the Internet at home. By April 2001 the figure had risen to 26%. (Source: Continentalresearch.com.)

Did you know ?

It is possible to connect to the Internet via satellite – this may bring about a merging of the TV and PC.

Multimedia kiosks

BT have installed new pay phones in shopping centres, rail and Tube stations, airports and motorway services areas throughout the UK. These phones not only allow you to make a standard telephone call, they also allow users to access the Internet. BT have included 'hot buttons' on the touch screen to take users directly to entertainment, travel, recruitment, shopping and sports information sites. Alternatively, users can go straight to their required web site by typing the web site address using a special keyboard (see Figure 6.16).

Figure 6.16 *BT's new Internet-ready pay phones*

Data transfer speeds

Have you ever sat by the computer for what seems forever, waiting for a file to be downloaded from the Internet or for a web site to open? There are several factors that can affect the speed at which data is transferred.

- The speed of your modem, or the modem at the other end of the communications line. The faster the modem, the quicker data will be accessed.
- Your phone line – an ISDN line, or ADSL – will offer far quicker access times.
- The size of the file being transferred – graphics, for example, take far longer than plain text.
- The amount of memory on your PC – browsers use up a great deal of memory storing details of the sites you visit.
- The numbers of users online at the same time as yourself. If you are surfing during the evening and at the weekend you will often suffer slower download and response times. Also, the time of day will affect download time – America goes online at approximately 3 pm UK time.
- The site you are visiting may be very busy.
- The amount of bandwidth available – bandwidth is the term used to describe the amount of data that can be transferred at one time via a communications line. The more bandwidth available, the faster the data will be transferred. Fibre optic cables will have a higher bandwidth than traditional telephone lines.

Key points

Data transfer speeds are apparent to the user by:

- the time it takes the web server to respond to a request to view a web page (response time), and
- the time it takes for a PC to load a web page (download time) once the request to view a web page has been responded to.

Did you know?

If you are sending an e-mail with an attachment which is a large file, it is sensible to compress the file using file compression software such as WinZip. This will save data transfer time.

Finding a web site 1

Activity

Try going to the following companies' web sites by guessing their address:

- Tesco
- Topshop
- Virgin Radio.

Activity

New top level domains are being introduced all the time. See how many different ones you can find in addition to those listed opposite.

Did you know

Many search engines or subject directories have pages specifically for the UK. Try looking at uk.altavista.com or uk.yahoo.com. Use sites such as these when you want to search for topics in the UK only.

If you know the address of the web site, you can go directly to it by typing the address in the address box and clicking 'Go'. If you are uncertain of the address of a company or organisation, try guessing. As organisations will try to incorporate their name in the address, it is often very easy to correctly guess their address. It is not necessary to type 'http'. You will recall that the web address is constructed in a uniform way, so if you want to find the web site of ITV, you can try enter www.itv.co.uk. You have probably guessed that their domain name will be ITV, and that they would use 'co.' as their top level domain and that as they are in the UK, their national TLD will be '.uk'.

Useful top level domains to know are:

.co indicates a company

.com a commercial organisation

.org generally refers to a charity or non-profit-making organisation

.ac indicates a university, college or academic department

.sch indicates a school

.gov indicates a government department

.net refers to a network-related site

.mil indicates a military site

.tv refers to the latest domain for television web sites.

Searching the web

As you have probably already discovered, there are millions of web sites, and it is sometimes quite hard to find the information you want. If you want to find a particular company, or piece of information, you will need to use a search tool, known as a **search engine** or **subject directory**. Using a search engine you can type in a few key words and you will be presented with a page of links to sites matching your criteria. Search engines are indexes which work by key words and context and I am sure you are familiar with popular search engines such as AltaVista (www.altavista.com), Ask Jeeves (www.askjeeves.co.uk) and UKplus (www.ukplus.co.uk).

Subject directories are similar to search engines, but are smaller collections of Internet files grouped by subject headings. These files are not rated for relevancy by software, but by humans. These are ideal if you wish to research a general topic and you want to avoid all the irrelevant files that search engines can find. An example of a search directory is Yahoo.com (see Figure 6.17).

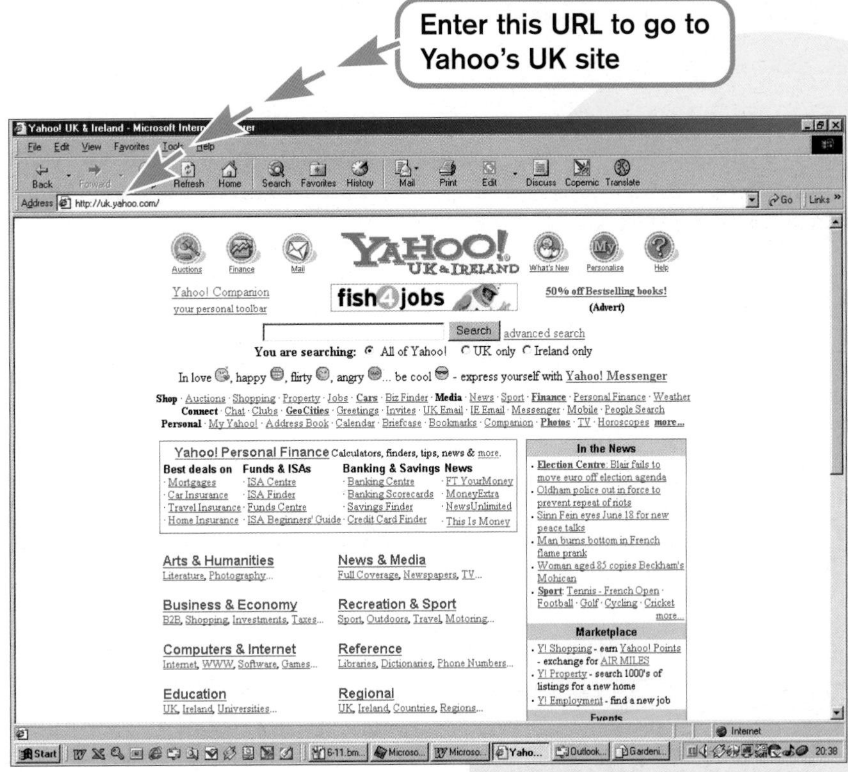

Figure 6.17 *Yahoo subject directory*

Tips for successful searching

As mentioned earlier, sometimes searching can be difficult because if you do not narrow your search in some way, you can be presented with a large amount of irrelevant information. There are ways to overcome this. Each search engine or search directory may differ slightly in techniques you can use, so do look at their help pages for tips.

- Use lower case instead of capital letters (upper case). Searches in all capital letters will produce results that are in capitals only, whereas lower case will produce results in both upper and lower case.
- Put a phrase in quotation marks. Pete and Sandra wish to find out if their range of teak garden furniture is priced competitively. If they enter the phrase 'teak garden furniture', it will extract information on web pages containing that specific phrase, rather than a web page containing any of these individual words.
- Some search engines, like Ask Jeeves, will allow you to type in direct questions. For example, Pete and Sandra could type in 'Where can I buy teak garden furniture?'
- Pete and Sandra can limit their search further by the use of operators (*and*, *or*, *not*, +, –). They could type *teak +garden +furniture –sheds*, or alternatively they could type *teak and garden and furniture not sheds.* They must type in the words using the correct spacing. This search will produce all sites listing teak garden furniture but exclude any with a reference to sheds.

Did you know ?

You can also use a 'meta-search' engine to search the WWW. These do not own a database of web pages themselves, but send your search simultaneously to several individual search engines and their databases of web pages. An example of a meta-search engine is Copernic, which you can download for free from their site at www.copernic.com.

Finding a web site 2

Cache

All the time you are online your browser is storing copies of the pages you have recently used in an area called '**cache**'. If you wish to return to a page you visited before, click on 'Back' until you reach the page you require. Because the computer does not have to go back to the web, but simply has to look into its internal cache, the page will appear quickly. You can click on the Forward button to return to the previous web page you were on.

Caching pages will save a lot of time and money if you are paying for online time.

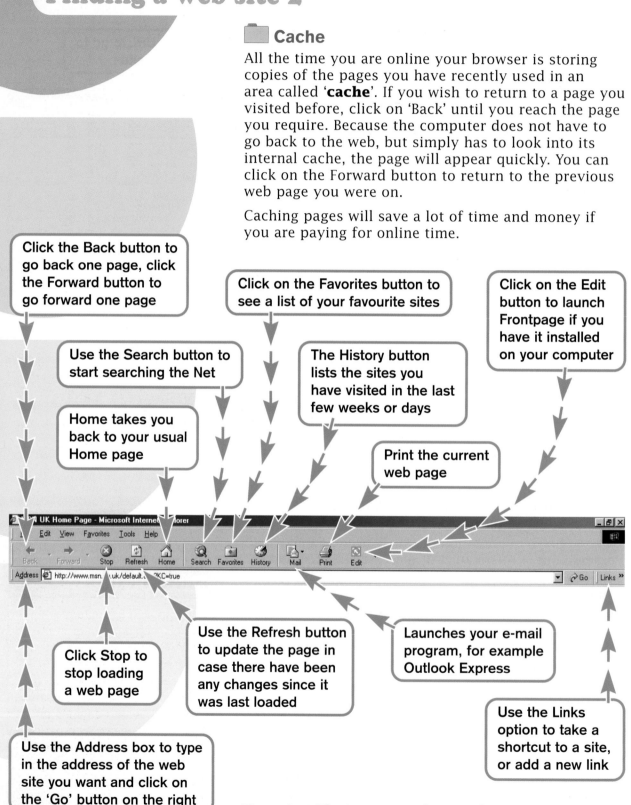

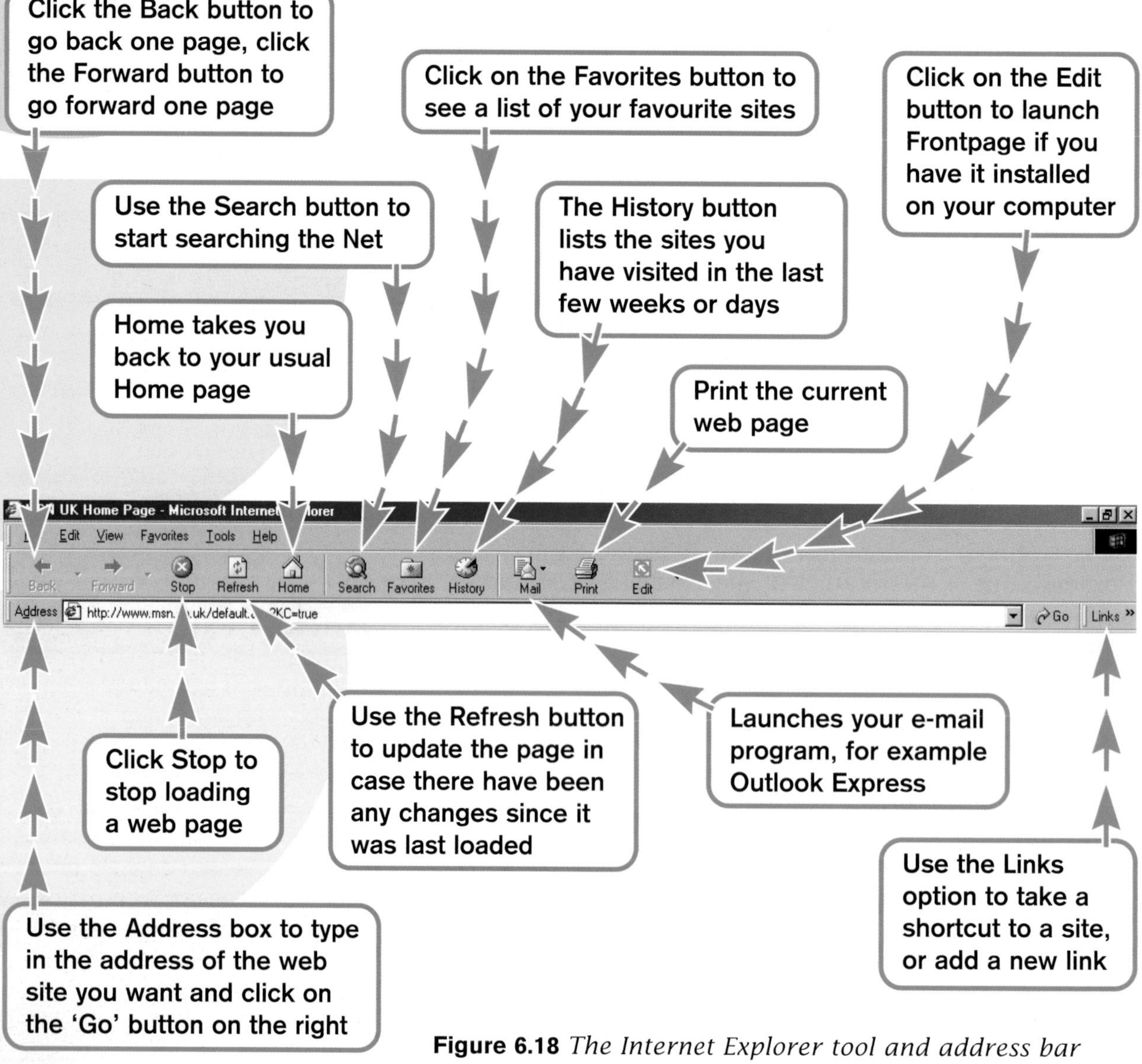

Click the Back button to go back one page, click the Forward button to go forward one page
Click on the Favorites button to see a list of your favourite sites
Click on the Edit button to launch Frontpage if you have it installed on your computer
Use the Search button to start searching the Net
The History button lists the sites you have visited in the last few weeks or days
Home takes you back to your usual Home page
Print the current web page
Edit View Favorites Tools Help
Back Forward Stop Refresh Home Search Favorites History Mail Print Edit
Address
Go
Links
Click Stop to stop loading a web page
Use the Refresh button to update the page in case there have been any changes since it was last loaded
Launches your e-mail program, for example Outlook Express
Use the Links option to take a shortcut to a site, or add a new link
Use the Address box to type in the address of the web site you want and click on the 'Go' button on the right

Figure 6.18 *The Internet Explorer tool and address bar*

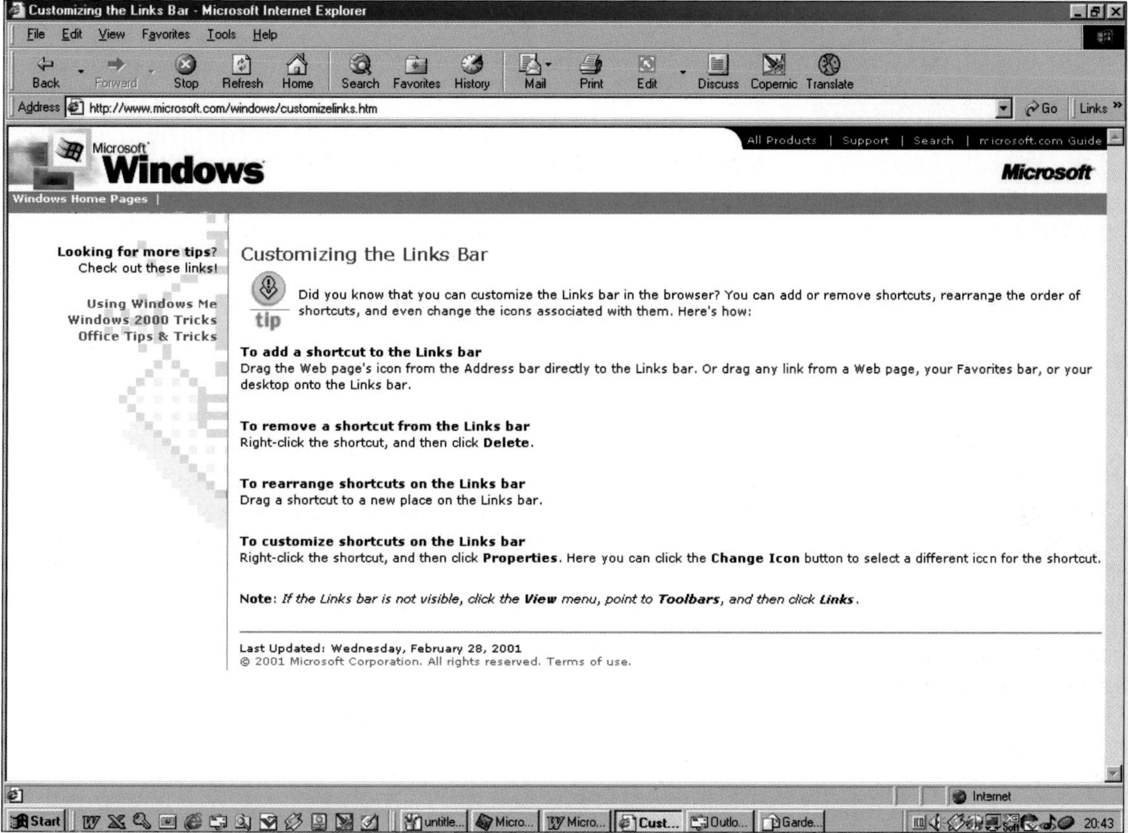

Figure 6.19 *Creating a link*

Favourites

You can bookmark your **favourite** sites. You can create folders and file these bookmarks, in the same way as you organise and save your files on your hard drive.

Links

You can create shortcuts called **links** to go to your favourites sites (see Figure 6.19). This works in a similar way to bookmarking a site and adding it to your favourites, but accesses the site in a slightly different way. It can be a marginally faster way of going to a frequently used site.

History

The browser will store a history of all the web sites you have visited over the last few days or weeks. This can be helpful if you have forgotten to bookmark a particularly useful site.

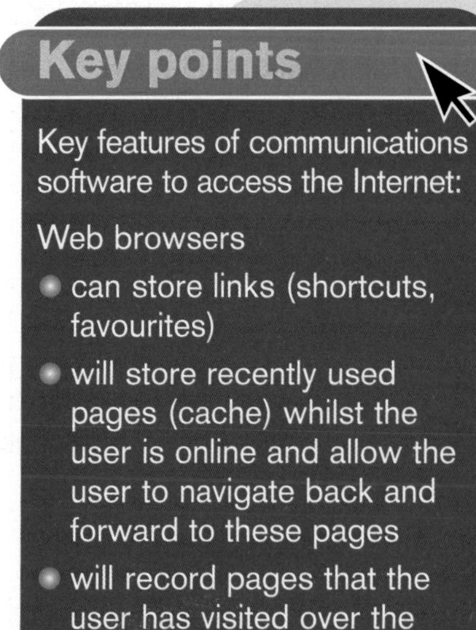

Key points
Key features of communications software to access the Internet:
Web browsers
can store links (shortcuts, favourites)
will store recently used pages (cache) whilst the user is online and allow the user to navigate back and forward to these pages
will record pages that the user has visited over the last few days or weeks.

Other services available on the Internet 1

Activity

Make a shopping list of six different items, such as books or CDs, that you or your family would like to buy for a special occasion such as Christmas. Investigate how much they cost in the local high street shops – make a note of how much time you spent doing this. Now research how you would buy these items on the Internet and compare how long it took you surfing the Internet to do this and how much the items cost. Which method was the most time-consuming? Which method did you prefer?

Did you know

The Hamamatsu 3-D body scanner has been developed by Japanese scientists to scan your body and store your measurements. The scan can be stored on a personal smart card which you will be able to use in high street stores adopting the new technology, and means that you will not have to waste time trying on clothes. It also can be stored on the Internet and will allow you to try on clothes in a virtual changing room before you decide to but it!

Let's look at other services available on the Internet.

ICQ (I Seek You)

With ICQ software you can engage in instant messaging without going to a chat room. The software will let you know if any of your friends are online and you can have a real-time chat.

Advertising on the Internet

Most businesses and organisations acknowledge that the future of their organisations will become increasingly dependent on the Internet. They can use the Internet to advertise their services for a relatively small investment by ensuring that their web site is included on a search engine. We will be looking at designing a web site for Greenfingers in the next chapter. When Pete and Sandra publish their site, they will need to ensure that when people are surfing the net for garden centres, their site will be included in the search results. This is done by submitting their web site address (URL) to a particular search engine's database.

Many companies put on advertisements known as 'banner advertisements' which appear when you are uploading information from the Internet. There are even sites which use a type of free advertising called a 'banner exchange'. These sites let different web sites trade advertisement banners.

Advertising on the Internet, therefore, is an excellent way of reaching an extremely wide, worldwide, audience.

Shopping

When you shop on the Internet, the location of the shop does not matter. Amazon Books is an example of a huge success story for online shopping. Amazon originated in the USA with only a web site and a warehouse. It now has a web site here – www.Amazon.co.uk – where you will find just about every book you can think of. Because Amazon has fewer running costs, such as premises, heating, sales staff, they are able to offer books at a lower price. However, at the time of writing, many e-commerce sites are currently not making as much they expected, and some are even closing down. In 2000 online purchases accounted for only 0.66% of retail sales and are estimated to increase to 5% by 2005. (Source: *The Sunday Times*, 11 March 2001.)

Supermarkets, such as Tesco and J Sainsbury, allow customers to order their groceries online and have them delivered to their homes. Although the number of people buying online is still not large, Sainsburys' average online transaction is about £100, which is four times the average in-store transaction. (Source: *The Sunday Times*, 11 March 2001.) Pete and Sandra could set up a shopping facility on their web site for their wholesale and retail business. They will need to ensure that customers are confident about the security of the site when customers pass details of their credit or debit cards to pay for purchases. Security on the Internet is discussed later on in this section.

Key points

Common Internet services include:

- World Wide Web – the WWW itself offers such services as advertising, customer support, distribution of software, e-commerce, online storage.
- E-mail.
- Newsgroups.
- Chat rooms.

Online auctions

You can also buy and sell goods through online auctions. A well-known auction site is www.ebay.com. Read the description carefully to ensure that what you are bidding for is actually what you want when making a bid.

Finding a job

When Greenfingers need to recruit staff, they often use a recruitment agency. Some agencies now use the Internet to advertise their current selection of jobs. As you can see from Figure 6.20, if you are looking for a new job, visiting an agency's web site is an ideal place to start. Reed's web site attracts over half a million visitors each month and Reed will even keep potential applicants updated with the latest job vacancies by sending them an e-mail or text message. In 2000, Reed sent 700,000 text messages and two million e-mail alerts to job seekers.

Financial services

Many banks and building societies now offer their services online. They usually offer better rates than traditional banks and building societies. Examples include Egg (a Prudential company) and Smile (part of the Co-operative Bank).

Figure 6.20 *Reed Recruitment Agency's web site*

Other services available on the Internet 2

Activity

List the reasons why you think Pete and Sandra should consider connecting to the Internet. What will be the benefits for their business? Do you feel there are any disadvantages?

Did you know ?

For personal and non-profit use, home users can download a firewall called Zone Alarm from Zonelabs.com in order to protect their machines.

Mailing lists

Sometimes when you are looking at a web page, you will see a invitation to join a mailing list. By joining a mailing list, you can have information on a topic of interest to you, sent by e-mail. Alternatively, there is a web site called www.liszt.com which is a directory of mailing lists, where you can search for a mailing list on a particular subject in which you are interested.

Distribution of software

You can download software from the Internet. Sometimes this is free, or it can be software that you are purchasing from a company such as Microsoft. The Internet is a great source for free software that you can download to your own computer. If you have a problem with a virus, you can use the Internet to search for a solution. Remember that the Internet is the easiest way for viruses to be spread, so always download files with caution and use a virus checker.

Customer support

Many companies offer a service to give support to their customers online. This can be by way of a 'Help' option, and usually the site will give the facility for users to e-mail their questions.

Security on the Internet

The user has to correctly identify themself by correctly answering all the questions

Closed lock to show a secure site

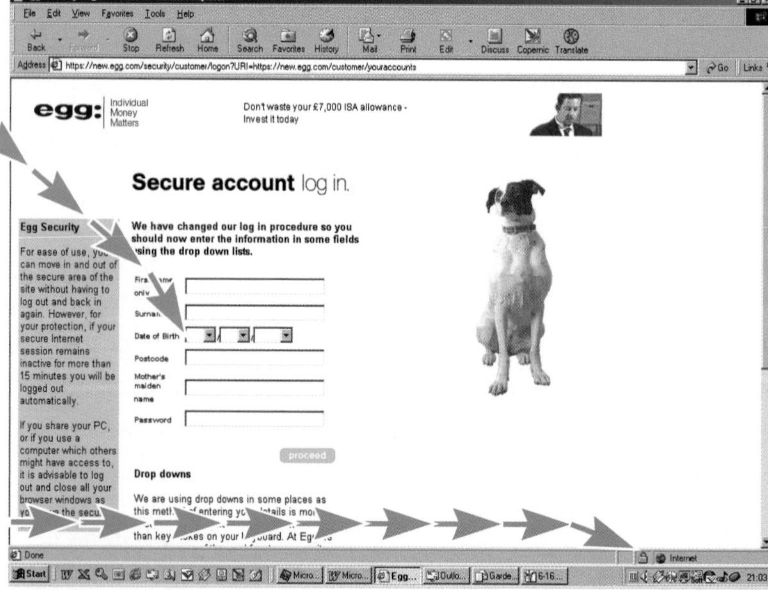

Figure 6.21 *The Egg login screen*

Many people are concerned about security aspects when conducting business on the Internet. A web site that is secure will show a closed lock at the foot of the screen.

A technique called **data encryption** is used by secure web sites. Encryption is used to encode the data before it is sent across the Internet. Each secure web site will have its own unique way of unscrambling the data; this is known as the *decryption key*. Keys of this type have been mathematically proven to be safe and secure.

A secure web site will also require the user to prove that they are who they say they are.

Both business and home users who use the Internet to transfer or receive personal details, such as credit card numbers, also need to protect themselves against hackers. You have learnt about hackers in Chapter 1. A piece of software called a **firewall** is used to prevent unauthorised people gaining access to data.

Online storage

You can save your files to an online storage company's computers (known as a virtual hard disk) just as you would to your own computer's hard disk. Whilst you are online, you can access these files as if they are saved on your own computer. It is an ideal way of backing up important files and also of sharing files with people throughout the world. Files are *uploaded* to the virtual hard disk and *downloaded* far more quickly than it would take by attaching them to an e-mail. They are even scanned for viruses free of charge by the online storage provider. Files can be accessed wherever you are in the world without the need of having your own computer, in a similar way to accessing e-mail from a Hotmail account.

Online learning

The Internet is increasingly being used in education. Earlier in this chapter you looked at the BBC's web site which provides extremely useful materials to help you with your studies – this is an example of online learning. Another example of online learning is the government's new initiative called 'Learn Direct'. Students can register and take courses from home, at a Learn Direct centre or wherever they can access the Internet. The advantage of online learning is that you do not have to attend a college or training school, but can study in the comfort of your own home.

Key points

Advantages and disadvantages of the Internet as a source of information.

Advantages:

- It is readily accessible from any computer, as long as the correct equipment is available.
- The information you find is up-to-date.
- The amount of data available is almost endless.
- Search engines and search directories enable you to narrow down your hunt for specific information.
- E-mail response means that you can send a message almost instantaneously throughout the world.
- The information can be presented by a variety of different media – graphics, sound, animation, text (multimedia).

Disadvantages:

- The cost of the equipment needed to access the Internet.
- The cost of the actual connection to the Internet – ISPs, ISDN, ADSL, etc.
- The difficulty in finding information required, despite the use of search engines.
- The time spent waiting for information to download.

Test your understanding

Fill in the gaps

1 LAN stands for _________ _________ _________ and WAN stands for _________ _________ _________.

2 A LAN consists of a group of computers which are li_________ together over one _________ geographial area.

3 A WAN allows a user to c_________ between computers located in a di_________ town or co_________.

4 The computers or workstations in a WAN are connected by t_________ li_________, s_________ or mi_________.

5 The central point of a star network is the s_________ or h_________.

6 The following are required to form a LAN: c_________; w_________s; n_________ i_________ c_________s; One or more s_________s; a n_________ o_________ s_________.

7 A c_________ r_________ is a facility on the Internet which allows you to hold typed c_________ with people throughout the w_________.

8 A modem is a device which converts d_________ signals from a c_________ to signals that can be sent down a t_________ line.

9 D_________ t_________ is the name given to how long it takes a PC to load a web page once the request to view the web page has been responded to.

10 Your web b_________ will store copies of the web pages you have recently used in an area called c_________.

Multiple choice questions

11 Which **one** of the following statements is false?
a) The advantage of a LAN is that data is stored separately on each workstation.
b) A LAN is a group of computers linked together with an organisation's own cabling.
c) A powerful computer to which the workstations are connected to is called a server.
d) A network has the advantage that peripherals such as printers can be shared.

12 Which **one** of the following is an advantage of a star network?
a) It is the simplest network topology to install.
b) If one computer fails, it does not affect the rest of the network.
c) It does not rely on a server.
d) It is economic in its use of cable.

13 Which **one** of the following is required to connect a PC to a network?
a) Workstation
b) Network interface card
c) Modem
d) File server.

14 Which **one** of the following is false?
a) You cannot make a telephone call whilst a fax is being sent from the same telephone line.
b) An e-mail can be sent to several people simultaneously.
c) It is cheaper to send a letter than an e-mail to Australia.
d) You will usually be informed if an e-mail does not reach its destination.

15 The ability to send text-based messages between offices over a network is known as:
a) Videoconferencing
b) Fax
c) E-mail
d) Newsgroups.

16 Which one of the following is not required in order to connect to the Internet?
a) Internet service provider
b) Modem
c) Virus checking software
d) Web browser.

CHAPTER 7

Presentation

In Chapter 6 we looked at how networks and the Internet could help Pete and Sandra's business. This technology can assist Greenfingers in communicating with customers, suppliers and staff. However, how they use the latest technological developments to present their business will have a major influence on the business's success. In this chapter we will be considering ways of presenting information, firstly by using a presentation package, and then by using web pages.

What do we mean by a presentation? At school or college your teacher may present information using an overhead projector and slides – that's a presentation. A computer in a tourist office that has been set up to show a series of pictures about an event or tourist attraction, is also a presentation. A web site, consisting of several web pages about a company, product or event, for example, is also a presentation. As we discussed in the last chapter, the web is a very cheap way of advertising. It allows a company to publish a brochure without paying a firm to print it. Nor does the company have to pay for extensive distribution of a brochure as it has the potential of being seen by people throughout the world. Once Pete and Sandra have created their web site, they will be able to update it as much as they like. They will also be able to consider selling their products online.

You can use PowerPoint to create computerised presentations. You can create a series of slides that includes many professional features, and finally having completed your presentation you can incorporate it onto a web site by using hyperlinks. You will learn about hyperlinks later in this chapter. You can even save your PowerPoint presentation as a web page.

We will start by looking briefly at PowerPoint and some of the features it offers, and then move on to looking at creating a web site.

Tips for creating a good presentation

Did you know 

All Microsoft Office applications use the same dictionary file to check spelling. If you add a word to the dictionary in Word, Powerpoint will also recognise it.

Did you know 

Clip art, unlike other pictures, is not defined as a series of dots. Clip art is defined by mathematically defined lines and curves. Therefore, a clip art picture doesn't have a natural size. This means that you can adjust the clip art picture to any size you want, and the computer will draw the lines and curves to that size without losing any of its details or looking grainy.

Activity 

Pete and Sandra have asked you to create a PowerPoint presentation for Gardening Jobs for the Month. Use PowerPoint to design this presentation. Your teacher will be able to supply you with instructions to help you.

PowerPoint features

PowerPoint is the most popular presentation package. It has many features that can enhance a presentation. You can:

- Make your text move, slide, and scroll.
- Rotate text.
- Include clip art and graphics.
- Use WordArt to design a logo for Greenfingers, similar to the one used in this book.
- Add lines and shapes, fill the shapes with colour, outline them and make them three-dimensional. There are 150 different shapes from which to choose!
- Use special shapes called *callouts* to include text within the shape.
- Include digitised film clips into a presentation.
- Include sound, either just little highlights of sound or a complete narration.
- Use animation to control how objects, such as pictures or text, are brought onto the slide.
- Finally, you can control the way PowerPoint changes the display from the preceding slide to the next slide by setting the *slide transition*.

PowerPoint is a very versatile package and it is very tempting to try to incorporate as many different features as possible within a presentation to show off your newly acquired skills. Doing so can distract from the actual content of the presentation.

Remember to:

- Plan the content of the presentation first. Your aim is to have a clear and understandable presentation. Add any special features after you have created the basis of the presentation and try to avoid using too many of these features at one time.
- Proof read your presentation carefully – silly spelling or grammatical errors will spoil the end result. It is important to remember that when we are proof reading, we unintentionally read what we expect to see.
- Avoid using too many technical terms or abbreviations with which your audience may be unfamiliar.
- Ensure that each slide should have one aspect that draws the audience's attention first – headings are best in a larger font than the remainder of the text.

Remember that you will need to use a font size that people will be able to read easily. Font size 12 or 14 may be okay for a handout, but you would need extremely good eyesight to read the words if you are sitting at the back of a room!

- Avoid using all capital letters – these are more difficult to read. When you are out and about, look at road signs – you will notice that they are usually in a combination of upper and lower case letters rather than all capital letters.
- Take care when using colours. Sometimes too many or the wrong colours can make a slide difficult to view – if you cannot view an object easily in the Black and White option from the View menu, then they will not be easy to view in full colour.
- Use words prudently. You may have heard the saying that a picture is worth a thousand words – this is very true and you may find, for example, that pictures or graphs are a much better way of communicating than text.
- Make sure that if you are going to use preset timings for the transition of slides, the timings are set at a realistic pace. Changing slides too slowly can be just as irritating as slides changing too rapidly.
- Keep the content interesting and to the point – a presentation that gives information overload may bore the audience and you will lose their attention.

Key points

- A good presentation is a well-designed one.
- Don't be tempted to use too many different features in one slide or presentation – it will result in a confusing and muddled outcome.
- Take care when using fonts and colours.
- Proof read the presentation carefully.
- Pictures are a good way of communicating information.

Activity

Look at the slide shown in Figure 7.1. Do you think it is well-designed? Compare it with the slide shown in Figure 7.2. Which do you consider is the better way of presenting information?

Figure 7.1 *Activity example 1*

Figure 7.2 *Activity example 2*

Web site design

Activity

Find a page of the Internet that interests you – preferably one that does not have too many pictures on it. Read the page to familiarise yourself with its contents. Is there a hyperlink? What happens when you click on it?

You can see how the page has been constructed with HTML code by viewing the source code through the View/Source or Document Source from the menu of your web browser. (This facility might not be available through all Internet service providers – if not, try clicking the right mouse button or ask your teacher.) The source code is what the author used to enable you to see the finished page as he or she intended when it was designed.

It probably looks very complicated because it will have been written by an expert in HTML and will have been designed to include many advanced concepts. Can you pick out some of the text you read amongst the coding?

Copy some of the coding, paste it into a Word document and print it out. As you read through this section see if you can identify the HTML codes in the print-out. It is better to copy and paste the code rather than print it direct from your web browser so that you don't end up with pages and pages of code.

Having created a PowerPoint presentation, we will now look at designing a web site for Greenfingers. Before we begin, we need to consider what a web site actually is.

HTML (hypertext markup language)

A web site is a collection of related web pages, a web page being an electronic document that can contain text, images, forms, graphics, and other multimedia such as animation. Web pages are created with **HTML** (**hypertext markup language**) and then viewed via web browsers such as Internet Explorer or Netscape.

Hypertext markup language is the code used to write pages for the web. This code is in the form of *tags* which surround blocks of text to indicate how the text should appear on the screen so that it looks the same when viewed through any web browser.

To explain it simply, the author of a web page designs the page and links all the material together using HTML. When the page is viewed (either by the author or someone viewing a published web page), the web browser software interprets the HTML language and displays the text exactly as the author intended.

It enables you to create *hyperlinks* within the text, so that when you click on a hyperlink you automatically jump to another part of the page or another page on the web. A hyperlink might be a word, a button or a picture.

Most word-processing software today enables you to produce HTML scripts without the need to understand the coding. You can also use authoring tools, such as FrontPage or DreamWeaver. We will be looking at this method of creating web pages later in this chapter. However, it is important to know the basic concepts of HTML, so we will be looking at how Pete and Sandra can create a web page by coding them manually.

In order to create a web page, Pete and Sandra will need:

- A simple text editor (like Notepad) to write the HTML coding or a dedicated HTML text editor, for example Allaire's HomeSite. There are many alternatives that they could use, including dedicated authoring tools such as Microsoft FrontPage, or DreamWeaver. They could also use standard application software such as Microsoft Word which includes a Save As HTML option, which automatically inserts HTML tags into a document and makes it web-ready. There are also many online wizards which will guide you through a step-by-step process.

- A web browser – a dedicated software application that will enable you to browse the web and view your own web pages.
- To learn the codes (or tags) used to format and structure the text.
- Finally, and perhaps most importantly, good design and presentation skills.

Tags

Did you notice words or letters inside the < and > marks in the document code you viewed in the activity? These are known as **tags** and are the way the web browser knows how we want the document to appear. For example, they tell the web browser where to start a new paragraph or print a line of text. They usually come in pairs with the second tag of the pair beginning with a slash symbol /. As an example the <h1> and </h1> tags indicate where a main heading begins and ends.

The first tag of any document is <html>, which tells the web browser that you are beginning a page of information written in HTML. The closing tag </html> is put at the end of the document.

Structure of an HTML document

There are always two parts of an HTML document: the head and the body. The first part of any document is always the **head** tag, which is bracketed as the <head> and </head> commands.

In the head area there are several tags that can be included. The most common is the document's title, bracketed by the <title> and </title>. The body of the document begins after the head: <Body> </Body>. The body will contain all the parts of the web page displayed in a web browser's viewing window.

Did you know

Sometimes word-processing applications such as Microsoft Word or WordPerfect are less effective for HTML than using a basic tool such as Notepad. This is because advanced word processors tend to create formatting in documents that interferes with HTML coding.

Activity

Look at a range of web sites on the Internet. Look at them critically. Do you think they are effective in presenting information? Are they easy to use? Are they well designed? How long did they take to download? Remember we learnt in the last chapter that files take longer to download when they include graphics and other multimedia. If a web page takes too long to download, there is the real risk that a visitor will lose interest and give up!

Key points

- Web pages are created using hypertext markup language.
- Tags are used to indicate how the text should appear on the screen.
- There are always two parts of an HTML document – the head and the body.

Creating a web page using HTML 1

What to type	Why
<html>	This indicates the start of an HTML page
<head>	This indicates some header information
<title> Greenfingers Garden Centres </title>	This indicates the text that will appear in the title bar at the top of your web page
</head>	This indicates the end of the header information
<body>	The start of the main part of the web page
<h1> Greenfingers – Southborough's Premier Garden Centres</h1>	A heading in the largest font size
<p> Pete and Sandra Wellings started their garden business in Seaford 15 years ago. Greenfingers now have branches in Dulton and Newford. They have built up a reputation for high quality plants and merchandise at excellent prices.	The <p> tag tells the browser to start a new paragraph </p> Indicates end of paragraph
</body>	Marks the end of the body of the web page
</html>	Indicates the end of the HTML page
<b>	</b> Displays characters in **bold**
<i>	</i> Displays characters in *italics*
<center><</center>	Everything between these tags is centred
 	Allows you to type words onto a new line

Table 7.1 *Explanation of html tags*

You are now going to create a very basic web page.

Before you start you will need to load your text editor. This is probably Notepad, which you will find by choosing Start, Programs, Accessories in Windows Me, 98 or NT. Check in your text editor to see that Wordwrap is switched on (Edit/Wordwrap). Key in the text shown in Figure 7.3, exactly as you see it. Look at Table 7.1 for an explanation of each line of code.

It is a good idea to create a new directory or folder with a suitable name, like 'Web Pages'. Save all files related to a web site in this folder (e.g. files you may want to link, graphics, files, sound files, etc.). You must save your file in the text editor with the file extension .htm.

Did you know ?

It is possible to write an HTML document as a long single line <html><head><title> Greenfingers Garden Centre</title>, etc. – but this is not good practice. It is much easier to work with if it is written as an orderly list as shown in Figure 7.2.

To view your page, open your web browser and select File/Open. Click on the Browse button and choose the file from the folder where you saved it.

Did you notice that the line endings in the web browser are not the same as those in your text editor? Browsers ignore extra spaces, tabs and new lines created by pressing the Enter key when you are writing the text in your text editor. How text is displayed will depend on the browser and the size of the VDU that a user has.

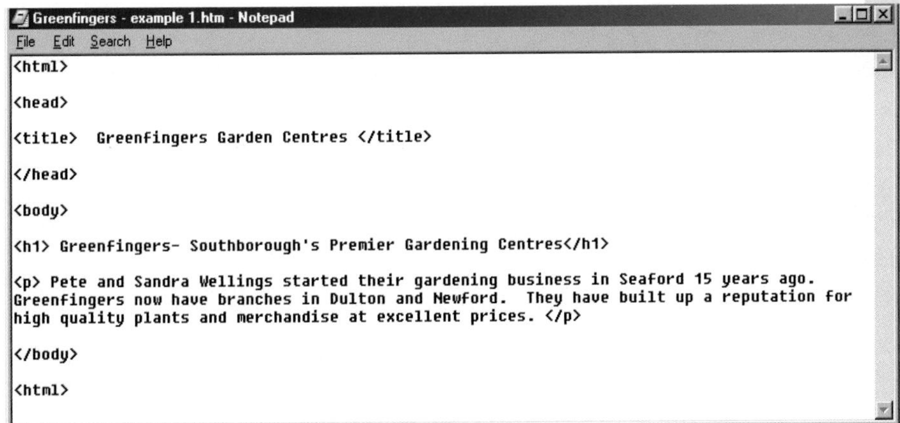

Figure 7.3 *The initial text*

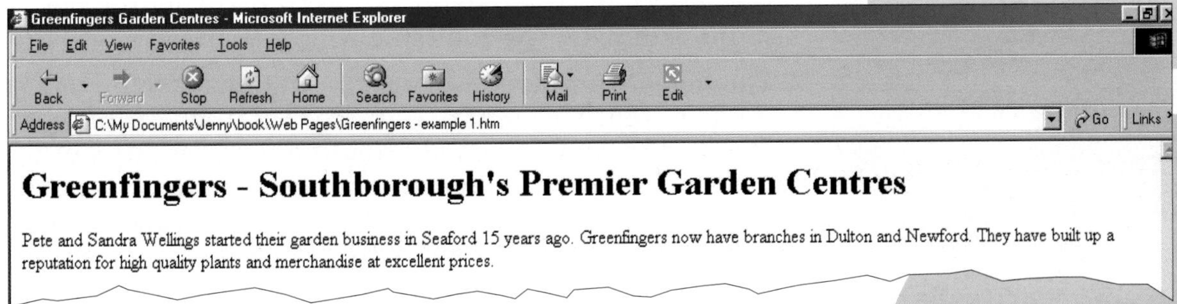

Figure 7.4 *The text viewed in a web browser*

Comment tags

If you want to write something in your HTML page that you don't want to appear on your web page, you use a **comment** tag. The tag that turns the comment on is <!-- and the tag that turns the comment off is -->. A comment is something you would use to add a note to remind you or someone else who is looking at your program about something important that you don't want to forget.

Did you know ?

Although most tags normally come in pairs, this is not always the case. The <br> tag, used to create a line break to create larger gaps, comes on its own. Also the </p> tag (end of paragraph) is optional.

Creating a web page using HMTL 2 / web site features

Key points

- You can use Notepad as a text editor to write HTML.
- HTML should be written in an orderly list.
- All files relating to a web page should be saved in one directory or folder created specifically for the web site.
- Comment tags can be used to add notes to your code.
- The colour of fonts and the background of a web page can be changed using designated codes or colour names.
- Font sizes and type can be changed.
- It is best to avoid using strange fonts as they may not exist on the computer of the person viewing a web page.

Activity

- Update your web page so that it includes some new code.
- Experiment with changing the font names and sizes.
- Try changing the background colour and font colour.
- Remember to save your updated web page!

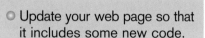

Changing the colour of the background and fonts

You can include within the <body> tag different attributes for the style of the text on the web page.

For example, by inserting the following text in the <body> tag in your html script, you can change the background to Pale Weak Yellow and font colour to Green on your web page.

```
<body>
<body text = Green BGColor = ffffcc>
<h1>Greenfingers – Southborough's Premier
Gardening Centres</h1>
```

Changing the font type and size

Apart from the headings, which you will remember come in sizes from H1 (the biggest) to H6 (the smallest), it is possible to increase the font size of standard text. The default size is 3, by using the tag <font size = 4>, the font size will be increased.

The default font type is Times New Roman, so by using the tag <font face = Arial>, the font on the web page is changed to Arial. When altering the font, beware not to use strange fonts as they may not exist on the computer of whoever is viewing your page. If they don't the browser will choose the 'next best' view.

Hyperlinks

In the last chapter you learnt that all the documents on the World Wide Web are connected by **hyperlinks**. When you move your mouse pointer over a hyperlink, the arrow changes to a pointing hand, and clicking on the mouse button connects you to the link. A hyperlink may be text, a button or a picture. You can create a hyperlink to one of your own documents or to a page on a different web site altogether. HTML anchor tags enable you to do this. Greenfingers could, for example, create a link to the Royal Horticultural Society.

An anchor tab for the Royal Horticultural Society would look like: <a href="http://www.rhs.org.uk"> Royal Horticultural Society </a> To simplify this: the first letter **a** indicates it is an anchor and **href** tells us it is a hypertext reference. The http://www.rhs.org.uk denotes the place you will go to when you click on the hyperlink. The **text** of the hyperlink will be word(s) you display on your page to indicate the link, in this case Royal Horticultural Society. Finally, the </a> shows the end of the anchor.

You can also insert hyperlinks in a document that enable you to jump to a different place on the same page. The place in the page you jump to is called the **target**.

This tag could, for example, be placed at the bottom of your web page, so that the user can click on it to go straight back to the top of the page.

Graphics and images

Pictures included in a web page can create more interest, add impact and help get your message across. They may come from ClipArt, they may be something you have drawn or scanned yourself or something you have downloaded from the web. A graphic feature might be flashing text, a moving image or animated clip.

Any picture to be stored on your web page must be stored on your hard drive in a graphics file format. The two formats that can be used with a web browser are GIF (pronounced 'giff' or 'jiff') and JPEG (pronounced 'jay peg'). A GIF (graphics interchange format) image is similar to a bitmap image and is made up of pixels (or dots). A JPEG (joint photographic experts group) file format is ideal for displaying photographic images because it can use over 16 million colours compared to 256 for GIF images.

Special software, called Shockwave, is available for producing animated graphics, videos and sound sequences. This software is designed to download quickly because a visitor to a web page does not want to wait a long time to see a full page. However, it is a very expensive and complex program that takes a long time to learn. At this stage you will find it interesting just to view examples.

You can include images recorded on a web cam onto a site. These can be still images that are refreshed occasionally or pre-recorded video footage. It is even possible to include a live link to a web cam. Many of you may have visited the 'Big Brother' web site, for example, to view in real time the antics of the house mates! It is worth remembering that including these aspects can seriously affect download times.

Did you know?

A useful web site to visit is that of the World Wide Web Consortium (WC3) at www.w3.org. This organisation is responsible for setting the formal standards of HTML. There have been several versions of HTML and at the time of writing the most current is HTML 4.01.

Did you know?

Some people, for example visually impaired users, use a text-only web browser. If you have included graphics on your web site, it is good practice to use 'alternative text' for images. The text will be displayed in place of the photo in a text-only web browser, or whilst the image is downloading.

Key points

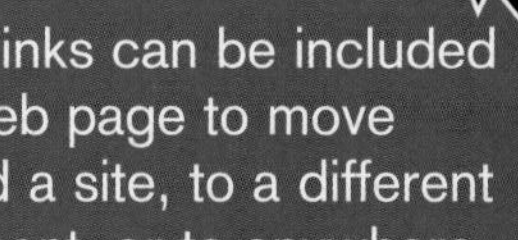

- Hyperlinks can be included in a web page to move around a site, to a different document, or to anywhere on the WWW.
- Graphics and images can be included in a web page. They can be animated or still.
- Pre-recorded or live images can be included in a web page, but download times will be affected.

Dedicated authoring tools

Did you know

When the standards for HTML were made, it was decided to make all aspects of it as safe as possible to ensure that a 'hacker' can't write code which will damage a visitor's computer. There are times however when you may need to write files on a web server or deal with data from fill-in forms. CGI allows this to take place as it provides a standard channel between the web page and special CGI scripts which are on the web server. A good example of a CGI script, which you have probably come across whilst surfing the net, is a counter which keeps count of the number of visitors to a page. You can download pre-written CGI modules that can be attached to your own code.

We have looked in detail at some of the programming code that enables you to create a web page. You can also use a word processor, such as Word, or alternatively use a dedicated authoring tool such as FrontPage Express, FrontPage or DreamWeaver to create web pages. When you create a web page using one of these alternatives, the software automatically inserts the HTML tags into the document. This makes developing a web page much easier and faster. These packages are often referred to as WYSIWYG (what you see is what you get) tools. This is because as you build the web page, what you see on the screen is the same as it will actually appear in a browser.

If you want to create a web page that includes more advanced features, such as tables or forms, you can easily do so using an authoring tool without having to learn the more complicated aspects of HTML or CGI. FrontPage Express comes free with Microsoft Internet Explorer 5.0 and is a good starting point. It is useful as it is integrated with the browser, but it does not come with all the features of the full version of FrontPage. However, as with other options, it offers templates and user-friendly commands for inserting graphics and links, and for formatting text. Using FrontPage Express or FrontPage, for example, you could create a basic page, similar to the one referred to earlier in this section, in a matter of minutes.

As you become more proficient with writing HTML, you will be able to view the code produced by an authoring tool and make alterations to improve the page direct into the code.

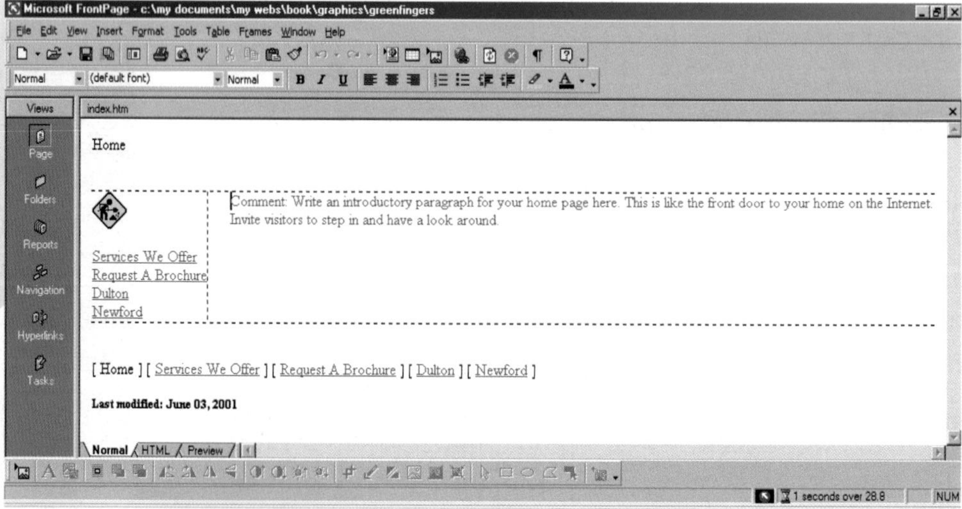

Figure 7.5 *An example Home Page template created using FrontPage*

Wizards

Before you begin creating a web site, you should plan on paper how you want the site to appear. Most authoring tools will include **wizards** to make designing a web site or page an easier process. Certainly, for the beginner, you can create a professional looking site by following one of the wizards provided. FrontPage Express will provide fewer options than the full version of FrontPage. A wizard will take you step by step through the process, giving you options from which to choose at each stage.

Your next step will be to build each web page in turn. However, unlike when you are coding in HTML, you will see screen prompts on how to continue.

You will see that there are three views: Normal, HTML and Preview. You use Normal View to edit the page, but you also have the option of viewing and editing the HTML code.

Once you have keyed in your chosen text, changing the font type, size and colour is far easier than in HTML. Simply select the text and change the font type, size and colour to options you prefer, just like you would do in Word.

Marquees

Marquees are scrolling text areas that will scroll across the screen repeatedly. They are useful for getting a message across. For example, Greenfingers could include a marquee in the banner area of their web site saying 'Southborough's Premier Garden Centres'. This would then appear on every page.

Themes

Another benefit of using an authoring tool such as FrontPage is that templates or **themes** are included, rather like the design templates supplied with PowerPoint. You can choose the theme for the entire web or for individual pages.

Tables and forms

Again, **tables** and **forms** can be created using an authoring tool quite easily by inserting a basic table structure in the first instance to create a table and by using a wizard to choose the design of a form.

Activity

- Investigate which authoring tool your school or college uses.
- What wizards come with the software?
- Which wizard would you choose to create your own personal web site?

Key points

- FrontPage allows you to build up the structure of a web step by step using the wizard.
- All files relating to a web site should be stored in one folder.
- You can edit the structure of a web in Navigation View.
- There are three ways to view a web page you are constructing: Normal, HTML and Preview. However, your Internet web browser will give you a better idea how your page will be viewed.
- A Page Banner will appear across the top of each page of a web site.
- Font types, sizes and styles can be easily changed.
- In FrontPage you can choose a theme that will apply to all pages.

Design considerations and publishing a web (uploading)

Activity

Look at six different web sites critically – decide with your teacher the ones you will be reviewing. Give each site a grade (Excellent, Good, Fair, Poor) for the following points:

- ease of use (are the instructions clear?)
- download time
- overall design
- ease of navigation round the site (did all the hyperlinks work?)
- up-to-date information (does the site give an indication of when it was last updated?)

Compare your findings with your classmates.

In this chapter we have looked at constructing a web site using a text editor and HTML and also using an authoring tool – FrontPage.

You will have realised that constructing a web site can be quite a simple process, especially when using an authoring tool such as FrontPage. However, it is also extremely important to make sure your web site looks good and is easy to use.

Design considerations

- Plan your site on paper before starting to construct it. You should draft a diagram showing how all the pages will link together and also how each page will appear.
- It is very tempting to use as many advanced features as possible. Just because you can include video clips and blinking text, it doesn't mean that you should! Sometimes too many features will detract from the information you want to convey.
- Don't use too many fonts on one page and stick to well-known ones. Not everyone will have the same fonts on their computer.
- Use graphics prudently. Too many will slow the download time and frustrate visitors.
- Make sure that the site is easy to use and any instructions are clear.
- Pilot your site with a friend or colleague. They may point out something obvious that you have overlooked.
- Look at other sites – they can be a wonderful source of new ideas of what to do and, importantly, what not to do.

Publishing the web

In FrontPage, a web does not become a web site until it has been published and can be viewed by other people. A web host is the name given to the company that provides space on a web server for you to publish your site.

Your own ISP may offer limited space to publish your site. If you wish to publish your web created in FrontPage, you need to find out if your ISP supports FrontPage server extensions. FrontPage allows you to search for a suitable web presence provider (WPP) when you are ready to publish your web. The steps to upload a site can vary from one ISP to another, but it is normally quite a simple process.

Many companies will offer to publish web sites free of charge on condition that they put some of the advertising banners at the top of each page.

Alternatively, your school or college may have their own **web server** onto which you can publish your site.

You learnt more about domain names and how they are made up in Chapter 6. If you want your site to be found easily, you should buy a domain name. In the UK, Nominet is the domain naming authority. They maintain a central database of all domains ending with .uk. If you want to find out if a particular domain name is available you can use one of the many specialised search sites, such as www.simply.names.co.uk. As more and more companies and individuals are purchasing domain names, different top level domains are being introduced. For example, '.gb.com' could be purchased if '.uk' or '.com' are unavailable.

Initially Pete and Sandra wanted to register Greenfingers.com as their URL, but unfortunately the name had already been purchased. As you can see in Figure 7.6, a further search revealed that Greenfingers-gardening.com is still available, and therefore they could purchase this as their URL.

Key points

- It is extremely important to design your site on paper before you even turn the computer on!
- Look at other web sites for ideas.
- Pilot your site with a friend or colleague.
- In FrontPage terminology, a web does not become a web site until it has been published.
- Publishing a web site is sometimes referred to as 'uploading'.
- Your ISP needs to support FrontPage extensions if you have created your site using FrontPage.
- Buy a domain name if you wish your site to be easily found.

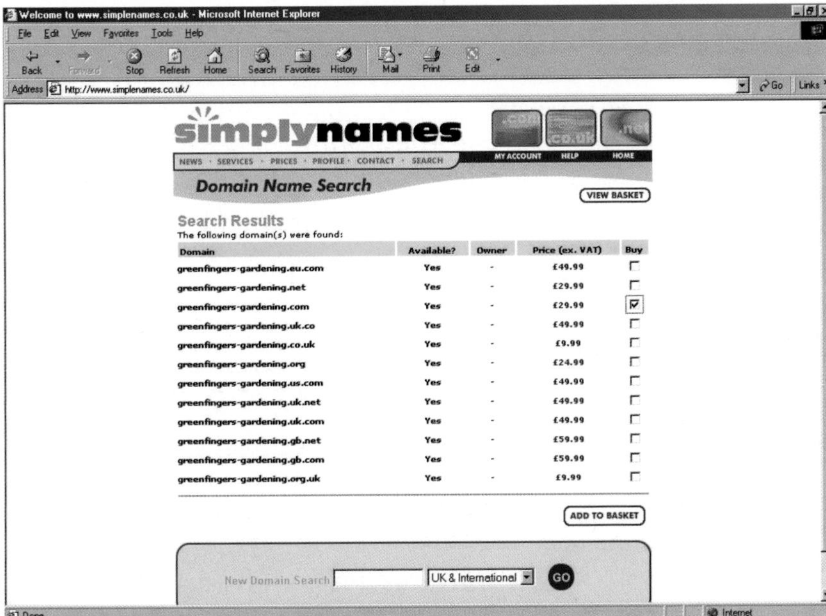

Domain	Available?	Owner	Price (ex. VAT)	Buy
greenfingers-gardening.eu.com	Yes	-	£49.99	
greenfingers-gardening.net	Yes	-	£29.99	
greenfingers-gardening.com	Yes	-	£29.99	☑
greenfingers-gardening.uk.co	Yes	-	£49.99	
greenfingers-gardening.co.uk	Yes	-	£9.99	
greenfingers-gardening.org	Yes	-	£24.99	
greenfingers-gardening.us.com	Yes	-	£49.99	
greenfingers-gardening.uk.net	Yes	-	£49.99	
greenfingers-gardening.uk.com	Yes	-	£49.99	
greenfingers-gardening.gb.net	Yes	-	£59.99	
greenfingers-gardening.gb.com	Yes	-	£59.99	
greenfingers-gardening.org.uk	Yes	-	£9.99	

Figure 7.6 *Buying a domain name*

Test your understanding

True or False?

1 Microsoft FrontPage is an example of a text editor.

2 The head tag is always the first part of an HTML document.

3 An HTML document is best written as an orderly list.

4 Browsers ignore extra spaces, tabs and new lines created by pressing the Enter key when you are writing text in your text editor.

5 A tag in an HTML document always comes in pairs to denote the beginning and end of the text to be formatted.

6 There are three ways to view a web page in FrontPage: Normal, HTML and Preview.

Multiple choice questions

7 Which one of the following **may not** improve the appearance and ease of use of a web site?
a) Clear instructions to the user.
b) Several different fonts on one page.
c) Graphics used carefully.
d) Avoiding the use of a large number of different features on one page.

8 Why is it important to use graphics prudently when designing a web site?
a) The ISP may not support the file format of the graphics.
b) Graphics are difficult to place on a web page.
c) Too many graphics may slow the download time of a web site.
d) The visitor's monitor may be too small to display the graphic properly.

9 FrontPage Extensions are:
a) wizards which enable you to create a web page in FrontPage
b) a hyperlink to help files
c) extra files needed on an ISP server which operate advanced web components such as forms created with FrontPage
d) a method of adding web pages to a web site.

Find the mistakes

Look at the following HTML script. There are 10 deliberate mistakes. See if you can find them all.

question.htm - Notepad

File Edit Search Help

```
<htm1>

<head>

<title>  Greenfingers Garden Centres - Dulton Branch <title>

</haed>

<body>
<body text = Green BGColour = ffffcc>
<h1><centre> <font face = Arial> Greenfingers Garden Centres - Dulton Branch </centre></h1>

<h3>
<br> Goldcrest Way
<br> DULTON
<r> DU7 2DX
<br>
<br> Tel: 083 1882 5487
<br> Fax: 083 1882 7845
<br> E-Mail dulton.greenfingers@userve.co.uk</h2>
<p <font size = 4>Pete and Sandra Wellings are pleased to announce that the Dulton Branch
opened on 2 April 2001  </p>



</boody>

</html>
```

CHAPTER 8

Spreadsheet modelling and simulations

In Chapter 4 you saw how a spreadsheet program could be used by Greenfingers to do financial tasks such as working out costs and sales of plants.

In this chapter, we will be looking at how a spreadsheet can be used as a **computer model**.

The term **model** probably makes you think of:

- a fashion **model,**
- a **model** car**,**
- an architect's **model** of new buildings.

A computer model is a computer program used to represent or behave like a real situation. The computer model must have **data** and a **set of rules** which control the way in which the model works.

As well as using spreadsheet software, computer models can be set up using simulations including **virtual reality** and **expert systems**.

Mathematical modelling 1

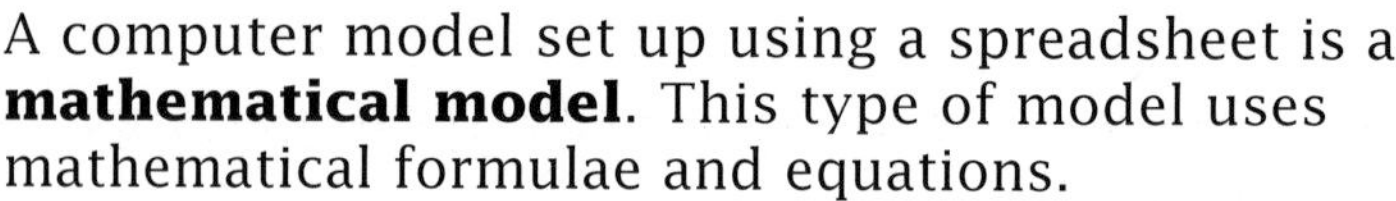

A computer model set up using a spreadsheet is a **mathematical model**. This type of model uses mathematical formulae and equations.

The use of a spreadsheet for modelling can be: quite simple, e.g. a budget plan for your holiday, or extremely complicated, e.g. the government's balance of payments model.

A spreadsheet model is based on the use of:

- different values of **input data**
- **formulae** which define the **rules** of the model
- **output** data which will vary according to the values of the input data.

The **output data** can be displayed as a:

- graph
- table
- spreadsheet worksheet.

Uses of spreadsheet modelling

A business such as Greenfingers could use spreadsheet modelling to help with the analysis of sales and profits by varying the value of the input data, e.g. selling price, to see the effect on the output data, e.g. profit/loss.

Pete and Sandra will need to have details about:

- Company sales – what is being sold and in what quantities.
- Profit/loss – how much money is being made/lost.
- Cash flow – how much money is being made/lost each week/month, etc.

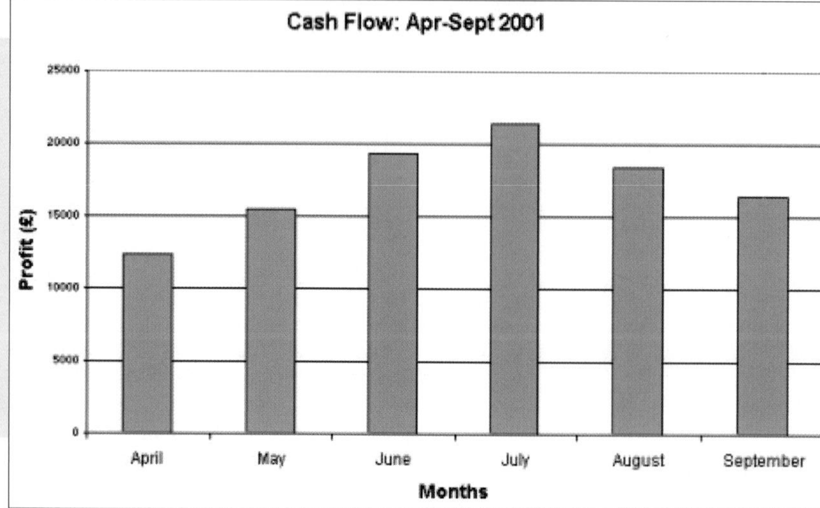

Figure 8.1 *Cash flow analysis graph*

They will also need to be able to predict what their sales and profits might be.

They could also use the model to investigate how they could reduce the company's costs and improve its profitability.

What if

Pete and Sandra could use a spreadsheet to investigate '**What if**' situations.

For example:

- **What** would happen to the sales **if** the price of all plants was decreased by 10%?

  They would have to consider:
  - Would sales increase because the selling price has gone down?
  - Would the profit be decreased because the selling price has fallen?

They could use a spreadsheet to investigate or **model** the different circumstances by:

- changing the values of the input data – e.g. reduce prices by 10%

  and
- checking the effect of these changes on the output data – e.g. what would happen to the income from sales.

In a simple example, they could use the spreadsheet for Bedding Plant Sales to investigate the effect of changing the price per unit of the bedding plants. Figure 8.2 shows the sales of bedding plants for April to July.

	A	B	C	D	E	F	G	H	I
1			GREENFINGERS WHOLESALE NURSERY						
2				Bedding Plant Sales					
3	**Bedding Plants**	**Price**	**Apr**	**May**	**June**	**July**	**Total No.**	**Total**	**Average**
4	Ageratum	0.06	8000	12593	15633	7550	43776	2626.56	10944
5	Begonia	0.09	6500	9353	11610	5610	33073	2976.58	8268
6	Busy Lizzie	0.06	5470	11600	14400	6960	38430	2305.80	9608
7	Geranium	0.23	6450	7932	9846	4760	28988	6667.29	7247
8	Lobelia	0.07	8685	10585	13140	6350	38760	2713.20	9690
9	Marigolds	0.08	5380	7801	9684	4685	27550	2204.01	6888
10	Petunia	0.18	7300	9425	11700	5655	34080	6134.43	8520
11		**Monthly**	**47785**	**69289**	**86013**	**41570**	**Grand**	**25627.88**	

Figure 8.2 *Sales of bedding plants*

Mathematical modelling 2

Pete and Sandra decide to investigate what might have happened to sales if the price per unit for all bedding plants had been reduced this year by 10% during April to July.

They use the spreadsheet and find that total sales has fallen to:

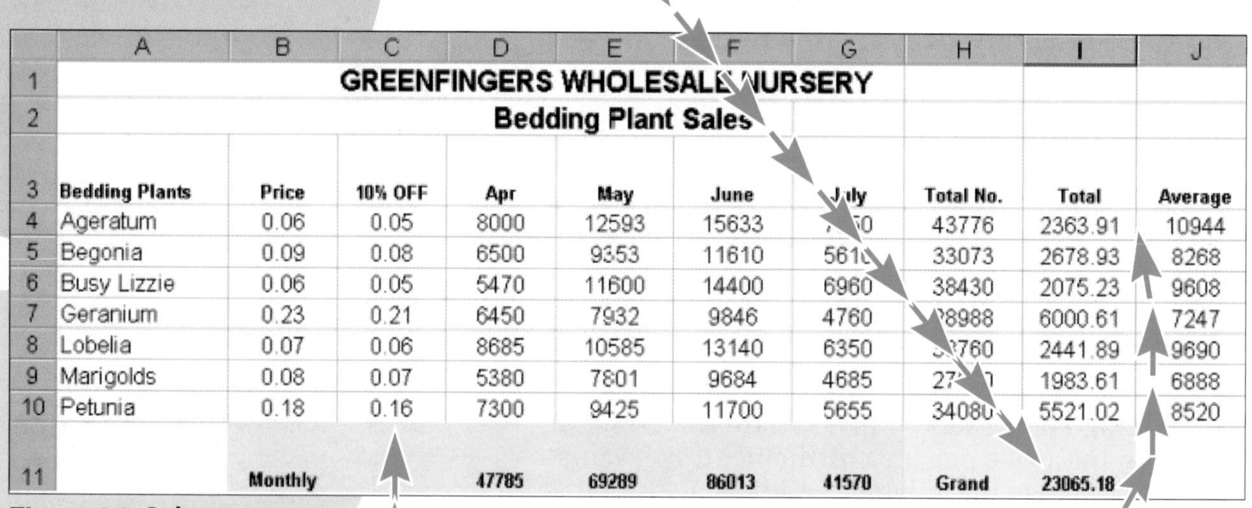

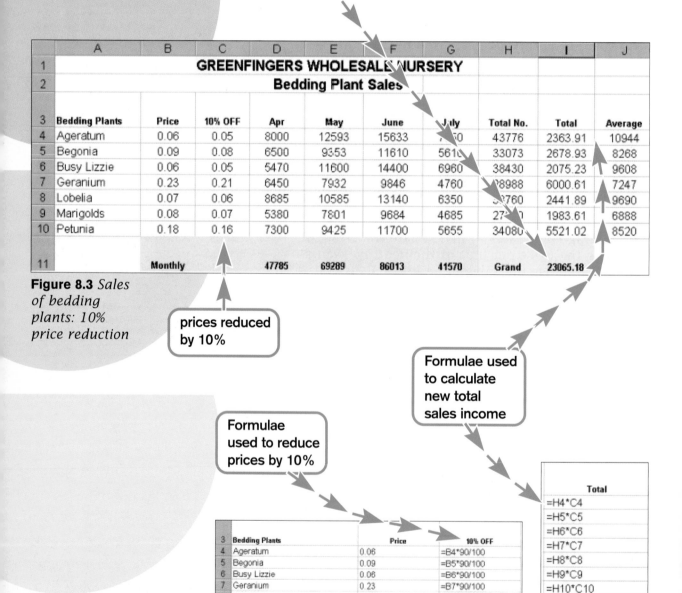

	A	B	C	D	E	F	G	H	I	J
1	GREENFINGERS WHOLESALE NURSERY									
2	Bedding Plant Sales									
3	Bedding Plants	Price	10% OFF	Apr	May	June	July	Total No.	Total	Average
4	Ageratum	0.06	0.05	8000	12593	15633	[illegible]	43776	2363.91	10944
5	Begonia	0.09	0.08	6500	9353	11610	[illegible]	33073	2678.93	8268
6	Busy Lizzie	0.06	0.05	5470	11600	14400	6960	38430	2075.23	9608
7	Geranium	0.23	0.21	6450	7932	9846	4760	[illegible]	6000.61	7247
8	Lobelia	0.07	0.06	8685	10585	13140	6350	[illegible]	2441.89	9690
9	Marigolds	0.08	0.07	5380	7801	9684	4685	[illegible]	1983.61	6888
10	Petunia	0.18	0.16	7300	9425	11700	5655	34080	5521.02	8520
11		Monthly		47785	69289	86013	41570	Grand	23065.18	

Figure 8.3 *Sales of bedding plants: 10% price reduction*

prices reduced by 10%

Formulae used to calculate new total sales income

Formulae used to reduce prices by 10%

	Bedding Plants	Price	10% OFF
4	Ageratum	0.06	=B4*90/100
5	Begonia	0.09	=B5*90/100
6	Busy Lizzie	0.06	=B6*90/100
7	Geranium	0.23	=B7*90/100
8	Lobelia	0.07	=B8*90/100
9	Marigolds	0.08	=B9*90/100
10	Petunia	0.18	=B10*90/100

Total
=H4*C4
=H5*C5
=H6*C6
=H7*C7
=H8*C8
=H9*C9
=H10*C10
=SUM(I4:I10)

Figure 8.4 *Sales of bedding plants: formulae for 10% reduction*

However, they predict that if a 10% price reduction is given on all bedding plants, then the number of each type of plant sold would increase.

They assume that sales of each type of plant would rise by 20%, and that the Total Income would also increase.

	A	B	C	D	E	F	G	H	I	J	K
1			GREENFINGERS WHOLESALE NURSERY								
2					Bedding Plant Sales						
3	Bedding Plants	Price	10% OFF	Apr	May	June	July	Total No.	20% Increas	Total	Average
4	Ageratum	0.06	0.05	8000	12593	15633	7550	43776	52531	2836.69	13133
5	Begonia	0.09	0.08	6500	9353	11610	5610	33073	39688	3214.71	9922
6	Busy Lizzie	0.06	0.05	5470	11600	14400	6960	38430	46116	[illegible]490.27	11529
7	Geranium	0.23	0.21	6450	7932	9846	4760	28988	34786	[illegible]200.73	8697
8	Lobelia	0.07	0.06	8685	10585	13140	6350	38760	46512	2930.27	11628
9	Marigolds	0.08	0.07	5380	7801	9684	4685	27550	33060	2380.33	8265
10	Petunia	0.18	0.16	7300	9425	11700	5655	34080	40896	[illegible]625.22	10224
11		Monthly		47785	69289	86013	41570	Grand		27678.22	

20% Increase
=H4*120/100
=H5*120/100
=H6*120/100
=H7*120/100
=H8*120/100
=H9*120/100
=H10*120/100

Figure 8.5 *Sales of bedding plants: formulae for 20% increase in income*

Goal seek

Pete and Sandra have decided that they need to have a total sales income of at least £30,000.

This is called their **goal**.

They can use a feature of their spreadsheet called **'Goal Seek'** to set this as their target.

The spreadsheet program can vary the value in **one specific cell** until a formula that is dependent on that cell gives the 'target' result required.

Activity

- Model the effect on the total sales of a 12% price reduction and a predicted 25% increase in the number of each type of plant sold.
- Check to see if your spreadsheet program has a 'Goal Seek' feature.

  If it does, investigate how Pete and Sandra might meet their target for an income of £30,000.

Key points

- A computer model is a computer program used to represent or behave like a real situation.
- A spreadsheet model is based on the use of:
  - different values of **input data**
  - **formulae** which define the rules of the **model**
  - **output data** which will vary according to the values of the input data.
- The output data can be displayed as a graph, **table** or **spreadsheet worksheet**.
- A spreadsheet is often used to investigate **'What if'** situations.

Simulations 1

Did you know ?

In February 2001, for the first time in 20 years, an outbreak of foot and mouth disease occurred on a farm in Northumberland. This disease, which affects pigs and cattle, is highly contagious and quite deadly. Infected animals have to be slaughtered. The virus is released in a mist of droplets. Scientists used computer modelling to predict the likely spread of the disease. By comparing information from earlier outbreaks against the known weather conditions, they were able to identify the possible infection area.

A **computer simulation** is a program which models a real-life system.

Examples of simulations include:

- a flight simulator
- computer games
- scientific experiments
- weather forecasting
- economic models
- virtual reality
- expert systems.

A flight simulator

A flight simulator is used to familiarise trainee pilots with a plane before they undergo expensive and possibly dangerous real training flights.

The flight simulator is a model of an aeroplane cockpit equipped with the controls and instrument panel to simulate the movements of the actual plane. The windows of the 'plane's' cockpit are replaced by computer screens. These simulate life-like events which alter as the trainee pilot controls the 'plane'.

Virtual-reality simulation (see page 191) has made it possible to model everyday, real-life events such as emergency situations, e.g. an engine on fire, landing at sea or flying in poor weather conditions, e.g. a severe storm.

Figure 8.6 *A computer game*

Computer games

Popular computer games include being a football manager or driving a racing car.

These examples are simulations of a real event. However, some games are not a model of a real situation. Many computer games, especially space and battle games, are based on fantasy which is made to appear real.

Science experiments

Scientists use computer models to simulate such things as the effect that global warming might have on the environment and world population growth during the next decade.

Weather forecasting

Services such as the Meteorological Office use very sophisticated computer models of the Earth's atmosphere to predict the weather and to provide weather forecasts.

Numerical modelling is the process of obtaining an objective forecast of the future state of the atmosphere. The process begins with analysing the current state of the atmosphere by taking a previous short-range forecast and using observations to amend this forecast so that the best guess of the current true state of the atmosphere is obtained. A computer model is then run to produce a forecast.

Economic models

The government, the Treasury and the Bank of England use economic models to investigate and predict what will happen in the economy.

The effects of varying the bank base rate could be modelled to see what might happen to the balance of payments and employment statistics.

Virtual reality

A **virtual-reality (VR)** system enables a person to move through and react within an environment simulated by a computer. The person feels that he/she is actually in the world which has been created by the computer. These **'virtual worlds'** are created by mathematical models and computer programs.

Figure 8.7 *A virtual garden*

Did you know ?

VR emerged in 1960s simulators that taught pilots how to fly by using head-mounted displays with tracking systems.

Simnet (simulator network) was used for interactive, real-time training to prepare troops for combat in the Gulf War of 1991.

Key points

Features of virtual reality:

- User feels part of environment.
- User experiences the model through a range of senses, e.g. sight, sound, smell, etc.
- Devices used:
  - Stereoscopic helmet (HMD – head-mounted device) to allow 3D visual/hearing.
  - Hand glove for touch sensations to control model.
  - Tracking device so user knows whereabouts in building.
  - Joystick to navigate around environment.

Simulations 2

Walking through the 'virtual garden"

Views of the 'virtual garden'

Figure 8.8 *The virtual reality 'walk through' garden*

The virtual reality controls panel works like a games joystick, allowing the garden to be 'walked through' in different directions. The garden can also be viewed from a range of heights and angles as shown in these scenes

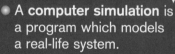

Key points

- A **computer simulation** is a program which models a real-life system.
- A **virtual-reality (VR)** system enables a person to move through and react within an environment simulated by a computer.
- In an **expert system (ES)**, a computer program is used to simulate the expert person's knowledge and experience of a particular situation.

Simulations using VR are very different from other computer-generated simulations because they need the person to use equipment which transmits sights, sounds and other sensations to the user.

- The most common use of VR is in computer games where the game player experiences the computer-generated game as though it was happening in real life.
- It is also used in the design of 3D environments such as rooms in buildings or, as for Greenfingers, a 'virtual garden'.
- Surgeons can plan and practice an operation on a 'virtual patient' in order to learn how to operate before actually performing the operation.

The illusion of 'being there' is called **telepresence**.

Software such as LandDesigner 3D by SierraHome can be used to investigate a range of garden landscapes, plants and garden furniture. Once a landscape has been designed, it can be 'walked through' on screen, just as it would be in real life.

Expert systems

A person who knows lots about a particular topic is often called an **expert**.

In an **expert system (ES)** a computer program is used to simulate the expert person's knowledge and experience of a particular situation. An expert system is also known as a **knowledge-based system (KBS)**, as the system depends upon the knowledge of the expert!

An expert system is usually made up of:

- a knowledge base (information about the situation)
- an inference engine (this analyses the information) and
- an end-user interface (this accepts inputs and generates outputs).

Expert systems do not use normal programming techniques. Instead artificial intelligence (AI) is used.

An expert system is special in that it:

- is about one particular situation or problem
- asks the user questions and receives answers from the user
- responds to the user's answer – it is **interactive**.

It can be used in medicine, for example, where the computer asks the patient about their symptoms and offers a range of answers. Doctors can also use it to help them determine the possible causes of illness, from which they can make the correct diagnosis and treatment.

Expert system at Greenfingers

An expert system is one of the most useful tools for helping growers with the day-to-day integrated decision support needed to grow their crops.

For example, Greenfingers could use an expert system to determine the best spacing for the growth of fruit trees. The computer would take into account soil type, slope, trailing system, cultivar, equipment width and root stock.

The expert system enables the producer to minimise economic risk and maximise profits. The user interacts with the program in a natural language similar to written English.

Activity

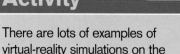

There are lots of examples of virtual-reality simulations on the Internet.

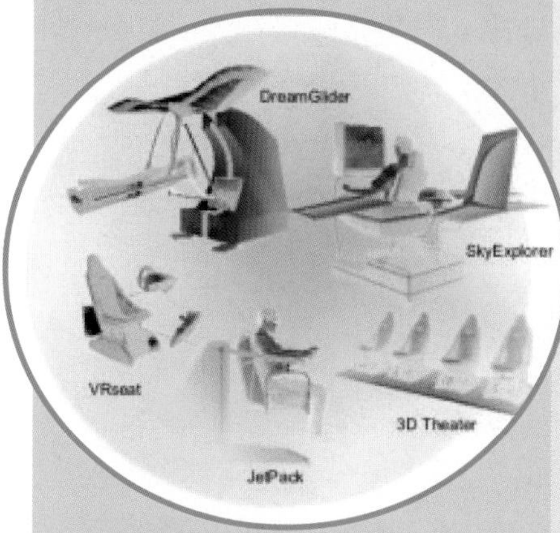

- Go to the site: http://www.dreamality technologies.com/ Investigate each of these virtual-reality simulations.
- Go to the site: http://www.bbc.co.uk/ history/multimedia zone/3ds/index.shtml to see some virtual reality reconstructions of historical events.

  You will need to download the plug-in: Cosmo Player 2.1 – please check with your teacher.

  This is a free plug-in which can be downloaded and installed on your computer. (It's a big download, so expect a delay the first time you look at these reconstructions on any computer.)

Why are models and simulations used?

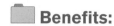

Benefits:

- **Safety**

  A safe environment can be used, e.g.:

  - A computer model of a nuclear reactor could be used to investigate the effects of altering conditions in the reactor.
  - In a flight simulator, a pilot can make mistakes without the danger of being hurt, killed or damaging expensive equipment.

- **Economic**

  - Expensive mistakes can be avoided by modelling and testing to see if the product works, before creating a full-size, real-life product.
  - In a flight simulator, a pilot can be trained without the cost of actually flying.

- **Time saving**

  - In science some real-life experiments can take days, weeks or longer to be completed. A computer simulation of the experiment can model the same experiment in seconds or minutes.

- **A range of conditions can be used**

  - Modifications to the original design can be made easily and the results quickly found out. For example, the effects of changing the input data on a model used by the Treasury for the Budget could be investigated to see what the effects would be for the economy.

Limitations:

- There are differences between simulation and reality. No model can fully match reality. For example, in a flight simulator, it is not possible to build in every possible reaction that the pilot might make when faced with a real-life situation.
- The accuracy/usability of output data from a model depends on the reliability of the input data and the rules the model is based on.

  For example, putting poor data in or using a badly designed model will give poor results.

Data, rules and time in a model

As we have already seen, a model must have input data and a set of rules by which it operates.

Data is the numbers which are fed into the model, e.g. the amount of fuel in a car.

Rules are built into the computer program and are used to generate an output value, e.g. the rate at which fuel is used at different car speeds.

If the data or rules are changed, then the model will behave differently. For example, the amount of fuel could be altered or the rate at which fuel is used could be changed.

The **time** in which a model operates will vary depending upon the type of model being used. A model may operate in **real time**, that is at the same rate as the real-life event. Other models may work more slowly or more quickly than the actual event.

Real-time models include:

- driving instruction using a simulator
- a flight simulator.

A model working **more slowly** than the real-life event would be:

- an action replay of a car crash when shown in slow motion.

A model working **more quickly** than the real-life event would be:

- a television weather forecast showing the weather for the next few days.

Stages in producing a model

1 Analyse the problem.

2 Design the model.

3 Make the model.

4 Test and adjust the model.

5 Validate the model.

6 Use the model.

Activity

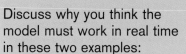

Discuss why you think the model must work in real time in these two examples:

- driving instruction using a simulator
- a flight simulator.

Test your understanding

Fill in the gaps

1 A computer model is a p__________ used to behave like a real situation.

2 A m__________ m__________ is set up using a s__________. This type of model uses f__________ and e__________.

3 A spreadsheet model uses i__________ data, f__________, which define the r__________ and o__________ data.

4 Output data can be displayed as a g__________, a t__________ or a s__________ w__________.

5 W__________ i__________ investigations using a s__________ are useful for investigating business situations.

6 A c__________ s__________ is a program which models a r__________ system.

7 V__________ r__________ enables a person to react within an environment created by a computer.

8 ES stands for e__________ s__________, which is a c__________ p__________ used to s__________ the expert person's knowledge and experience. This system is also known as a k__________ b__________ s__________.

9 A f__________ s__________ is used to train pilots without using a real aeroplane.

Multiple choice questions

10 A computer model is:
a) a computer program
b) an input device
c) an output device
d) a piece of hardware.

11 A computer model must be **validated**. This means:
a) inputting data
b) designing the system
c) checking that the model works correctly
d) analysing the problem.

12 When a model works at the same rate as the real-life event it is working:
a) as a spreadsheet
b) as an expert system
c) in virtual reality
d) in real time.

13 Another name for an expert system is:
a) virtual reality
b) a knowledge-based system
c) a simulation
d) a goal seek.

14 The first stage in making a model is to:
a) design the model
b) test the model
c) analyse the problem
d) validate the model.

15 A computer model used to predict the weather uses:
a) a computer game
b) an economic model
c) real time
d) numerical modelling.

16 An example of a computer game based on fantasy is:
a) a football manager simulation
b) fighting an alien spaceship
c) designing a garden
d) using a flight simulator.

CHAPTER 9

Data logging and control

In this chapter we will look at the way Greenfingers controls:

- the growth of plants in the greenhouses
- parking in the car park

and

- the selection of items from the warehouse shelves.

If plants are to grow well in the greenhouse, conditions such as temperature and humidity must be controlled. Similarly, the number of cars in the car park must be checked to avoid overcrowding.

In both cases data is needed, e.g. the temperature and humidity of the greenhouses and the number of cars entering and leaving the car park. This data is obtained using the process of data logging. **Data logging** is the automatic capturing and storage of data for use at some time in the future.

The data can be used by computer systems to control the conditions in the greenhouses and the number of cars entering the car park. These are examples of **computer control**.

We will look at the process of data logging and how it is used in the greenhouses. Next we will consider computer control and its application in the control of the conditions in the greenhouses and the arrangements for car parking.

Finally, we shall look at how computers can control robots in the selection of items from warehouse shelves.

Data logging 1

Did you know ?

Water can exist as ice (solid), water (liquid) or gas. As a gas, water can be steam or exist as **water vapour** in the air. Water vapour in the air is called humidity.

Greenfingers has greenhouses in which plants are grown for sale. To allow the plants to grow successfully the air temperature, light and humidity levels inside the greenhouses must be kept within certain **pre-set limits**. Similarly, the dampness of the soil must be kept within a certain **range** of values. A **computer control system** is used to keep the different conditions in the greenhouses within the pre-set limits.

The entry of cars to the car park at Greenfingers must be **controlled** so that no more than the **maximum number** of cars is allowed in at any one time to avoid the car park becoming overcrowded. A computer control system is used to detect cars entering and leaving the car park in order to make sure that the number of cars in the car park at any one time does not exceed the number of parking places.

In both the case of the greenhouses and the car park a system of data logging is used.

What is data logging?

Data logging is the automatic capturing and storage of data for use at some time in the future.

Features of data logging are:

- a computer system is used to collect (or **record**) the data **automatically**
- data is collected **over a period of time**
- **no human is required** to supervise the data collection as it is done automatically by a computer system.

Why use data logging equipment?

Data logging is used because:

- data can be logged over very short or very long periods of time without human intervention
- readings taken by the computer system are much more accurate and quicker than those taken by a human
- data can be obtained in dangerous and inhospitable environments, e.g. on the top of a mountain where weather conditions are monitored

Key points

Data logging is the automatic capturing and storage of data for use at some time in the future.

Features of data logging are:

- a computer system is used to collect (or record) the data automatically
- data is collected over a period of time
- readings taken by the computer system are much more accurate than those taken by a human
- data can be obtained in dangerous and inhospitable environments
- the data can be processed quickly into tables and graphs.

- recording data is a repetitive, boring and time-consuming task for a person. A computer can free the person to do other, more interesting jobs
- recorded data can be automatically downloaded onto a central computer using telephone lines or satellite links
- the data can be stored, usually on a backing store, for later use
- the data can be processed quickly into tables and graphs. This may happen continuously as the data is being collected or at some later time. Data can be analysed at a convenient time
- from the results of data capture/analysis, tables and graphs can be printed.

Figure 9.1 *A computer doesn't mind doing the boring jobs!*

Sensors

The data logging process is monitored by a **sensor**. A sensor is an **input device** used to **measure a physical quantity**. Sensors measure changes in environmental conditions.

There is a vast range of types of sensor, far too many to mention in detail here. However, some of the most common ones are:

Key points

- A sensor is an input device used to measure a physical quantity.
- Sensors measure changes in environmental conditions.

Sensor	Used to measure/respond to	Where used
Heat	Temperature	Greenhouse
Humidity	Water vapour (humidity) in the air	Swimming pool, greenhouse
Infra-red	Infra-red radiation, e.g. body heat	Security/alarm systems
Light	Light level	Greenhouse
pH	Acid/alkali levels e.g. acid rain, pH of soil	Environmental experiments
Pressure	Pressure	Pressure pads at traffic lights to measure traffic flow
Smoke	Smoke in the atmosphere	Fire alarm systems
Sound	Sound	Security/alarm systems
Tilt	Angle of tilt	To prevent a crane from falling over when lifting a large load
Touch	Detects if one object bumps into another	Computer-controlled robots

Table 9.1 *Types of sensors*

Data logging 2

Remote logging

Sometimes data has to be collected away from a computer using a **data logger**. This is a device pre-programmed to automatically collect and store data.

The data logger would be brought back, connected to a computer and the data downloaded from the data logger to the computer for display, storage and analysis. This is called **remote data logging**.

For example, if an experiment is done 'in the field' to record the pollution level in a pond, a data logger would be needed that could measure and store data until the unit is brought back and the data downloaded onto the computer.

Data loggers need to withstand harsh conditions, so they need to be robust. They would need to be waterproof if used in or near a pond or river, resistant to acids and alkalis if collecting data in a chemical plant.

Data logging in the Greenfingers' greenhouses

Sensors measure the temperature, light intensity, humidity and the dampness of the soil. If the plants are to grow well, each one of these measurements must be kept within **pre-set limits**. Computer control is used to make sure measurements are always within the pre-set limits. (This is discussed in more detail in the section on computer control.)

Types of data

The physical quantity being measured can have many different values. The sensors in the greenhouse produce **analogue data**.

For example, a light sensor or **light-dependent resistor (LDR)** could be used in the greenhouse to measure the amount of light inside the greenhouse throughout the day and night.

Did you know

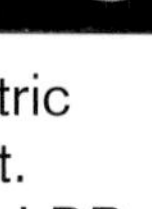

An LDR has a small electric current running through it. As more light falls on the LDR, the resistance to the flow of the current gets less, so more current flows through it.

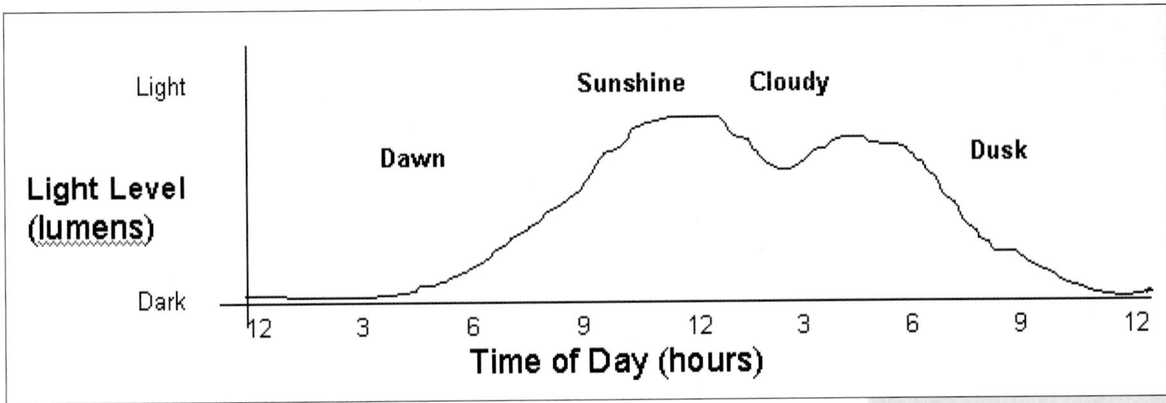

Figure 9.2 *Measuring light inside a greenhouse*

This data is then sent to the computer for processing, but a computer cannot understand analogue data. Computers can only work with **digital signals**. So, the analogue data must be converted to **digital data** which the computer can process.

An electrical device (an **interface**) called an **analogue-to-digital converter** (**ADC**) is used to change the analogue data into digital data. The varying voltage of the analogue signal is converted into digital pulses.

The ADC is connected between the sensor and the computer's **input–output port** and is called an **interface**.

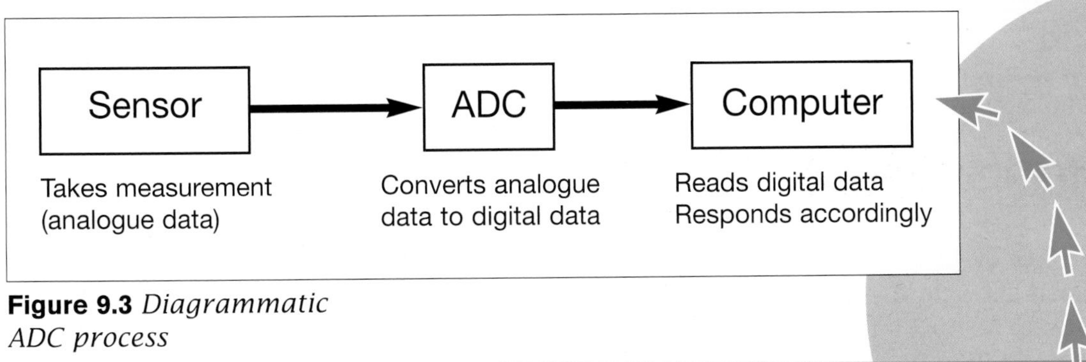

Figure 9.3 *Diagrammatic ADC process*

In computer control (see later), this process will need to be reversed to take the digital signal from the computer to an output device or actuator that requires an analogue signal. In this case a D to A converter is used.

Data logging 3

Digital data

Digital data consists of a series of pulses of electricity. At any time there are only two **states**, either there is a pulse of electricity or there is not a pulse. The electricity is either flowing or not flowing – it is ON or OFF.

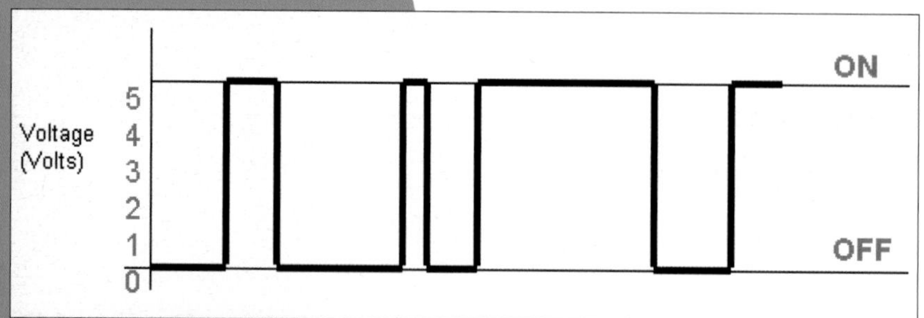

Figure 9.4 *Digital data*

A computer accepts digital signals as a series of 1s and 0s

ON = 1

OFF = 0

Did you know ?

A bit (or binary digit) is a 1 or 0 used to represent data.

A bit is the smallest unit of information recognised by a computer.

Bit pattern

The digital signals from the analogue-to-digital converter (ADC) are fed into the computer through a series of wires. At any moment in time, each wire will have a pulse (ON = 1) or no pulse (OFF = 0). The pattern of ONs and OFFs allows the computer to read the corresponding pattern of 1s and 0s. The pattern of 1s and 0s received by the computer is called a **bit pattern**.

The sensing of the light level in the Greenfingers' greenhouse would produce a bit pattern similar to the one below:

This is a simplified version showing only three wires from the ADC and so a 3-bit pattern is used.

In practice 16 or 32 bits would be used allowing the voltage range to be split into many more parts than 8.

This would give far greater accuracy in the converted readings.

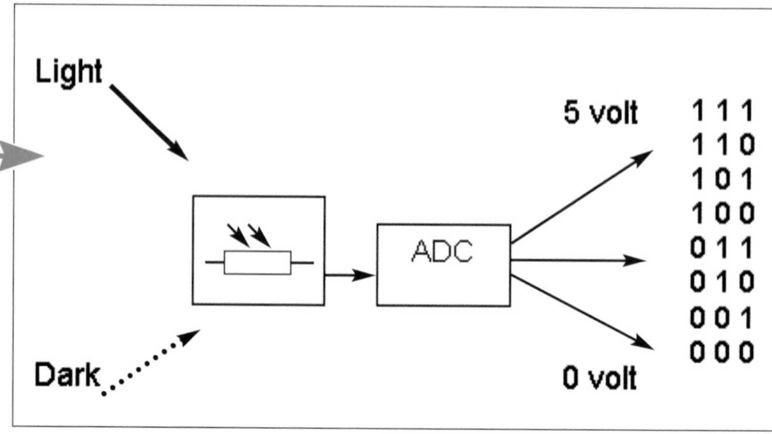

Figure 9.5 *A bit pattern*

Period of logging and time interval

When a data logging system is being set up, there are two very important decisions to be taken.

1 For how long will the logging take place?

Will data be recorded over a few seconds, days, weeks or even longer?
This is called the **period of logging**.

2 How often will a measurement be taken?

Will a measurement be made every one-thousandth of a second, once a minute, once a day?

The time between measurements is called the **time interval** or **frequency of sample**.

This affects how many measurements are made in the period of logging and so affects the amount of data which is available for analysis.

If the time interval is too long and the period of logging short, there will not be enough data to analyse.

If the time interval is too short and the period of logging long, there will be too much data!

Decisions about the period of logging and time interval will depend upon what is being logged.

Key points

- Most sensors produce analogue data.
- Computers can only work with digital signals. So, the analogue data must be converted to digital data which the computer can process.
- An electrical device (an interface) called an analogue-to-digital converter (ADC) is used to change the analogue data into digital data.
- The period of logging is the length of time over which data is recorded.
- The time between measurements is called the time interval or frequency of sample.

Stages in data logging

1. Set up data logging equipment.
2. Set up the period of logging.
3. Set the time interval (frequency of sample).
4. Collect the data.
5. Save the data, e.g. store on hard disk.
6. Analyse the data.

Control 1

Control systems monitor environmental conditions using **sensors**. These conditions can be changed using **actuators**.

An actuator is an output device which carries out an action upon an instruction from a computer. It generates signals to make other devices take some sort of action, e.g. a motor to open blinds.

A simple control system will usually consist of:

- a sensor
- an interface: a piece of hardware, maybe with some software, used to connect two parts of a system to allow communication. (The interface can convert data from one form to another, e.g. ADC.)
- a computer
- an actuator
- a feedback loop.

Types of control system:

- **Dedicated control systems**, such as those found in washing machines and dishwashers. These have built-in programs stored in a microprocessor.
- **Computer control systems** can be re-programmed and so are more flexible.

Control systems have: an input, a process and an output, as shown in the diagram.

Did you know ?

Signals sent by a computer to a device such as an actuator are **control signals**. Control signals are sent by the computer through an **output** port.

INPUT	PROCESS	OUTPUT
The data collected by the sensor. **Input devices:** **Heat sensor** (thermistor) **LDR** **Switches** e.g. push/reed/tilt.	The **process** will take place either in the interface box or in the computer system itself. Analogue signals will be converted to digital signals. **Processing software** such as **Logo** will control output devices.	**Output devices** include: Lights, sprinklers, loudspeakers, VDU, printer. An example of an **actuator** is a motor which can close the blinds in a greenhouse.

Figure 9.6 *Features of control systems*

In order to be able to act upon an input signal, the computer must be programmed how to respond. A **control program** must be written and installed on the computer. The computer will then react according to the level of the input signal received. It will decide whether or not to send an **output signal** to an output device.

For example, if the input shows that too much light is coming into a greenhouse, compared to the pre-set limits, the computer will send a signal to the actuator to close the blinds.

This process is constantly repeated with signal values being constantly fed back round the system through the process of **feedback**.

The control system is quite often designed using a **flow chart**.

A flow chart can be used to explain how the control system operates (see also page 216). A simple flow chart as in Figure 9.7 on page 206 can be drawn using these symbols:

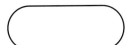

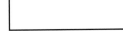

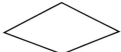

Start/End

This is used at the start and end points of the flow chart

Process

This shows an operation or action, e.g. 'Check input value'

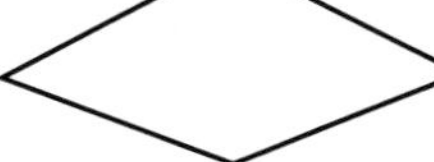

Decision

This contains a question, e.g. 'Is input value within required range?'

Why is computer control used?

- Computers do not need to eat, rest or sleep.
- Computer-controlled machinery is very accurate.
- Quality of output is consistent.
- Data is processed very quickly by computers, so machinery in turn responds rapidly, working fast.
- Computer-controlled machinery can work in places which might be inhospitable or dangerous for humans.

One important point is that, although the initial cost of installation of a computer-controlled system is high, operating costs are low when compared to the payment of workers' wages.

Key points

- Control systems monitor environmental conditions using sensors.
- Control systems have:
  - an input
  - a process
  - an output.
- A control program must be written and installed on the computer.
- A feedback control system uses the value of the output signal to affect the input signal.

Control 2

Feedback

In a simple control system a processor sends a signal to an output device which then takes some action. In most control systems the computer receives a signal back.

A **feedback control system** uses the value of the output signal to affect the input signal. Such a system uses a **feedback loop** involving the environment being monitored, a sensor to measure changes in that environment, an interface to convert signals, a computer to process the data and a computer-controlled output device to make appropriate changes.

The flow chart shows the cycle of sensing, processing (comparing to pre-set limits) and reaction (doing something if the input value is out of the range).

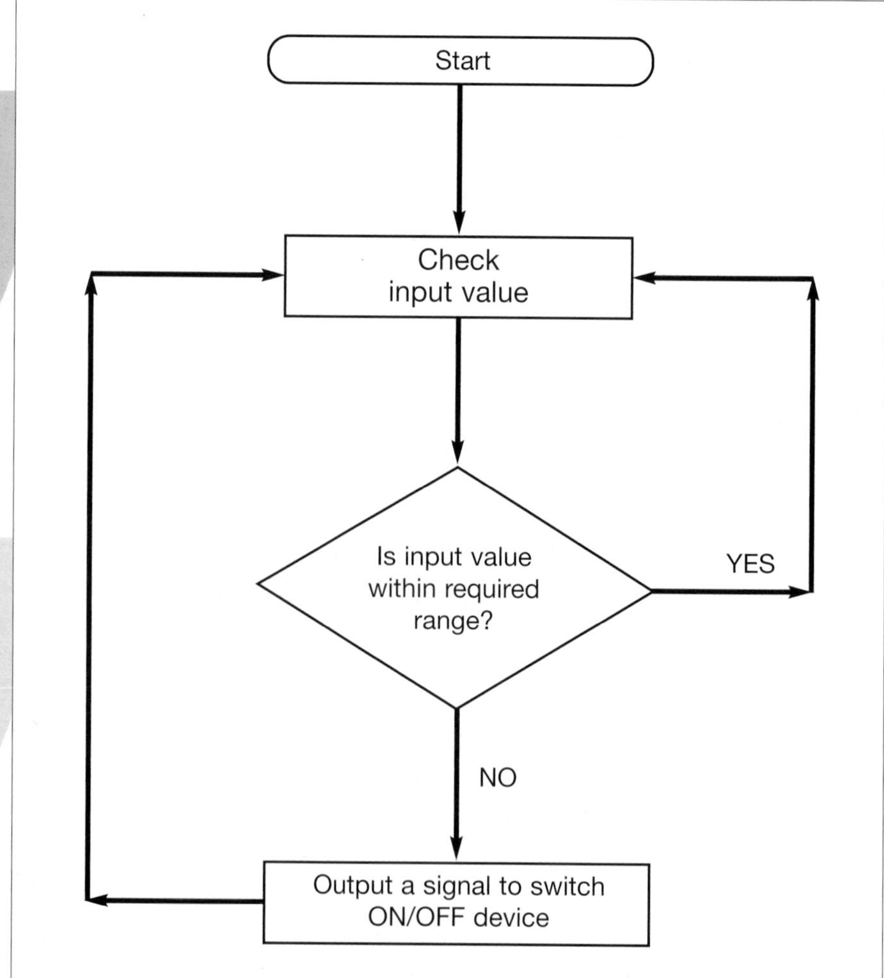

Figure 9.7 *The feedback loop*

Computer control in the Greenfingers' greenhouses

Each greenhouse needs to be kept at constant temperature and humidity. In addition, the amount of light entering the greenhouse and the dampness of the soil are also controlled – see Figure 9.8.

Each of these quantities will have a **pre-set range**. Limits will have been set and programmed into a computer. If a value is sensed to be outside of the pre-set range, then the computer will send a signal to activate a device in order to effect a change, bringing the value back in range.

Heat sensor
measures air temperature

Light sensor
measures light intensity – how much light is in the greenhouse

Humidity sensor
measures how much water vapour is in the air

Soil sensor
measures the dampness of the soil

To control temperature
- Fans switched ON/OFF
- Windows OPENED/CLOSED
- Heater switched ON/OFF

To control light
- Lights turned ON/OFF
- Blinds OPENED/CLOSED

To control humidity
- Water sprinklers turned ON/OFF

To control soil dampness
- Water sprinklers/hose pipe turned ON/OFF

Figure 9.8 *Computer-controlled greenhouse*

The data for temperature is captured by a **heat sensor** and the data for humidity by a **humidity sensor.** The computer receives the readings from both sensors. If the reading is analogue, then it is converted into digital format by the ADC.

The computer checks to see if readings are within the pre-set ranges.

For example, for temperature:

IF temperature too low	THEN	fans turned OFF *or* heaters turned ON *or* windows CLOSED
IF temperature too high	THEN	fans turned ON *or* heaters turned OFF *or* windows OPENED

The humidity would be checked in a similar way.

The computer would be programmed to **repeat** the process of taking sensor readings **at regular intervals** and then to act appropriately. This process would carry on for 24 hours a day, all year round.

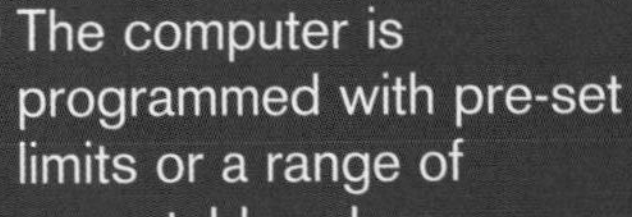

- The computer is programmed with pre-set limits or a range of acceptable values.
- If values are out of range, then the computer sends a signal to a device to bring values back into range.

Control 3 Real-time processing

Real-time processing

Real-time processing comprises:

- Input data from a sensor sent to a computer.
- A computer to process the data.
- Control signals sent back **instantaneously.**
- An action appearing to happen immediately – or in **'real time'**.

The advantages of real-time processing are:

- Very fast response to inputted data.
- The output can be used to alter and improve the input.

Unfortunately, for effective real-time operation a computer must be **dedicated** to the task being performed. The computer runs the same program all the time. It cannot be used for any other task.

Computers running in real time must have sufficient processing power and speed to handle extreme situations. For example, if, simultaneously, lots of people try to book tickets for an event, the computer system must be able to cope with the demand without crashing or making a mistake!

Examples of real-time processing systems:

- Missile guidance system
- Industrial and manufacturing processes
- Intensive care of patients in a hospital
- Airline reservation booking system
- Electronic point-of-sale system.

Greenfingers uses a computerised, real-time system for recording goods sold at the tills. As soon as an item has been bought by a customer, it is immediately recorded as being sold and the number on the stock database is reduced. There is always an up-to-date and accurate record of the stock items which are available for sale.

Greenfingers' car park

The entry of cars to the car park at Greenfingers must be controlled in real time if the car park is not to become overcrowded. The car park control system would operate as below:

- A **sensor** would register that a car has approached the entrance to the car park.

The sensor could be a **pressure mat** placed at the entrance.

A signal would be produced if a car goes over the pad.

The pressure pad sensor is a **digital** sensor because it is either **ON** or **OFF**.

- The signal data would be passed on to the computer.
- The computer would have been programmed with the maximum number of cars allowed into the car park at any one time, i.e. the total number of parking spaces in the car park.
- The computer would have counted the number of cars which have **entered** the car park.
- The computer would have recorded the number of cars which have **left** the car park.
- It would then compare the number still **IN** with the total number of parking places.
- **IF** the number still **IN** is less than the total number of parking spaces **THEN** a sign saying **SPACES** is displayed

and

- the car is allowed in.

But

- **IF** the number still **IN** is equal to the total number of parking spaces, **THEN** a sign saying **FULL** is displayed

and

- the car is not allowed in.

The following flow chart shows the condition for a car being allowed/not allowed into the car park.

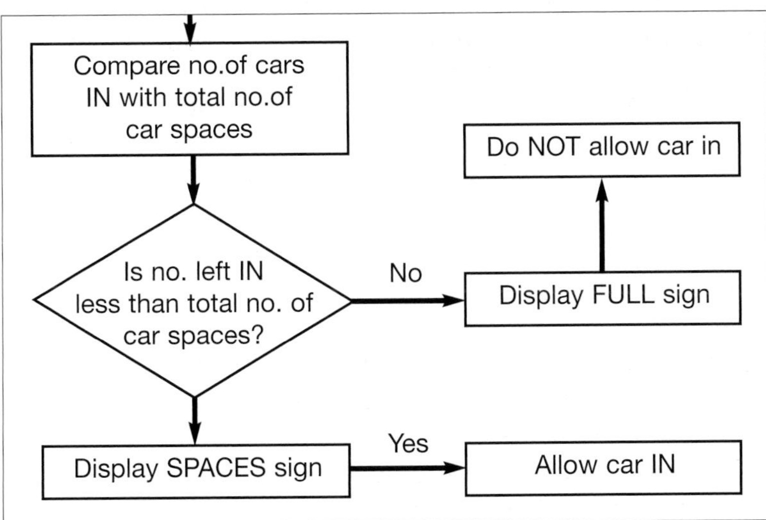

Figure 9.9 *Simplified flow chart of car parking system*

Key points

In real-time processing input data is processed very quickly to allow the output to have an immediate effect on the input.

Activity

Investigate what other type of sensor might be used at the car park entrance. Would this sensor be analogue or digital?

Robots 1

A **robot** is a device which is **programmed** to undertake a task.

Robots take many forms and are used in a variety of situations. As with the control systems described earlier, the use of robots has a number of advantages:

- They can work 24 hours a day, all year round without getting bored or needing a break.
- They can work faster than humans. As a result, productivity is higher than with human employees.
- The output is of a consistently high quality.
- They can work to greater degrees of accuracy than human workers.
- They can work in conditions which would appear hostile or dangerous to humans.

Unfortunately, robots are extremely expensive to buy and install. They could also be expensive to maintain. Also they are not as adaptable or versatile as people. They are usually built and programmed to do one particular job.

If a robot malfunctions (goes wrong), it cannot think for itself. If this happened on a production line in a factory, and it was not noticed, a robot might produce lots of faulty goods.

The financial cost of installing robots must be balanced by an increase in productivity and financial gain for the company.

From the workers' point of view, there is always the fear that the introduction of robots will cause unemployment. On the other hand, workers can be freed from boring and repetitive tasks. They can be retrained to do something more interesting.

A robot comprises:

- A sensor to monitor a change in the robot's environment – for example, its position or direction.
- A microprocessor to process the data from the sensor.
- An actuator or actuators to make the robot move or to allow the robot to operate an external device

Using robots at Greenfingers?

Greenfingers is looking to expand the size of its warehouse to store a much larger range of plants and garden furniture. On a visit to a large garden warehouse staff from Greenfingers saw the use of computer-controlled robots to collect items from the warehouse shelves.

The robots were used to move to different parts of the warehouse and then to select items from the shelves before returning with this stock to the despatch area.

To move around the warehouse the robot was built with a light sensor. This sensor enables the robot to follow a white, painted line on the warehouse floor.

If the robot is on track and is following the white line correctly, the light level received as an input will be within a **pre-set range**. The robot is allowed to carry on with its journey.

However, if the light level falls below the lowest value in the pre-set range, this means that the robot is veering off track. The robot's processor receives the signal about the low level of light and immediately, in **real time**, makes adjustments to the direction of the robot until it is back on track.

The movement of a robot is under the control of its microprocessor. Signals are sent to the microprocessor either along a cable connected to the robot, or by radio/microwaves.

Programming robots

A robot must be programmed before it can carry out a task. A **program** is a **set of instructions** given to the robot to tell it how to perform the task.

The robot can be programmed by someone:

- inputting the set of instructions or program for the steps in carrying out the task

  or

- by getting the computer to 'learn' what is required to complete the task. In this case, a person would actually do the task leading the robot through it. The computer would remember or record the sequence of steps and would then be able to perform the task unaided.

Robots performing different tasks will each need a separate program.

Computer programs are written in a code that the computer can understand. There are many different codes or **computer languages** which can be used.

Key points

- A robot is programmed to undertake a task.
- A program is a set of instructions.
- Computer programs are written using a computer language.

Advantages of using robots:

- They can work 24 hours a day, all year round without getting bored or needing a break.
- They can work faster than humans. As a result, productivity is higher than with human workers.
- The output is of a consistently high quality.
- They can work to greater degrees of accuracy than human workers.
- They can work in conditions which would appear hostile or dangerous to humans.

Disadvantages of using robots:

- Robots are extremely expensive to buy, install and to maintain.
- They are not as adaptable or versatile as people.
- If a robot malfunctions (goes wrong), it cannot think for itself.

Robots 2

Example 1

Instead of using a sensor to follow a line on the warehouse floor, the robot could be programmed to move around using the computer programming language **Logo**.

Logo has a set of commands which can be used to instruct a robot.

To move the robot in the warehouse, the robot would be programmed with a set of commands telling it how far to move and in which direction.

Area where a customer's ordered goods are stacked on shelves

To move the robot from A to B this program could be used.

FORWARD 2

LEFT 90

FORWARD 20

RIGHT 90

FORWARD 17

LEFT 90

FORWARD 3

FORWARD 2 means move forward 2 metres

LEFT 90 means turn 90 degrees anti-clockwise

Despatch area where goods are collected by customers

Robot

Figure 9.10 *A program for moving a robot across the warehouse floor*

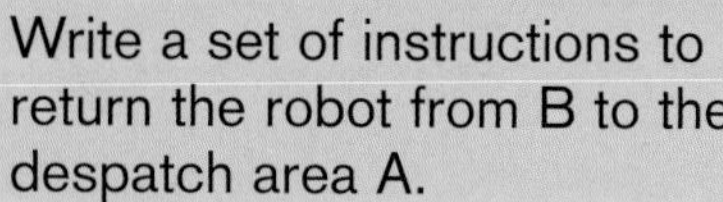

Activity

Write a set of instructions to return the robot from B to the despatch area A.

Example 2

In Example 1 the robot followed a set of instructions to move to an area where the required goods were stacked. The robot must now collect the goods from the shelves.

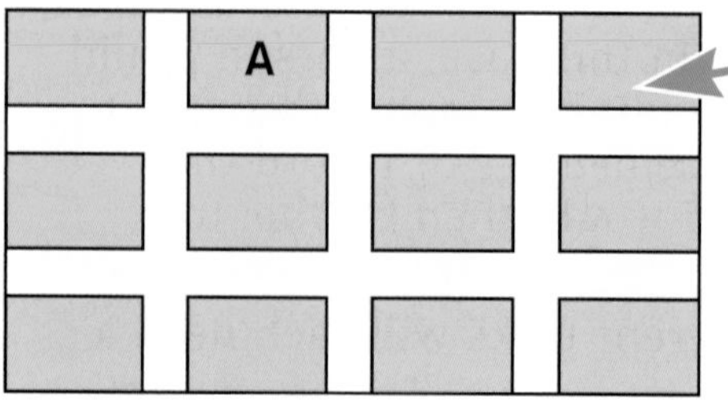

The robot must collect the item labelled **A.**

Robot

Figure 9.11 *Robot collecting goods from a shelf*

One program could be:

```
START
UP 3
LEFT 2
PICK UP
RIGHT 2
DOWN 3
END
```

The robot has now collected the item from the shelf and is ready to return to the despatch area.

Sensors in robots

As we have seen, a light sensor can be installed in a robot to assist the robot to follow a line on the ground.

Sometimes a sensor is included to assist with safety. For example, a 'bump sensor' is used to detect when the robot has bumped into another object. If this happens, the robot is programmed to stop moving forward in a way which might be dangerous.

It will then follow instructions to turn away from the obstruction and move forward again, hopefully finding a safe direction in which to travel.

Microprocessors

The control systems and robots used at Greenfingers use microprocessors.

A **microprocessor** is an integrated circuit or 'chip' which contains the central processing unit (CPU) of the computer. The control programs used in the control systems and by the robots are stored in a microprocessor.

Many household devices, such as a video cassette recorder and a microwave oven, use a microprocessor.

Key points

Control programs are stored in a microprocessor.

Activity

Look around your home to see how many devices are controlled by a microprocessor.

Test your understanding

Fill in the gaps

1 A computer control system is used to keep conditions within p__________ l__________.

2 Data logging is the a__________ capturing and s__________ of data for use at some time in the future.

3 A s__________ is an i__________ device used to measure a p__________ q__________. It measures c__________ in the e__________.

4 When data is collected away from a computer a d__________ l__________ is used.

5 An a__________ is used to generate signals to make another device move.

6 Many sensors produce a__________ data, but a computer can only accept d__________. So an i__________ called an a__________ to d__________ c__________ must be used.

7 The patterns of 0s and 1s received by a computer is called a b__________ pattern. B__________ is short for b__________ d__________.

8 When setting up data logging it is important to consider the p__________ of l__________ and the t__________ l__________.

9 Control systems have an i__________, a p__________ and an o__________. The computer must have a c__________ p__________ installed.

10 Control systems are often designed using a f__________ and most have a f__________ l__________.

11 When a control system responds immediately to an input it is said to work in r__________ t__________.

12 A r__________ is a device which is p__________ to undertake a task. A p__________ is a set of instructions.

13 A m__________ contains the c__________ p__________ u__________ of a computer.

Multiple choice questions

14 A sensor is used to:
a) change the environment
b) measure changes in the environment
c) turn on a fan
d) convert signals from analogue to digital.

15 Data logging does not require a person to be on hand to collect data. This means that it is better than using a person because it is:
a) cheaper
b) slower
c) quieter
d) more accurate.

16 A sensor used to measure the temperature of a greenhouse is called a:
a) pressure sensor
b) thermometer
c) heat sensor
d) infra-red sensor.

17 A robot could be programmed using the computer language:
a) Lego
b) Logo
c) Leggo
d) Letgo.

18 A feedback control system uses:
a) the value of the output signal to affect the input signal
b) the value of the input signal to affect the output signal
c) the value of the pre-set limits to affect the input signal
d) the value of the input signal to affect the pre-set limits.

CHAPTER 10

Systems analysis and coursework

Most business today use computers. From time to time these companies need to upgrade their systems. Similarly, companies that don't use computers come to realise their potential and decide to set up a system from scratch. They are about to embark on information systems projects. A large, complex project might involve a team of IT professionals for many months, even years. A smaller project will involve fewer people and will take less time. No matter how large or small an information systems project, the stages that have to be followed before reaching a conclusion are very similar.

- **Investigation**. Why does the user need to change the present system and, in general terms, what is required from a new system?
- **Analysis**. Looks in more detail at what a new system should provide and what hardware and software will be needed.
- **Design**. A detailed breakdown of the input, output and processing that will be required together with the user interface of the new system.
- **Implementation**. Following detailed design, the new system is put in place, tested, user documentation prepared and users trained to use it.
- **Monitoring**. Ongoing maintenance and development of the system.

In this chapter we are going to take a brief look at what is involved at each stage in the process and consider what we have learnt in relation to Greenfingers Garden Centre.

Following on from this we will see how the same processes can be applied to your coursework.

Diagrams 1

We will start by looking at data diagrams and their construction as they are an important part of systems analysis and will be referred to throughout this chapter.

Diagrams are used by systems analysts to provide a graphical style for describing computer systems (see page 205). They provide an easy-to-understand overview of the system and by using symbols can show:

- the devices to be used
- the order of tasks to be carried out in the new system
- the media used for input, storage and output
- the files used by the system.

You may recognise some of the symbols below from the flow chart on page 135 that has been used to illustrate the production of gas bills. The symbols you are most likely to use are shown below:

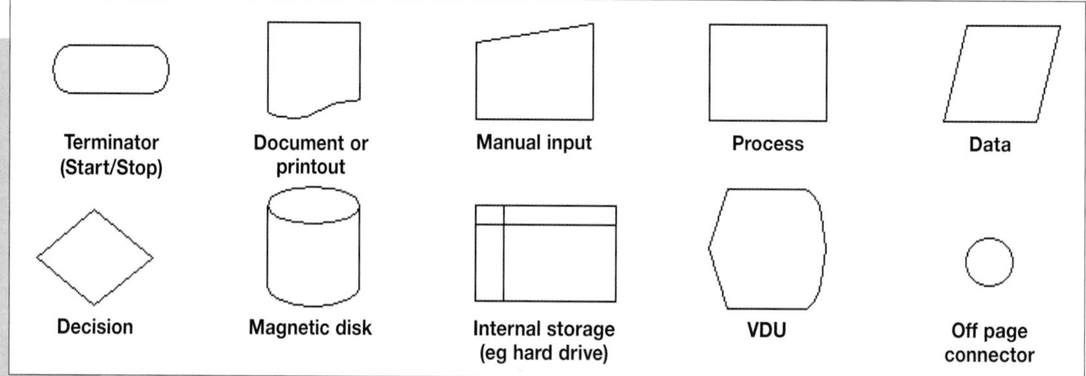

Figure 10.1 *Most frequently used symbols*

You will find all these symbols in AutoShapes on the Drawing toolbar in Microsoft Word.

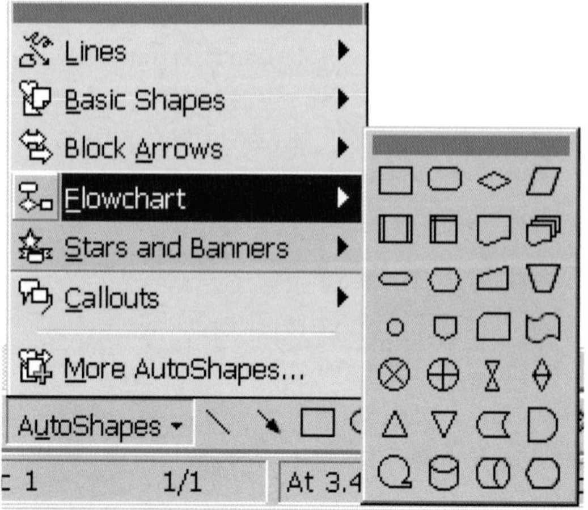

Figure 10.2 *Symbols on the Drawing toolbar*

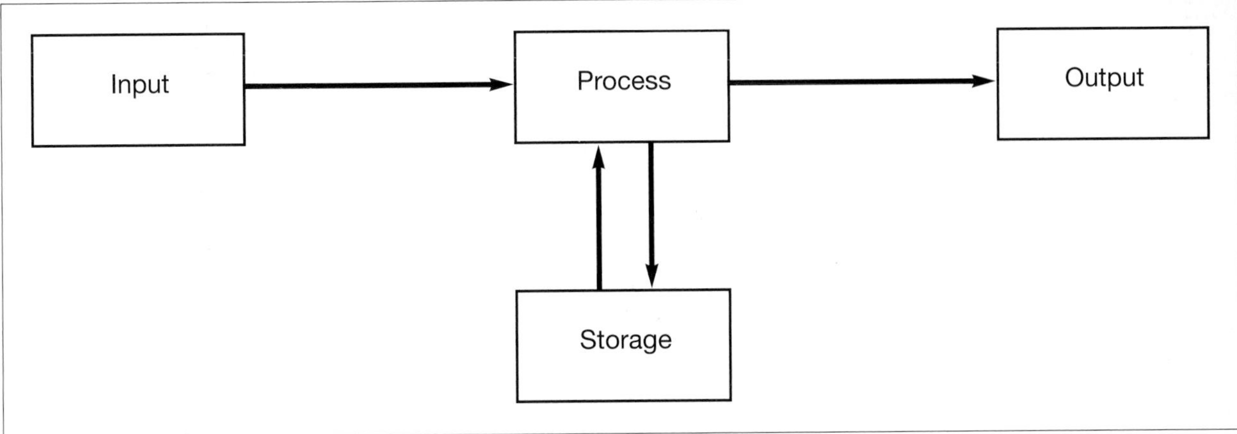

Figure 10.3 *The information processing cycle could be represented like this*

Handwritten draft
Keyed in
Saved on hard drive
Processed in Word
Saved on floppy disk
Document printed

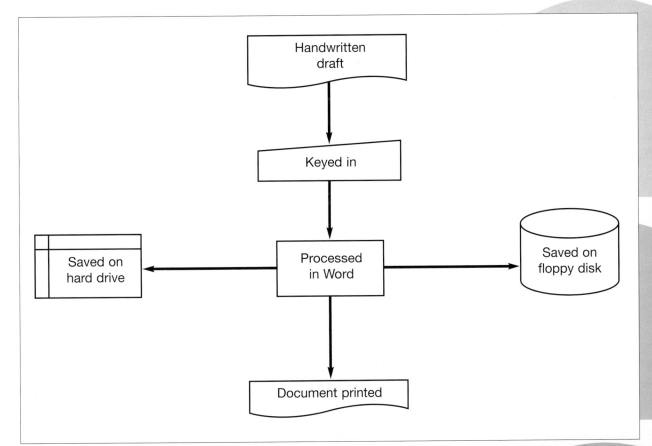

Figure 10.4 *Diagram showing the word-processing operation of editing text, saving and printing*

What we have shown you here are very simple ways of illustrating computer systems. When you move on to study IT at A level, you will learn how to produce more complicated diagrams.

Diagrams 2

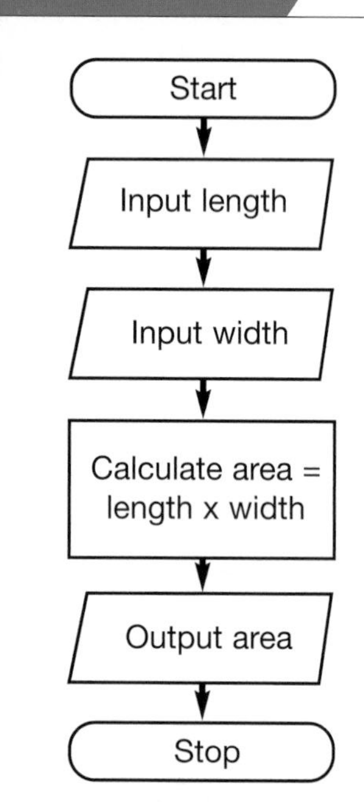

Figure 10.5 *Diagram illustrating algorithm*

Algorithm

Before a computer program can be written to work out a particular problem, it must be broken down into small steps (or instructions) that will offer a solution to the problem. These instructions are known as an **algorithm**. An algorithm is a set of instructions that, if followed exactly, will lead to a solution. For example, if you want to buy a new carpet for a room you calculate the area by multiplying the length by the width. If you think about this in terms of input, process and output you would produce an algorithm like this.

1 Input the length of the room.

2 Input the width of the room.

3 Calculate the length multiplied by the width.

4 Output the answer.

An algorithm can be illustrated diagramatically and Figure 10.5 represents the algorithm we have just described. The arrows indicate how one step leads on to the next. The algorithm assumes you know the length and width of the room. If it had included the question 'Do you know the length of the room?' you would have had to make a decision – Yes or No. Figure 10.6 shows the same diagram, but this time it includes decision boxes which give you the option to answer Yes or No.

Imagine you have been given a large pile of index cards which contain girls and boys names and ages. You have been asked to sort through them and make a list of girls over the age of 12. What are the steps you would follow to achieve this? Figure 10.7 typifies your actions.

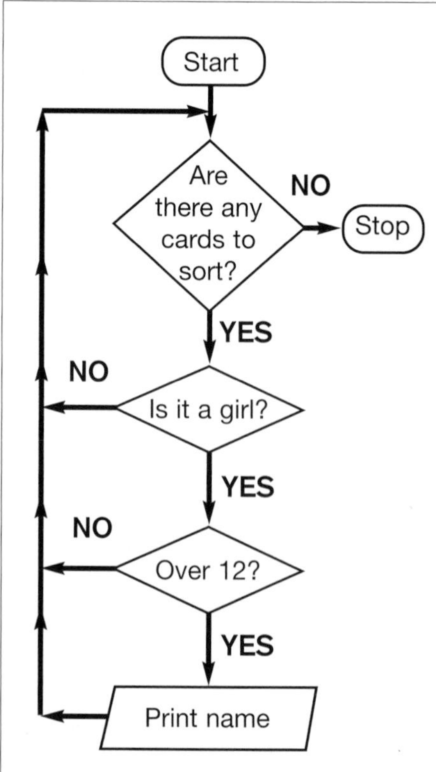

Figure 10.6 *Diagram for sorting information*

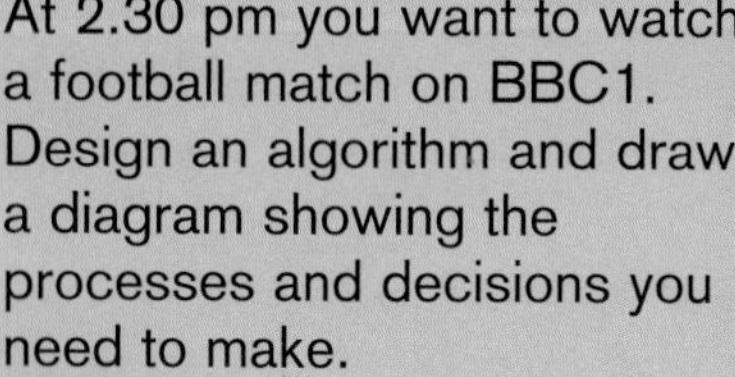

At 2.30 pm you want to watch a football match on BBC1. Design an algorithm and draw a diagram showing the processes and decisions you need to make.

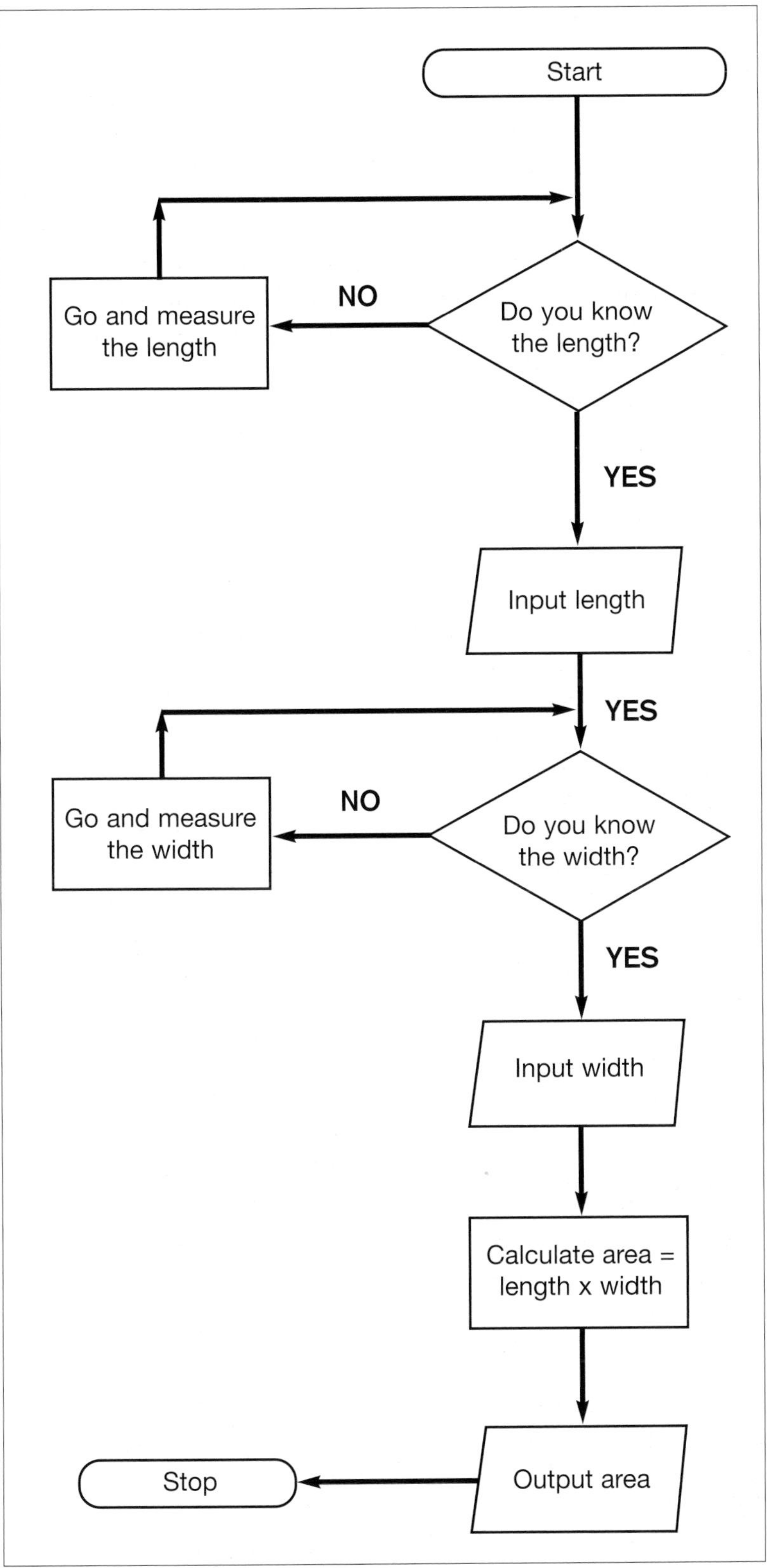

Figure 10.7 *Diagram with decision boxes*

Activity

The following list represents the steps you need to take to make a cup of tea. Put the list in the right order and produce a diagram using the symbols in AutoShapes.

1 Take tea bag out of cup
2 Put tea bag in cup
3 Pour boiling water in cup
4 Stir
5 Add sugar?
6 Boil the water
7 Add milk?
8 Fill kettle
9 Ready
10 Fetch cup.

Systems analysis 1

Figure 10.8 *Systems analyst observing Rose Garland working in Greenfingers' office*

Investigation

What are the reasons that might prompt the need for a new system or an overhaul of an existing system? Technology is constantly moving forward and you saw in Chapter 2 that the power of the computer has increased in leaps and bounds over the last few years, for example: faster processors and increased memory; flat screen monitors that take up less desk space; in many cases laser printers have replaced the need for dot-matrix printers. Software is constantly evolving too. As an example, Microsoft Word has been available in three versions over the last five years – Word 6, followed by Word 97 and now Word 2000! No doubt Microsoft is already well advanced in developing the next version. Methods of communication are also changing rapidly. The use of e-mail means that more staff must have individual access to computers. In the coming years more and more business will be carried out over the Internet and the arrival of teleworking, laptop computers and mobile telephones mean 'the office' can be situated anywhere.

If an organisation wishes to remain competitive it must keep its systems up-to-date and any one of these reasons might force it to re-evaluate its existing arrangements. Whatever the reason, once a decision has been taken that a new system is required, an investigation must be made to determine whether the new system is technically feasible and whether it is economically viable, i.e. will the costs of installing the system reduce overall operating costs and increase productivity or performance in the longer term?

Feasibility study

This investigation is usually referred to as a **feasibility study**. A feasibility study looks at the existing business practice and any problems associated with it. Its purpose is to consider in general terms what the new system should achieve and whether the current system could be modified to meet the new needs. If a new system is considered necessary, an estimate of the overall cost and a time scale for implementation would be given. The feasibility study will be considered by the management of the company who will make the final decision on whether to proceed to the next stage.

If we return to Greenfingers Garden Centre, they have several reasons for installing a new system:

- The existing hardware and software is out of date.
- The business is expanding into new, larger premises at Seahaven.
- They are going to open two new garden centres at Dulton and Newford.
- They will be selling a wider range of products.
- They will be employing more staff.

The fact that they are about to move into new premises and open the two new branches provides the perfect opportunity to bring their systems up-to-date.

Analysis

A detailed analysis of the current system would be carried out by a systems analyst whose role would be to take the feasibility study one step further by conducting a detailed examination of the individual components of the proposed system. This would include:

- Investigation of hardware and software currently in use and proposals for replacing it.
- Observation of current work practices to see how jobs are done now and what improvement could be achieved.
- Interviews with staff at all levels to find out what they want from the new system or a survey of existing staff by questionnaire.
- Study of existing business documentation such as forms, invoices, etc.

Following this detailed review of the existing work practices, the systems analyst will be in a position to outline the objectives of a new system – the input, process and output. He/she will use a series of data-flow diagrams to illustrate the way data flows within the current system and to show how it will flow in the new system. Diagrams would be made to illustrate input screens and the format for documents that will be output from the new system. In addition, he/she will update the original estimate for the overall cost of the system and the time-scale for implementation.

The analysis report is passed on to a team of system designers and will contain all the information necessary for them to work on the detailed design of every aspect of the new system prior to its implementation.

Activity

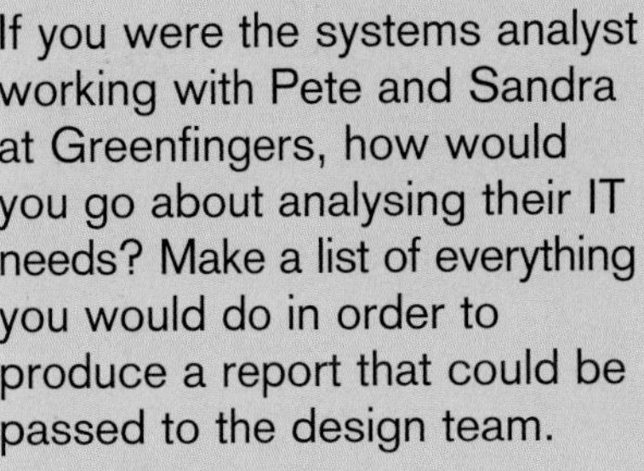

If you were the systems analyst working with Pete and Sandra at Greenfingers, how would you go about analysing their IT needs? Make a list of everything you would do in order to produce a report that could be passed to the design team.

Look at page 227 to see if your ideas matched ours.

Activity

Pete and Sandra have called you in to advise them on the best ICT solutions to meet the needs of the expanding business. Think back over everything you have learnt about IT in the earlier chapters of this book and use this new expertise to come up with an outline proposal for Greenfingers Garden Centre. Share your ideas with your teacher and the rest of your class and see if their ideas match yours. You will find our solution on page 226.

Systems analysis 2

Design

It is only after detailed analysis that the design of the new system can begin and each stage must be thought about in great detail. A systems designer usually undertakes this stage of the project, although sometimes the systems analyst will continue his/her work.

Output

The intended output from the system will determine the processing capability needed by the rest of the system and is therefore the first stage in the design process. Output might be to a VDU or a control device such as a heater or motor. Alternatively, the output might be the production of documents or the design of reports from a database. The systems designer will need to know what information should be displayed and, in the case of document production, how many documents will be required and how often. Test plans will be drawn up prior to implementation of the system to check the final output meets the original criteria.

Input

Having ascertained the output, the systems designer will need to think about what data needs to be input into the system and how. If manual input is required, how will the user interact with the system? Will a data-input screen need to be designed? Manual input might be through a keyboard whereas automatic input might be via a bar-code reader or sensor. If data is to be input into a database, a breakdown of data will be needed to establish the data type, and the volume of data to be handled so that an estimate can be made on the storage capacity required.

Software

The system will need an operating system and software in order to process the data. Very large organisations might have software programs specially written for their individual purposes but this is a very expensive and lengthy process. Most companies will be able to use standard application software that has been written by software houses and designed to meet the needs of a variety of users. The advantage of this is that they can start to use it immediately and it is very much cheaper. If 'off-the-shelf' software is being used, the designer will produce detailed notes of any system configuration that might be necessary. For example, the design and structure of folders/sub-folders, macros or templates or the creation of spreadsheets or databases. Test data will be designed to ensure the new system works as it is meant to. The systems designer must also consider methods to ensure security of data.

Hardware

The systems designer is responsible for specifying the number and type of workstations to be provided, together with printers and other peripheral devices. He/she will also decide whether a local or wide area network is necessary and will advise on security measures to protect the hardware.

When the designer has finished, he/she will provide a set of documentation including:

- System diagrams.
- Written descriptions.
- Specimens of data input and output documents.
- Data-input screens.
- Diagrams representing directory/folder structure, etc.

The completed design will provide sufficient detail to enable other members of the team to implement the new system in full.

Activity

The systems analyst's report on Greenfingers Garden Centre included the following:

> '... Discussion with the office manager identified a need for a new system to record the hours worked by part-time staff. The long-term objective is to issue staff with magnetic swipe cards but budget constraints have forced this to be deferred. As an interim solution it has been agreed that staff will complete a monthly time sheet. Data from this will be entered manually into the system to calculate monthly pay and a pay slip will be produced. The data required will include the employee's name, staff number, branch, month and year, together with a record of the days worked and the start and finish times. ...'

As the systems designer you must produce the specimen data input document described in the analyst's report. Remember to provide enough detail to enable your design to be produced exactly as you picture it.

When you have finished your design, swap with a friend and see if you can each produce what the other has designed. Look on page 228 (Figure 10.10) to see if your design is anything like ours.

Systems analysis 3

Implementation

As we have already seen the design specification will be so explicit that implementation is just a question of following the design instructions – a little bit like assembling a model or furniture piece by piece. During this stage lots of things will be happening at the same time:

- Hardware and software will be purchased.
- Networks installed.
- New programs written or existing software configured.
- The system and/or software tested using the test plan.
- User documentation written.
- Staff trained.

Figure 10.9 *An office being refitted with computer equipment might involve new cabling, repositioning of workstations or office moves*

Activity

How do you think Greenfingers Garden Centre will implement the initial phase of their new system? If you recall, the systems analyst's recommendations included the installation of a wide area network, new computerised office systems and electric point-of-sale terminals. Discuss a possible outcome in small groups and then compare your ideas with the rest of your class.

If a complex program is being written, the program will be split into small parts and a team will work on each part in isolation, bringing the whole program together at the end. However, as we have seen it is more likely that configuration of 'off-the-shelf' software will take place and the team will create the spreadsheets, databases, macros and templates recommended by the designers and will produce the documentation to accompany it.

User documentation

User documentation is provided for the people who will be using the software to help them deal with everyday problems. It will include instructions to perform special functions within different software applications, such as using any macros or templates that have been designed, and illustrations to help and reassure users.

Technical documentation

Technical documentation is written to explain the technical set-up of the system so any future modifications can be carried out with the minimum of disruption.

Testing and training

When the hardware has been installed it will be tested to make sure it all works and that communication has been established between all the devices. Similarly, any configuration to software will also be tested. New spreadsheet and database files must be checked to ensure they produce the results expected before they are brought into use.

Staff must be trained to ensure they know how to use the new systems. An investment in training will help eliminate problems and stress when introducing the new system.

New software systems are seldom implemented directly in case there are any serious errors that need to be rectified. More often they are run in parallel to the old system for a period of time or phased in slowly, section by section. No business can afford to be without their computer system, nor can it afford to lose data, so these measures are taken to ensure there is no disruption to the day-to-day operation of the company.

Monitoring/evaluation/maintenance

During the design and implementation stages, everything possible would be done to ensure a smooth transition but it is only when the new system is in use that any minor errors may come to light. For example, there might be a coding error that has to be rectified or changes may be needed to input screens or printed reports. The checks are carried out to ensure the system has met the original requirements, is working properly and is easy to use. The system is being monitored and evaluated and this is an ongoing process because at any time the computer user may need slight modifications or additions. If the system has been well designed any future modifications will be quite straightforward, enabling it to meet the changing needs of the business for several years to come.

Exactly the same process would take place at Greenfingers Garden Centre and they would then be able to move on to the next phase in their programme of development and expansion.

Key points

Any project to install a new computer system or upgrade an existing system will go through the following processes:

- Investigation. Establishing whether a new system is necessary, exactly what it will be used for and whether it is a viable proposition.
- Analysis. Breaking the problem down into parts and studying each part in detail.
- Design. Solutions to each part of the overall system will be designed.
- Implementation. The design proposals are put into effect, tested and user documentation prepared.
- Evaluation. The final stage in the process checks that the original requirements or objectives have been met, are working properly and whether any modifications are necessary which is an ongoing process.

Conclusions 1

What conclusions will be arrived at for Greenfingers Garden Centre?

Investigation

The investigation, or feasibility study, would be carried out in association with Pete and Sandra Wellings. At this stage of the process they would probably reach an outline decision to replace all the existing hardware and software with a new computer network so that all three centres would have access to the same data.

Other areas they might wish to consider in more detail are:

- The use of electronic point-of-sale terminals in the sales areas to record sales and monitor stock levels.
- The introduction of a computerised database to record stock details.
- The introduction of computerised office systems, including word processing, spreadsheet, database, and e-mail and the configuration of the software.
- The installation of a computer-controlled telephone system.
- A system for automatically recording the hours worked by part-time staff.
- Automatic calculation of salaries and payment of salaries by BACS.
- Establishing a web site.
- The introduction of a computerised presentation to provide customers with information about the jobs they should be doing in the garden at any particular time of the year.
- System security.
- The introduction of a computer-control system to maintain environmental conditions in the greenhouses.
- The introduction of a computer-aided design system for garden design.
- The introduction of a computerised database of plants and plant care for customer use.

Analysis

The systems analyst working with Greenfingers Garden Centre would need to make several visits in order to understand how the business was run at the present time. The ideas raised at the feasibility stage would be looked at in greater detail and some might be put on hold until a later date. A lot of time would be spent in discussion with Pete and Sandra and as a result, a list of priorities will become apparent which the systems analyst would develop. He/she would spend time with Rose Garland in the office and Salim Hassan in the shop to see what their jobs involved and to find out what ideas they might have for the new systems. Copies of invoices, order forms, letterheads and any other business documentation would be required by the systems analyst to help him/her formulate the objectives of the new system. The final budget for the new system would need to be agreed and a time plan for implementing the new system specified.

The report from the systems analyst would be passed on to the design team so that each element of the system could be planned in detail. In the case of Greenfingers Garden Centre the report might recommend phasing in the new system as follows:

- Install a wide area network linking all three garden centres.
- Test the new system initially in Seahaven and then bring Dulton and Newhaven online as they open.
- Introduce computerised office systems, including word processing, spreadsheet, database, e-mail and a computer-controlled telephone system.
- Introduce a database system to record customer details.
- Use electronic point-of-sale terminals in the shops to record sales and monitor stock levels.
- The introduction of a computerised presentation to provide customers with information about the jobs they should be doing in the garden at any particular time of the year.
- Establish systems for hardware and data security.

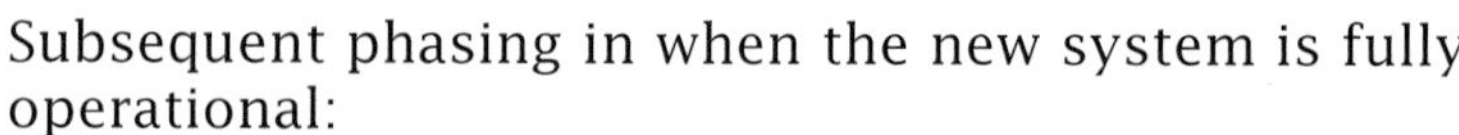

Conclusions 2

Subsequent phasing in when the new system is fully operational:

- A method of automatically recording the hours of part-time staff.
- Automatic calculation of salaries and payment of salaries by BACS.
- Development of a web site.
- The introduction of a computer-control system to maintain environmental conditions in the greenhouses.

Further investigation into:

- The introduction of a computer-aided design system for garden design.
- The introduction of a computerised database of plants and their care for customer use.
- The possible future use of e-commerce.

Default Margins

Logo | Greenfingers Garden Centre / Monthly Time Sheet — Arial 14pt Bold

line

Arial 12pt Bold – Name ______ Branch ______ / Staff No ______ Month/Year ____/200_

Shade light grey

Bold –

Date	Time Started	Time Finished
1		
2		
3		
30		
31		

Signed ______ Date ______

Authorised ______ Date ______

Design

This is a possible design the systems designer might have produced from the analyst's report. Did your design include as much information as this one? If not, it was incomplete and might not have been implemented as you had intended.

For example, a detailed design will specify size of margins, style and size of fonts, line spacing, position and size of any graphics and an indication of where the graphic will come from.

Figure 10.10 *A possible design from the analyst's report*

Implementation

Greenfingers Garden Centre is moving into new premises and so the installation of the system can go ahead without any disruption to the business. Provision for cabling would be made during construction and new desks would be in place before the hardware was introduced. Security of hardware would be incorporated with the building security system. For example, alarms to rooms might be introduced and the hardware could also be secured to the desktop.

The hardware would be installed and an operating system compatible with a network would be needed. User accounts and passwords would need to be set up together with a suitable system for organising data files. Security of data would be a priority and anti-virus software would be installed.

The office would probably use off-the-shelf software such as Microsoft Office or Lotus Smartsuite for word processing, spreadsheet and database use, and would most likely purchase a business accounting package such as Sage. Configuration of the software would be carried out, such as the creation of databases, macros and templates. All software, including the use of e-mail, would be tested to ensure it produced the expected outcome. Staff would need to be trained to use the new software – this might be done in-house or through an outside training provider.

On the retail side of the business a database detailing stock would need to be set up and the electronic point-of-sales terminals installed. Provision for this would also have been made during construction and so would not disrupt day-to-day sales. Stock levels would need to be counted and entered into the database. Staff would be trained to use the EPOS terminals. Extensive testing of the system could take place before the business transferred from the old premises.

Once the Seahaven centre was operating smoothly the new sales teams from Dulton and Newford would spend time at Seahaven to learn the systems. In this way they would be fully trained when the two new garden centres opened and came online.

Test your understanding

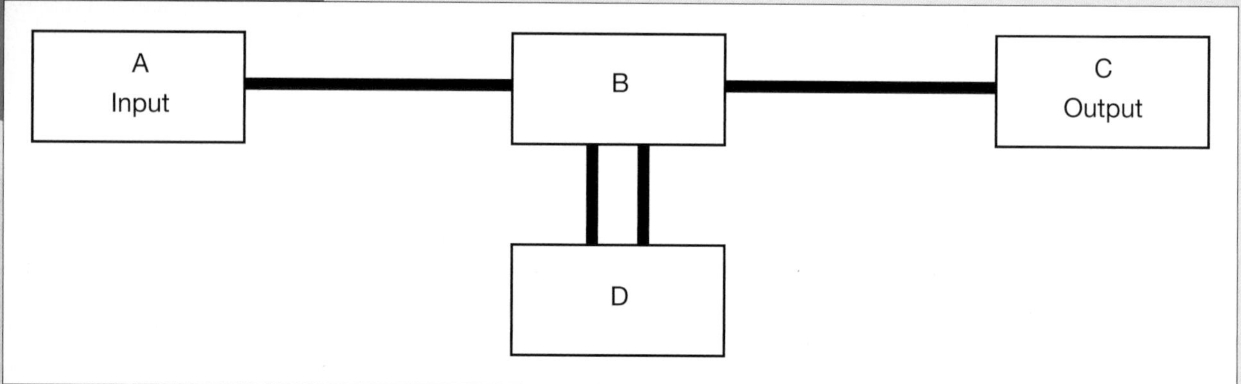

Questions 1–6 relate to the diagram above.

1 What is the purpose of B and D?

2 Indicate the direction of data flow between each component.

Answer questions 3–6 by choosing the correct words from a–l below.

3 Which two of the following does A represent?

4 Which two of the following does B represent

5 Which two of the following does C represent?

6 Which two of the following does D represent?

a) adding and subtracting
b) digital camera and floppy disk
c) mouse and sensor
d) plotter and VDU
e) VDU and mouse
f) keyboard and graphics tablet
g) tape and hard drive
h) sorting and searching
i) printing and microphone
j) sensor and printer
k) speaker and printer
l) floppy disk and hard drive

Complete sentences 7–11 using the correct phrase from a–e below.

7 Systems analysis means ______________________

8 Monitoring means ______________________

9 Systems design means ______________________

10 Implementation means ______________________

11 Systems diagrams and flow charts
are a means of: ______________________

a) putting the solution in place and testing it
b) describing a computer system in graphical style
c) breaking the problem down into parts and proposing a solution
d) checking that the solution is working the way the systems analyst intended
e) producing the instructions that will enable the solution to be put into action.

Are the following statements True or False?

12 Staff using the system are interviewed in order to produce a test plan.

13 Monitoring and maintenance is an ongoing process.

14 User documentation is written to help the systems analyst propose a solution.

15 The feasibility study looks at how the new system is performing.

16 The systems analyst tests that the system is working properly.

17 An algorithm is used to illustrate a new system.

18 Technical documentation is produced to help people use the new system or software.

19 The systems analyst outlines the objectives of the new system.

Coursework

The processes that we have been looking at are referred to as the information systems life cycle.

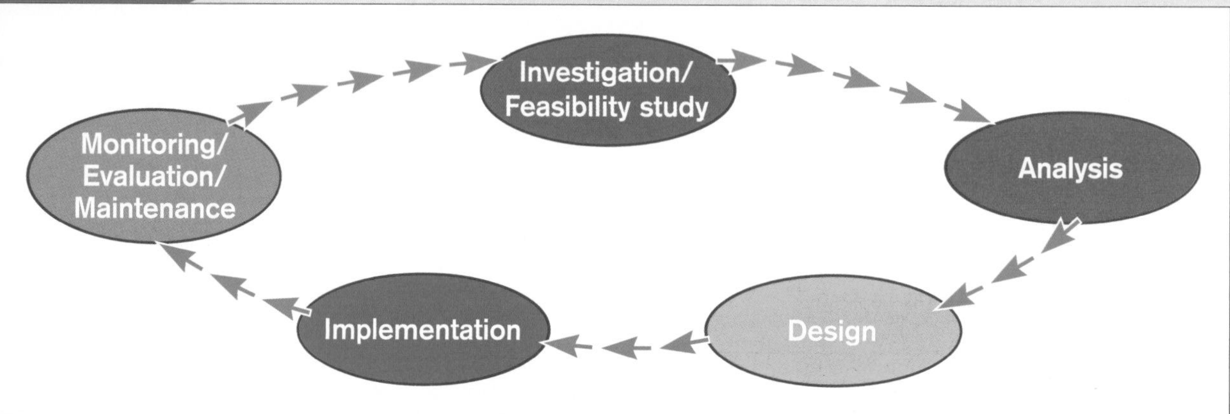

Figure 10.11 *The information systems life cycle*

During the coming months you will put together a collection of coursework that accounts for 60% of your final examination grade and you will be able to use the same processes to help you identify and solve four distinct problems for your coursework collection.

Planning your coursework

The four pieces of coursework added together account for 60% of the overall examination mark, so if you work hard on your coursework, it will make all the difference to your final grade.

Here are some general hints to help you with your coursework:

1. When you have agreed a topic with your teacher it is important that you plan your work carefully. An overriding consideration in planning your project must be the time and resources you have available to complete it. Your teacher will guide you on this and will make sure you don't embark on something that is going to be too big to finish. You must also bear in mind that you will still have work to do for the other subjects you are studying.
2. Don't waste time in class working on things that can be done away from the classroom. Use the time you have with your teacher to get any help you need.

3 - You should word-process your work and make sure it is presented clearly and accurately.
  - Don't rely solely on spelling and grammar checks. Proof read your work to make sure it makes sense.
  - Check that your headings are all the same style and that you have not changed font style in the middle of the text.
  - Use Print Preview before printing your work and check that your page breaks are in the right place.
  - Use the header and footer areas of the page for your name, page number and title of the work.
  - It might be helpful to insert the date and time so that you can assemble your print-outs in the right order.

4 Use folders/directories to keep all your project work together and save updates of your work regularly with different file names. In that way, in the unlikely event you find yourself with a corrupt file, you can revert to the previous version and you will not have too much work to repeat.

5 Make regular backup copies of all your data files as a safety precaution. Keep the backup disk in a safe place and don't use it as the only copy of your work in case you lose or damage the disk. It is sensible to save your coursework on the school or college system and on your computer at home too.

6 Keep all the print-outs of your work because you will need to hand in evidence to show how you have arrived at the solution to your project. A good project will always show that improvements have been made throughout the process. Keep the print-outs clean in a plastic folder.

7 Design a front cover showing the title of your project, your name and the date. It might be useful to save the design as a template so that you don't waste too much time reproducing the same thing for each piece of coursework.

On the pages that follow we are going to look at the process headings you will follow for your coursework.

Identify

Identifying a suitable topic for each project can be difficult, however your teacher will be able to help you choose something suitable. Ideally you should try and identify a 'real' user who would benefit from your project, but in reality the 'real' user might be another student in your class. What you are looking for is someone with a problem that can be solved with the help of IT 'tools' and it is important that you have a 'real' user who will be able to evaluate your finished project for you.

The 'problem' could be anything:

- The introduction of a computerised system to replace a task currently performed manually.
- The production of a newsletter or programme for a school event.
- The creation of a spreadsheet for the collection of data and the graphical presentation of the results.
- The use of an existing database to produce a mail-merge letter.
- Writing macros or producing templates.
- Creating a series of web pages.

Once you have identified a 'real' user with a problem, you will be able to prepare your statement 'identifying' the project. This is the first stage of your coursework and the statement will describe the user and the problem and provide some background information. It should also consider alternative ways of solving the problem and should justify the method you have chosen. Finally, you must explain what the user expects to be able to do when your project is finished – this is the project objective or the user requirement.

To make this easier for you, it might be helpful to make notes under a series of headings before preparing your statement. If you do this you are unlikely to forget to write something important. Ask your teacher to let you have copies of the prompt sheets we are using in this chapter and which are available in the Tutor's File.

IDENTIFY

What you will write under this heading is the equivalent of the feasibility study which looks at the existing business practice and the problems associated with it. You should describe in general terms what the new system should achieve and consider whether the existing system can be modified. Estimate the time-scale for completing the project.

Who is the 'real' user?

- Describe the person for whom you are working on the project. If relevant to the problem, describe the job the person holds or say what the connection between the person and the problem is. For example, the user might own a business, run a club, have a hobby, etc.

What is the current problem?

- Explain the problem and say in very general terms what you are being asked to do to solve it.

Why has this problem arisen?

- Provide some information about how the job or task is done now.

What is the objective or user requirement for this project?

- This is the first thing you must think about because everything else will follow on from the objective. Describe in some detail what the 'real' user wants to be able to do when you have finished the project. It is better to say 'the user would like a template he can use every month to avoid repeating calculations' than 'the spreadsheet will make things quicker'. In other words, quantify and justify your objectives.

What are the different ways this problem can be solved?

- Sometimes there might be more than one way to do the same thing. For example, a record of names and addresses could be produced in a database or spreadsheet. A newsletter could be produced in word-processing or desktop-publishing software. Give a brief comparison of the various ways.

What is the best way to solve the problem and why?

- Having compared the alternative solutions, you must decide the most effective way to solve the problem and give your reasons for coming to that decision. In other words, you must justify your choice. For example, you might have been limited by the software/hardware available to you or you might be more familiar with one software application than another. Whatever the reason, share it!

Analyse

Now that you have identified your outline plan, the next stage is to break it down into more detail. The first stage will be to collect together any information you need so that you can complete the project. This might involve visiting your 'real user' to interview him/her or you might need to design a questionnaire in order to collect data for analysis. You will need to prepare some initial sketches of input and output screen designs, spreadsheet layout, database fields, etc. The designs can be handwritten sketches without a lot of detail at this stage and should be checked with the user to ensure they match his/her requirements.

Before you can plan much further ahead you should prepare suitable diagrams to show the sequence of operations needed to solve the problem. These should relate back to the objectives or user requirements you specified when you produced your identify statement. The diagrams will help you identify the hardware and software you will need to complete the project. Once you have worked out the flow of data you can consider the input, processes and output of your project.

Data can be input by various methods but it must be checked for accuracy. How will you do this?

The processes will vary depending on the software you are using but you must specify the particular 'tools' that make the software appropriate for the project. List the formatting tools you will use in a word-processed project such as a report, for example page numbers, spell check, bullets, justification. In a spreadsheet you might need to change the column width, centre a heading across the spreadsheet, format numbers to percentages. In a database you might need to create a form, filter data, add combo boxes and calculated controls. If you are designing a series of web pages you will certainly include hyperlinks and probably graphics and font effects too.

The output will most likely be in the form of a print-out and you need to consider whether the output will always be the same. For example, do you need to set a spreadsheet to landscape and do you want the grid lines to print? Do you want multiple copies to be collated or printed in reverse order?

You should also specify the names to be given to directories and data files at each stage of implementation. What backup method will you recommend and how frequently should backup take place?

When you have the answers to all the questions on the following table, you are ready to prepare your report which, when finished, will provide sufficient detail so that you or someone else can work towards the design solution to your problem.

Once again, we have made notes against a series of headings that will help to remind you of the information you must provide in your Analysis Report.

ANALYSE

The purpose of this stage is to break the problem down into small parts and to plan each part in detail so you have all the information you need ready to move on to the design stage.

What information do I need to gather and where will it come from?

Look in detail at each part of the project and consider what information you need to have before you can begin the design. For example, what information do you need from a data-collection form? What fields are to be included in a database and what row and column headings should be in a spreadsheet? Do you need to research information before you can start? Include sketch designs but don't worry about including too much detail at this stage.

Show the data flow?

- Illustrate the sequence of steps needed to solve the problem with a diagram. Make sure your diagram relates to the user requirements or objectives you identified originally.

What hardware and software will be needed?

- You don't need to list the obvious components of your computer system, only those which are specific to your project, e.g. scanner, colour printer.

  If the coursework is 'Manipulation of a Spreadsheet', don't specify spreadsheet software but if you want to include clip art in your spreadsheet you should refer to it.

  If you are producing a word-processed report with a chart or graph imported from a spreadsheet, you should mention the spreadsheet but there is no need to refer to word processing.

Analyse/Design

How will I input the data?

- Will you use a keyboard, scanner, digital camera, etc.? Will the data be input manually working from a manuscript, data-collection form or will it be downloaded from a CD-ROM or the Internet? If you input the data manually how will you check the accuracy?

What processes will be carried out on the data?

- What will happen to the data once it has been input and what features (or tools) in each software application will you use? For example:

  Word processing – page orientation, font size and style, columns, tables, text boxes, WordArt, ClipArt, margins, borders, headers and footers, merge, templates, macros, etc.

  Spreadsheet – number format, borders, colour, formulae, charts and graphs, gridlines, etc.

  Database – field data types, range checks, input masks, indexes, validation or verification techniques, sorting, searching, forms, reports, etc.

How will the results of the data be presented or output?

- Will you need soft and/or hard copy of the data, and is it to be printed in black and white or colour? Will you need different output at different times? How many copies will be required? Do you need to design a particular style of report from the database?

How will I store and back up the data?

- Indicate the names you will assign to data folders and data files. Indicate the file names you will use at each stage of the implementation. Will you set the computer to save by default to a particular folder? Specify a method and frequency of backup, e.g. floppy disk, CD-RW, zip disk, tape.

How will the data be secure?

- Will you password protect files or make them read-only? Will you enable AutoRecovery and automatic backup?

DESIGN

The important thing to remember here is that you will not be using the computer to draw up your designs, only to produce notes!

Much of the work you do for this section of the project will be handwritten or drawn, but must be annotated to show the full detail. Until it is designed in full, you cannot transfer the design to the computer – save that for the next stage.

Your outline ideas from the Analysis Report will form the basis of the designs and you can now incorporate any feedback from your user. You will be able to see what we mean by this when you look at the sample coursework in the Tutor's File.

What detail should you include?

If your project involves a **spreadsheet** this is the time to indicate the formulae and specific details of formatting. For example, which cells should display 0.00 or £0.00 or %, should negative numbers appear in red? Should the row or column headings be in bold and should they be formatted to wrap the text, right align or centre it, etc.? Which columns need to be increased in width and where do you want borders and shading? All this detail will mean that anybody could pick up your design and produce the spreadsheet exactly as you intended, and in real-life computer design this is what actually happens. You must also design test data to test the formulae are correct and must indicate the results you expect the test data to produce.

Are you designing a **database**? This is the time to specify data types, validation rules and relationships. The layout of screen forms, reports and queries should be provided together with test data. Your test data should test extremes of data and, again, you should indicate what you would expect to happen in the test. For example, if you have a field set to accept data greater than 49 (>49) and less than 80 (<80) your test data might include 45, 48, 49, 50, 60, 75, 79, 80 and 81. What would you expect the results of the test data to show? You must also make sure that your test data will enable you to test your queries. For instance, if you have a query to show all girls over the age of 12, make sure you include test data with girls above and below the age of 12.

Design

If you are **word processing** a project, you would need to specify whether the page is landscape or portrait, single or double-line spaced plus the size and style of font you wish it to be produced in. Where will the data come from – a CD-ROM, the Internet or handwritten notes? Draw sketches to indicate where graphic images should sit in relation to the text or columns. Give an indication of the width of columns and the sizes of margins and also indicate how you will 'test' your project. In this case you would need to detail the use of the spell checker, print preview and proof reading.

If you are designing a **web site**, you should indicate your links to other pages/sites and provide a test plan for the links. Will you provide navigation buttons? Much of the information you need to provide for word-processed projects would apply to web sites, e.g. font styles and sizes, position of graphic images, etc.

You must also include full details of file names to be assigned to every stage of implementation and details of the backup and security procedures you will implement. The following checklist should help you to remember everything.

Remember!!

You will not be using the computer to draw your designs. They will be handwritten. Only use the computer to present your summary.

What are the original objectives of the system?

- It makes sense to list the objectives so you don't forget something. Number them and then check each objective against the checklist below to make sure you haven't forgotten something important.

1
2
3
4
5
6

	Objectives					
	1	2	3	4	5	6
Sketch design(s) provided						
Software to be used						
Page orientation						
Margins						
Font size, style and colour						
Position and size of graphics						
Line spacing						
Position/style of headings						
Text alignment						
Position of tables/columns						
Borders and shading						
Formulae						
Cell format						
Column width/height						
Field names						
Data types						
Primary key						
Validation rules						
Input screen layout						
Design of forms						
Design of queries						
Design of reports						
Hyperlinks						
Navigation buttons						
Test data						
User instructions						
Folder/File names						
Backup methods/security						

Implementation and evaluation

Implementation

At last we come to the exciting part of the project where you can get on and use the computer. You will probably spend as much, if not more, time on this part of your coursework as you have already spent in analysing and designing your solution. The evidence for this stage of your coursework will come from annotated hard copies showing the sequence of development in implementing and testing the design. You must remember to keep all the hard copies you print out. To help you assemble them in the right order when you hand your project in, it is a good idea to use Last printed in AutoText in the footer.

When you see something that needs changing on a print-out, write a note indicating what needs changing and why. This is called annotating your evidence and is essential if you are to earn the extended marks. Similarly, if the final version differs from the original design, include a note to say why the changes were necessary.

Make sure you check your work to ensure that all errors are corrected. Hand in the original print-outs and circle the errors you had to correct. You will not lose any marks if you made mistakes and corrected them, but you will if your work contains mistakes that you have not corrected.

You must also include evidence that you have implemented your test plan fully and annotated it to show how the expected and actual results compared.

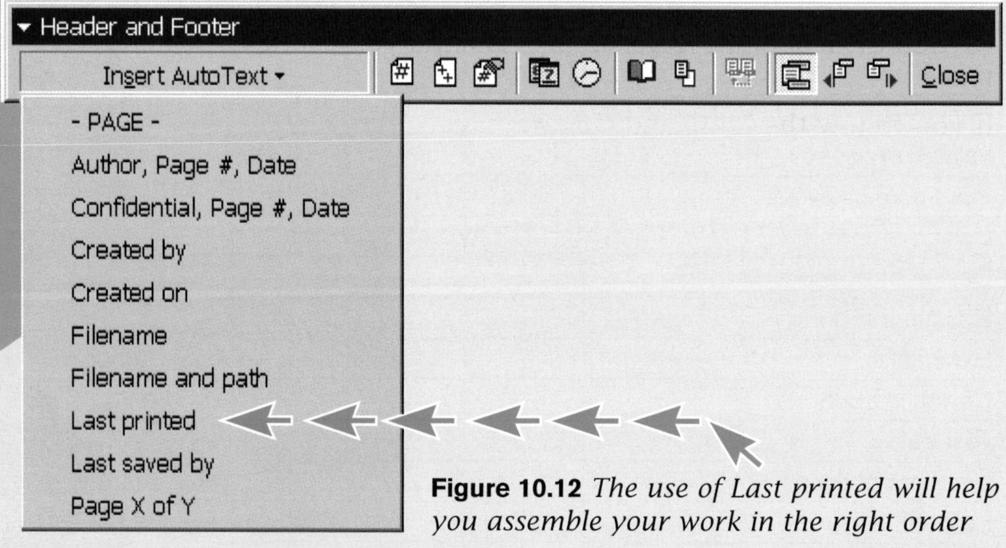

Figure 10.12 *The use of Last printed will help you assemble your work in the right order*

Make sure your user documentation is clear and understandable. Include screen prints wherever possible to reassure the users of your system that what they are seeing on their screen is what you intended.

Provide screen dumps as evidence you have saved the work with the file names and in the folder you specified.

Evaluation

The evaluation or monitoring of the project completes the information systems life cycle and this final process will help to identify any improvements or modifications that might be needed.

Your evaluation should refer to solving the problem and is **not** about using the software. It must relate back to the original objectives or user requirements of your project and should describe both what was successful and what went wrong and why. Suggest ways to avoid similar problems in the future or to improve upon the solution you achieved. You will not lose marks if your project didn't quite meet the objectives, providing you explain what went wrong and why and what you would do next time to avoid it.

One of the most important things to include with your evaluation is feedback from your 'real' user. This could take the form of answers to a set of written questions you have designed or a letter. The most important thing is that you indicate you have understood the comments and are able to provide written evidence of further improvements you could make.

If you follow the hints and tips we have suggested as you prepare your coursework you should manage to achieve a solid foundation towards your overall grade which you can take forward and build upon as you prepare for your written examination.

Good luck!

Sample coursework

Your teacher will be able to give you sample coursework to study and more hints to help you prepare your own work.

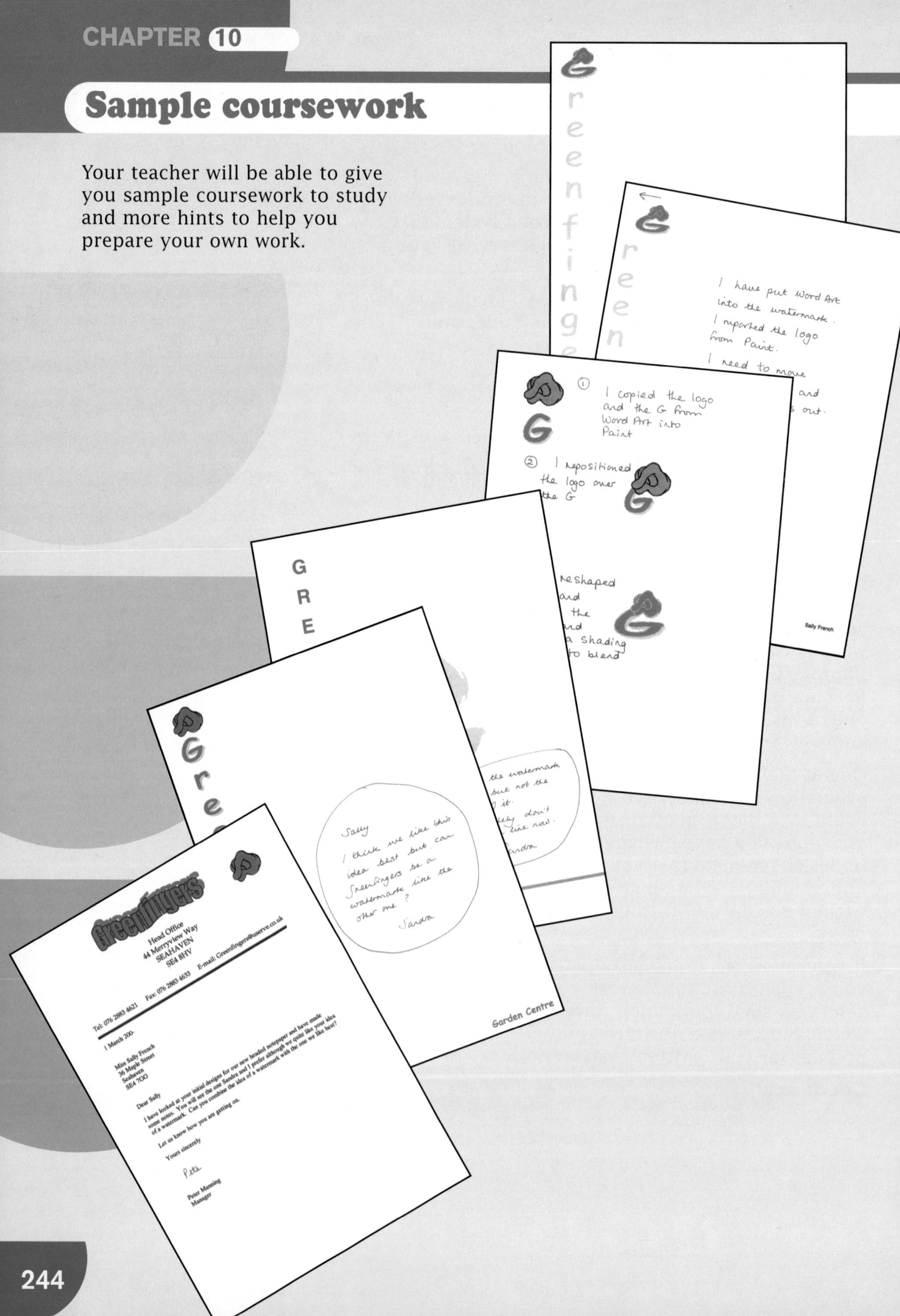

Greenfingers

Head Office
44 Merryview Way
SEAHAVEN
SEA 8HV

Tel: 076 2883 4621 Fax: 076 2883 4633 E-mail: Greenfingers@userve.co.uk

1 March 200-

Miss Sally French
36 Maple Street
Seahaven
SE4 7GG

Dear Sally

I have looked at your initial designs for our new headed notepaper and have made some notes. You will see the one Sandra and I prefer although we quite like your idea of a watermark. Can you combine the idea of a watermark with the one we like best?

Let us know how you are getting on.

Yours sincerely

Pete

Peter Manning
Manager

Index